Studies In

Includes Small Group Questions & Leader Notes

2 Volumes In 1

Volume One
"Our Father...Yours Is The Kingdom"

Volume Two
"Your Kingdom Come, Your Will Be Done"

See Tom's new book:

Our Divine Mandate

Completing Humanity's Great Commission

Revised – 2020

ISBN: 978-0-9984514-1-1

ENDORSEMENTS

"Tom Casey's book drives home the importance of the reality and presence of the Kingdom of God in the lives of God's people today, and helps us understand the tremendous Kingdom assets and prophetic resources Jesus has placed at our disposal as His representatives to this world. Grasping the fact that Jesus sent each of us to expand on the ministry He began when He was here, realizing that our interaction with the Holy Spirit is the most important relationship each of us has in this world, and embracing the training that God has for each of us to empower us to cooperate with Him in His prophetic activities on the earth, should motivate each of us to pursue and take hold of the Kingdom of God as a precious prize. Tom calls us to partner with Jesus as His Kingdom representatives, in this age, before He returns."

Mike Bickle
International House of Prayer of Kansas City

"Tom Casey's new book is a solid biblical, theological, and practical book that can help anyone who wants to better understand the Kingdom of God and its prophetic dimensions. I highly recommend it to everyone, but especially pastors and teachers who want to see an increase of the operation of the power of the Kingdom in their lives, and who want to see more prophetic activity in their lives."

Dr. Randy Clark
Founder and President, Global Awakening Network of Churches

"Tom Casey provides a welcome volume on the Kingdom of God by clarifying its meaning and significance. Inviting readers to participate more passionately in its advance, he awakens us out of complacency, challenging readers to appropriate the Kingdom authority that God has delegated to those who follow Christ. Through the power of the Holy Spirit and divine grace, we need more voices like Tom's, such that God's Kingdom will come and His will be done throughout the earth!"

Diane J. Chandler, Ph.D.
Associate Professor, Regent University School of Divinity

"I enjoyed reading Tom's book, "Studies In The Kingdom Of God". What touched me is the emphasis on The Father, The Son and The Holy Spirit as the source, the reason, the motivation, and the empowerment for us to join in the cause of extending and deepening the rule and reign of God in our lives and families, in order that all the families of the earth may be blessed by God."

Doug Brown
Director, E3 Leadership Group - Great Commission Network of Churches

"In this book Tom explains how the Kingdom is prophetic and as God's prophetic people, we are to take the Kingdom into our own spheres of influence. Right in the middle of our everyday life is where Jesus desires to be! It's where He makes Himself known and seen and felt through ordinary people like you and me. It is our heritage, our destiny to live with Him and in agreement with His heart at work, at home, at play in every sphere we touch, in every season of our lives. This tangible expression of Jesus is powerful and affects a change in the lives of many all around us as we live and move and have our being in Him."

Diane Bickle
Founder and President, Glad Heart Realty - Kansas City, Missouri

FOREWORD

What a novel idea! Who would have thought to identify and examine *the major theme in the ministry of Jesus* and apply it to real life? Traditional systematic theology books rarely even devote a page or two, out of hundreds, to the Kingdom of God. Even then, the Kingdom was identified only with the visible church (Catholic position), or to the "invisible church" (Protestantism), or a progressively Christianized future of the world (Postmillennialism and old Liberalism), as though there were nothing more to be said! The Kingdom of God was an invisible doctrine.

This progressive idea of the Kingdom of God, however, caught fire among secular academics. Immanuel Kant, Friedrich Schleiermacher and Albrecht Ritschl saw the Kingdom of God at the end of inevitable progress toward a world of ideal human relations in a perfect Christian society. This view of inevitable progress toward an ideal offered a template for the materialistic theories of Darwin's biological evolution and Marx's economic stages of class struggle toward communism.

American fundamentalism (1920s onward) reacted vigorously against the "modernist" (Liberal) idea of the Kingdom of God being a secularized "just society," which seemed a substitute for a need for grace, the work of the cross, salvation, and a final reign of Christ. More recently, a few (very few) standard works appeared, devoted to the Kingdom of God, but they were either detached, academic discourses (K.L. Schmidt, "*basileia*," in *TDNT*, John Bright, G. Vos, Ladd) or devotional books (Alva J. McClain, Martyn Lloyd-Jones, G.R. Beasley-Murray).

In every case, all of these views, traditional, philosophical, secular, academic or even devotional, filtered out *the very biblical essence of the Kingdom—power*. "The Kingdom of God does not consist of 'talk' but *dunamis* [miracle power of the Spirit]" (1 Cor. 4:20).

A generation ago, in a brilliant article in the tradition of the "biblical theology movement" from the 1930s onward, James Dunn showed this connection ("Spirit and Kingdom," *Expository Times*, Nov 1970). His ground-breaking work, however, seemed to threaten the theological establishment, who mostly ignored it. Dunn showed the centrality of the Spirit/Kingdom nexus when he wrote:

> "*Basileia* [kingdom] in fact is one of these words whose use by Paul seems inconsistent and confusing till we realize first that they are as extensive in application as the Christian life is long, and second that the Spirit is the link which binds them all together, bringing consistency and clarity to their usage. I refer particularly to: "resurrection," "redemption/ deliverance," "righteousness," "glory," "life," "salvation," "adoption."

Expanding on Dunn, the radical association of the kingdom and the power of the Spirit for today was introduced to the traditional theological community at a packed session of the Evangelical Theological Society Annual Meeting in Santa Barbara in 1970. This "Kingdom theology" connection appeared soon after as a substantial theme in John Wimber's popular theology of "power healing" course he taught at Fuller Seminary. Fuller professor Don Williams expanded and popularized this new theology in his *Signs, Wonders, and the Kingdom of God.*

In this exciting tradition, then, Tom Casey's new work provides us with a well-rounded view of the Kingdom of God, *as Jesus intended it*, by applying it in very real life experiences that identify closely with the kingdom power encounters of the New Testament.

Jesus and the writers of the New Testament, never intended for their writings to be simply a source for theological information, but rather, a training manual for the kingdom-empowered life of discipleship.

Tom Casey has caught the spirit and intention of the New Testament writers, which he has articulated in his important new work. I heartily commend this work to you.

Jon Ruthven, PhD
Professor Emeritus, Regent University School of Divinity
Author, *On the Cessation of the Charismata,*
What's Wrong with Protestant Theology

INTRODUCTION

The seed for this book was actually planted seventeen years ago, in 2000, as my Master's thesis, at the end of my studies at Regent University's School of Divinity. The thesis was titled, "*The Prophetic – Embracing, Introducing & Integrating It Into The Local Church*". It has long been a passion of mine to see the prophetic activities of the Kingdom of God embraced and integrated into the life of the local church. This thesis endeavored to address many of the misconceptions and issues concerning these prophetic activities and to state the case for moving these activities, normally relegated to external seminars and conferences, back into the life and experience of the local church where Jesus intended them to operate within their proper context and spiritual oversight.

At the time, God graciously provided me with seasoned, experienced assistance as I developed and wrote this thesis. Dr. Jack Deere served as my coach and mentor, as I prepared to write this thesis. Mike Bickle and the leadership at Metro Christian Fellowship in Kansas City, Missouri, and Rick Joyner and the leadership at Morningstar Ministries in Charlotte, North Carolina provided invaluable insight and guidance when it came to the practical application and governance of these prophetic activities within the local church environment. These three ministries were instrumental in making the communication of my thesis, and its message, possible. I want to take this time to, again, thank Jack, Mike, Rick and those from their ministry teams who gave of their time and experience to assist me with the content of that thesis document. Mike is now the Director of the International House of Prayer in Kansas City, Missouri.

Usually, when one completes his or her formal studies, these sorts of documents sit on the shelf in their home or office and gather dust. Yet, in regard to this thesis document, God wouldn't let me put it on the shelf to gather dust. Over the last sixteen years, God took a relatively obscure aspect of my thesis, the Kingdom of God, and expanded my understanding of it in regard to its reality, presence, nature, and activities on the earth, through His Kingdom people, the Church. What was once a confusing and little-known theological concept in my mind has become a real, tangible force in my life, as He has instructed and trained me in its powerful presence and operation on the earth. I couldn't keep this to myself.

This book, *"Studies In The Kingdom of God"* is actually two volumes in one. The first volume, *"Our Father…Yours is the Kingdom,"* discusses the reality and nature of the Kingdom of God, while the second volume, *"Your Kingdom Come, Your Will Be Done,"* discusses the presence and activities of the Kingdom of God on the earth in and through His Kingdom people. Both books give a scriptural and theological foundation for these various aspects of the Kingdom of God, while providing practical instruction and some real-life examples of those who have witnessed and experienced the activities of the Kingdom of God, throughout Church history and in today's world. At the end of each chapter you will find small group questions and leader notes, and suggestions for practical application of what is written.

Writing books like this is never easy because the Holy Spirit doesn't let you write and instruct on such a subject without, first, taking you through the classroom of life - to use your personal experience to transfer these scriptural and theological concepts from your head to your heart. This spiritual training and instruction doesn't happen overnight because the Holy Spirit is not in a hurry to do what is necessary to transform you into a person God can use to further the purpose and activities of His Kingdom on the earth. As a result, these are not simply theoretical, theological concepts and statements I am promoting, even though these necessary elements are included in the book. I have written this book to contain authentic, personal experiences and the Kingdom reality that these personal experiences bring to the lives of the people mentioned here.

The Kingdom of God did not come to promote the agendas, plans and purposes of the rich, famous, influential, and powerful on the earth, even though these individuals can experience the presence and activities of the Kingdom of God if they pursue it in the way Jesus instructed us. The Kingdom of God is for every follower of Jesus who sets himself or herself to pursue it with vigor, patience, tenacity and faith as if it was the only thing on this earth worth possessing. That is because the Kingdom of God is the only thing on this earth worth possessing, even if we possess nothing else. If we possess everything else but do not welcome, possess and experience the reality and presence of the Kingdom of God, we possess nothing of eternal significance.

Jesus tells us that the Kingdom of God is moving forward in the earth with great passion and determination and those who would take hold of it must do so with this same passion and determination, as a precious prize. Knowing what the Kingdom of God is and how it operates isn't enough. He also wants us to embrace and experience it, and its power, so we can be its eye-witnesses to those who live and work around us, within our personal spheres of influence.

Jesus said, *"If you love me, you will keep my commandments."* Experiencing and demonstrating the presence and activities of the Kingdom of God is the context in which Jesus made this statement. He commanded us to experience the Kingdom and to take this witness of the Kingdom to the world around us. We are to experience the reality and activities of the Kingdom of God in our lives so we can be living witnesses of His Kingdom to those around us, and to take the Kingdom into every area of society and the seven cultural kingdoms of this world. This must happen before Jesus returns and He has left us here, with His Spirit, ability and authority to do just that. The Kingdom of God is truly a precious prize. Let's discover it and pursue it as if we really believe it.

Tom Casey

SUGGESTIONS FOR READING THIS BOOK

This book was written with the expectation that it will be read and studied within a number of different environments, whether it is as an individual, or within a friendship study group, a discipleship group, a small group, or a home group. It can be studied together within a Sunday School class, a women's fellowship study group, a men's fellowship study group, or as a church's leadership team. It may even find its way into schools of ministry, Bible schools and seminaries.

The Kingdom of God was the main theme of Jesus' life and ministry when He was walking the earth. He proclaimed it everywhere He went and told those around Him that He was sent for this very purpose. Yes, He came to die for the sins of humanity but He also brought the presence and activities of the Kingdom of God with Him when he came. He also lived to instruct and train His disciples in the reality, presence and activities of the Kingdom of God while He was with us.

Therefore, it stands to reason that the Kingdom of God should be an important topic of study and a reality we should all earnestly desire to experience within our individual and corporate lives together. Jesus even told us that the Kingdom of God is moving forward in the earth with great passion and determination, and those who would take hold of it must do so with the same passion and determination, as a precious prize. If Jesus said that, then how can we, as followers of Jesus and His Kingdom people on the earth, desire and pursue anything else with the same passion and determination as we do the Kingdom of God.

With this in mind, I would like to make a few suggestions as to how this book can be read and studied by those who have a desire to not only understand what the Kingdom of God is but to, also, embrace it and experience the reality of it within the context of their daily lives. God created the human race within the context of community and this is the best environment in which the Kingdom of God can be understood and experienced. Studying and experiencing the Kingdom of God individually is a very worthwhile endeavor and there are some who will find themselves in a position where this is the only way they can pursue it. I heartily encourage you to set your heart on doing this and God will meet you in your desire and faith, to effectively teach and instruct you.

Yet, the optimum environment for pursuing, studying and experiencing the Kingdom of God is within community, with other followers of Jesus, and within an environment where there is experienced, spiritual oversight to be given to those who are studying and pursuing the Kingdom. There may not always be experienced, spiritual oversight available within the community of believers. We can't let that stop us from moving forward with what we know we need to do and what Jesus encourages us to do. God will meet us where we are when we exercise faith in His word and what He commands us to do, and He has commanded us to pursue and embrace the Kingdom of God as a precious prize.

We must all start at the beginning when it comes to learning about and experiencing the Kingdom of God and its activities. Even if we have been followers of Jesus for a number of years, we may not have the understanding of and experience with this aspect of who He is and what He has made available to us. This is why the Holy Spirit is here. He is here to come along side of us, each of us, as we seek to understand and experience the realities of God and His Kingdom. We can lean on and trust in the Holy Spirit's presence and ability to take us from where we are now, to where Jesus wants us to be.

This will not be a quick journey and it will not be without risk, difficulties and failure. We shouldn't expect it to be otherwise because Jesus doesn't expect it to be otherwise. He told us that in this world we will have difficulties. He also told us to be encouraged and cheerful as we embark on this journey because He has overcome the world and everything that would seek to discourage and hinder us.

So, set your hearts to embrace, understand and pursue the Kingdom of God as a precious prize. Set your heart to pursue and become intimately acquainted with the Holy Spirit because He is the most important person and relationship we have in this world, and He is the means by which we will grow and mature in our faith and in our journey to know and experience the realities of the Kingdom of God.

When it comes to you and those within your community of fellow believers in Jesus, encourage each other, even when you make mistakes and fail. You will make mistakes and fail in some of your attempts to hear the voice of the Spirit and to respond to what He is saying to you. Failure doesn't deter God from working in our lives and it shouldn't deter us from moving forward with God. This is why we need each other. We must encourage and help each other as the Holy Spirit guides us into these realities.

Those who are leaders among us must exercise grace and patience with those we lead just as the Holy Spirit gives grace and exercises patience with us, as He leads us in our own spiritual journeys. Leaders are called to serve the Body of Christ and there is no greater service to Christ than to guide, instruct and encourage those we are called to lead in their pursuit of the Kingdom of God.

We all have much to learn when it comes to embracing, pursuing and experiencing the realities of the Kingdom of God. There is no better place to start than where we are and with those fellow believers in Jesus that God has placed within our lives. Don't wait for a better time to begin this journey because there is no better time to begin than right now. May God bless us as we embark on this wonderful journey.

Tom Casey

Volume One

"Our Father...Yours Is The Kingdom"

Table of Contents

Volume Two

"Your Kingdom Come, Your Will Be Done"

Table of Contents

VOLUME ONE

"Our Father...Yours Is The Kingdom"

The Reality & Nature of the Kingdom of God

(1)

The Importance Of Responding To The Influences Of God

*"**Our Father who is in heaven**, hallowed be Your name, Your kingdom come, Your will be done on earth as it is in heaven. Give us this day our daily bread and forgive us our debts, as we also have forgiven our debtors. And do not lead us into temptation but deliver us from evil. **For Yours is the kingdom** and the power and the glory forever."* Mathew 6:9-13 (emphasis mine)

"Things which eye has not seen and ear has not heard, and which have not entered the heart of man, all that God has prepared for those who love Him." 1Corinthians 2:9

These are two wonderful passages of scripture. One, we know as *The Lord's Prayer.* The other is taken from 1Corinthians 2, where Paul is expounding on the wisdom of God, which He displayed through the death, burial and resurrection of Jesus and then expounded on, further, through the Holy Spirit. Both of these scriptures are indicative of the tremendous blessings and inheritance we have been given by our heavenly Father, as believers in Jesus and heirs of the Kingdom of God through Jesus.

After following Jesus, observing His lifestyle and participating with Him in His ministry, the disciples recognized that Jesus was a praying man and, even more significant, that God answered His prayers. As a result, they asked Jesus to teach them how to pray. They wanted to see the same results from their prayers that Jesus saw from His.

As Jesus began to teach them about prayer, modeling it for them, He started with the phrase, *"Our Father."* This phrase was not some ritual introduction to a formal prayer Jesus prayed every day, hoping that His Father heard it. Nor was it part of a spiritual formula to coax the Father to do something for Him. Jesus knew who He was praying to and He had established an intimate relationship and spiritual connection with His Father, as He grew from a small boy into an adult.

In this phrase, *"Our Father,"* Jesus acknowledged His relationship with His Father and called on this relationship for the purpose of personal interaction, fellowship, and co-laboring with Him, as Jesus engaged in His daily activities. Not only was Jesus recognizing His relationship with the Father, He was acknowledging the fact (by saying "**Our** Father") that this relationship with God as *Father* was available to all who pursued this same intimate relationship and spiritual connection.

In His model prayer, Jesus continued by making specific requests of the Father, not as "scatter shots", hoping to mention one that happened to "hit" on something that was already on the Father's agenda for that day. Jesus interacted and communicated with the Father concerning what He needed, as the Father's Kingdom representative to the earth and to humanity, as well as acknowledging the Father's character qualities and Jesus' devotion to His Father's will and purposes. Jesus' prayers communicated His love, honor and respect for the Father and what the Father means to Him, in His personal experience.

Effective prayer is not about saying the right words in the right way at the right time. It's about engaging in and expressing the realities of an intimate relationship that has been and continues to be developed over time, and drawing upon these relationship realities when the need or opportunity calls for it. Jesus modeled what prayer was to be like – not in word only but in heart attitude and in personal experience.

When we read or say the *Lord's Prayer* and we finish the phrase, *"…and lead us not into temptation but deliver us from evil"*, we tend to "coast" to the end of the prayer. We say or read the remaining words as if they are simply the formal closing to the prayer because (we assume) we have just completed the most important part. But, if we look carefully at what Jesus said following His requests, we discover that He expresses what He believes to be the foundational reality for why He knows His prayers will be answered.

The simple word *"for"* is the key. This small word *"for"* can also be expressed by the word *"because"*. Whatever follows the word *"for"* or *"because"* provides us with the premise or reason for the expectation that what was previously requested will be answered. What Jesus said after *"for"* is the reason He knows His prayer will be answered. What follows is, *"…Yours is the kingdom, and the power and the glory, forever."*

Focusing on, *"yours is the kingdom..."*, what does this phrase mean? In Jesus' mind, it is the foundational truth and reality for believing that His prayers will be answered by the Father. Not only is God Jesus' Father but ***His Father possesses the Kingdom***. If Jesus knew and declared that His prayers were going to be answered because God, His Father, possesses the Kingdom; it makes sense that this is also the foundational reason for why we can believe our prayers will be answered.

Now, concerning the second scripture, above, from 1Corinthians 2:9; the Apostle Paul in his first letter to the Corinthians reveals much of what God has given to us as our inheritance, as followers of Jesus Christ. Paul refers to this spiritual activity and inheritance, and the means by which God gave it to us (the death, burial, and resurrection of Jesus), as the wisdom that was hidden in ages past but has now been revealed to us by His Spirit. *"Things which eye has not seen and ear has not heard, and which have not entered the heart of man, all that God has prepared for those who love Him."* [1] This is not wisdom that has been hidden for a future age, though there is wisdom for future ages that He has kept hidden and has yet to reveal. This wisdom Paul speaks of is for and pertinent to this present age in which we live. To relegate this wisdom to the future, only, is to cut ourselves off from what God intends for us to know and experience now, in this age. Paul didn't say, *"...that God has prepared in heaven and in the ages to come, for those who love Him."*

In regard to these two scriptures, there are three questions we need to ask ourselves; 1) *"Do I know God as my Father, experientially, as Jesus did?"*; 2) *"Do I understand and experience the reality that my Father "possesses the Kingdom", so that I have the assurance that my prayers will be answered?"*; and, 3) *"Do I (predominantly) relegate to heaven and to the ages to come the unimaginable things that God, in His wisdom, has prepared for us who love Him?"* What we often consider to be a simple, formal closing to *the Lord's Prayer*, Jesus considered to be the foundational reality for why He expected His prayers to be answered. What we tend to relegate to "after we die", Jesus and the early church believers understood as relevant and available to them to experience in this life. The Holy Spirit has revealed these things to us, now, in this life and for this life.

When we observe in the scriptures, the lives of Jesus and the early church believers, we see the *truth* and *reality* of the Kingdom of God as being foremost in their lives, message and ministry. We see that the effectiveness of Jesus' prayer life and ministry activities depended on the reality of the *Kingdom of God* being present with Him where He lived.[2] We are told by Luke that when Jesus began His ministry, He went from village to village

---

[1] 1Corinthians 2:9
[2] John 11:38-44; Luke 5:17; Matthew 12:25-28

proclaiming the *Kingdom of God*.[3] When Jesus cast demons out of people, He declared that He did so by the *Kingdom of God*.[4] Jesus told His disciples that the *Kingdom of God* must be forcefully engaged and passionately embraced as a precious prize.[5]

When Paul neared the end of his life and he was being held under house arrest, he continued to preach the *Kingdom of God* to those who came to him.[6] When Jesus was teaching His disciples about the things that would take place before His return to the earth at the end of the age, He told them that this gospel or good news of the *Kingdom of God* must be preached throughout the world, as a *witness* to all the nations, and then the end of the age would come.[7]

This word *witness* (Greek. *marturion*) means to observe and experience something first-hand and to give testimony to its reality. In other words, to be a witness of the Kingdom of God we must observe and experience its reality first-hand in our lives and be able to demonstrate and give personal testimony to that reality. If we don't have that first-hand experience and observation, we aren't witnesses; we are simply giving hearsay testimony based on what we've heard from others who may or may not have experienced it. How can I demonstrate and give testimony as an eye-witness of something that I haven't observed or personally experienced? As we will see, the Kingdom of God is to be observed, personally experienced, and its reality demonstrated by the followers of Jesus. Otherwise, there is no real testimony of its reality and presence.

"Our Father…Yours is the Kingdom!" If this simple statement was the foundational reality for Jesus' life, ministry and relationship with the Father, how much more should it be for our lives? Sadly, many of us in the Body of Christ today have little or no understanding of the Kingdom of God, much less first-hand experience with its reality. We can't fully grasp and accomplish our purpose on the earth, as human beings and as followers of Jesus, without a clear understanding and first-hand experience of the reality of the presence of the Kingdom of God and its activities in our lives.

The New Covenant scriptures tell us that the gospel message of the Kingdom of God is good news.[8] Do we, as followers of Jesus, truly believe that the Kingdom of God is real, that its influence and activities are present

[3] Luke 8:1
[4] Matt. 12:28
[5] Matt. 11:12
[6] Acts 28:16-30
[7] Matt. 24:14
[8] Luke 4:43

with us, and that they are "good news" to us? In Psalm 19, King David, a believer in and lover of the Kingdom of God, boldly proclaims the affections of his heart when he declares his love and fascination for God and His Kingdom in these statements:

- *vs.7 - "the law of the Lord is perfect…the testimony of the Lord is sure."*
- *vs.8 - "the precepts of the Lord are right…the commandment of the Lord is pure."*
- *vs.9 – "the fear of the Lord is clean…the judgments of the Lord are true and righteous."*

David declares that everything God is, does and says is perfect, good and right. All of it is good news to him. These words aren't simply an intellectual agreement or an emotional reflection on David's part. David is convinced in His heart that these statements are true and are good news to him. He has observed and experienced them in his life and, as a result, has submitted himself including his lifestyle, beliefs and passions to God and His Kingdom. David has embraced the Kingdom in order to see this "good news" impact and guide his life. He has no reservations in believing and living according to these realities of God and His Kingdom.

The question is what do we think about these statements David made in Psalm 19? Do we share the same sentiments as David did about God and His decisions, words and actions? Do we agree with, embrace, and confess these same Kingdom truths in our lives? For instance, even if we don't understand all of the decisions and activities that God declares and carries out, do we love them, embrace them as precious and perfect, and consider them to be good news to us? Do we willingly submit ourselves to them, knowing that they are righteous and good because they come from God and His Kingdom? Or, do we doubt Him and them? Do we put up resistance to them because they don't seem to agree with what we think God is like or what we believe is true about God? Are we resistant to God and His Kingdom because what He does and says don't agree with what we think should be done or said; being different from how we would do or say it, or how we view ourselves, the world, and people around us? Does God's "worldview" seem to clash with our own?

How we respond to God's revealed nature, actions, words, and decisions may very well tell us what we truly believe about God and whether we consider the realities of His Kingdom to be good news. If our perception of God, His words and His activities are different from how God has revealed them to us, we may have a skewed perception of God, or we may not have truly embraced Him and His Kingdom with all of our hearts. There is nothing wrong with having and asking questions about what God says and does but once we are confronted with the truth of what He has revealed, how we respond could reveal the true condition of our hearts.

There is an important principle in the Bible we must understand. In Romans 1:18-32, Paul explains the process by which people become reprobate in their attitudes, thinking, and actions towards God. This act of *reprobating* is resisting or responding in unbelief (not responding in faith) to the influences of God in our lives, over time. It is the willing resistance to the revealed nature, attributes, will, purposes and activities of God, over time, as He directly or indirectly influences our lives. The longer we knowingly or unknowingly resist these direct and indirect influences and activities of God, the more calloused toward God we become.

We, by an act of our will, as we engage in the daily decision-making processes of life, can eventually become completely hardened in our heart and mind toward God.[9] We find it more and more difficult to distinguish the difference between good and evil. We can become so morally and spiritually blind and bankrupt, we will consider evil to be good and good to be evil. Paul tells us that God has and continues to reveal Himself and His Kingdom to us through what He has made, so that none of us has any excuse before Him.[10] This process of reprobating does not happen overnight but it does happen, if we consistently resist the influences of God in our lives.

We are told that Satan blinds the minds of the unbelieving.[11] We are also told that anyone can think and act in opposition to God and His influences, in his or her life, through unawareness and deception.[12] "*Without faith it is impossible to please God because everyone who comes to Him must believe that He is and that He is a rewarder of those who diligently seek Him.*"[13] Unawareness and deception do not excuse us from, and are not a defense against the consequences of resisting and rejecting the influences of the Kingdom of God in our life. In fact, unawareness and deception are the major reasons why we engage in the process of reprobating to begin with. This process of reprobating does not happen overnight; it takes time. God will continue to encounter and confront us with His Kingdom activities in order to get our attention, to turn us toward Him. This process of reprobating is slow but sure, if the influences of God are resisted or ignored.

---

[9] Ephesians 4:17-19
[10] Romans 1:20
[11] 2Cor. 4:4
[12] 2Corinthians 11:3; Colossians 2:8; Ephesians 4:22-27
[13] Hebrews 11:6

As followers of Jesus we need to recognize that we, too, can engage in this process of reprobating by not responding in faith to the influences of God and His Kingdom. We can resist God and His influence in different areas of our life. This spiritual activity of not responding in faith to the influences of God will slowly harden our hearts, deafen our spiritual ears and blind our spiritual eyes to what He wants to reveal to us or accomplish in our lives. The more we resist His influence the more difficult it becomes next time to discern and respond to His influence in those areas. He may determine that it is necessary to go as far as to "shock" us, through an activity of His Kingdom, to get our attention so we realize that He is endeavoring to influence our lives. God works in response to our faith and our faith response is a voluntary act on our part.

As an act of our will, we can embrace the activities and influences of God and His Kingdom in our life. Or, as an act of our will, we can resist or ignore these same activities and influences. We make decisions every day as to what we will do and not do with the physical influences and information we receive through our five physical senses. We also make decisions as to what we will do with the spiritual influences and information we receive from God and His Kingdom. We choose if, when, and how we will respond. God has sovereignly established it this way.

God created us with a free will and He will not violate our free will. If we resist and ignore God's activity and influences in our life, He will let us go down the path we choose. We can be reprobating in some areas of our life and not in others. These areas where we are unaware of or resist His influences can keep us from experiencing all that God has for us, as His Kingdom people.

Paul went so far as to pose the question directly to the Galatians, when they began to "move away" from their intimate relationship with the Holy Spirit and the activities of the Kingdom of God in order to embrace Jewish legalism, ritual, and faithless ceremony. Paul chastened them by asking them several questions, *"You foolish Galatians, who has bewitched you… did you receive the Spirit by the works of the Law, or by hearing with faith? Having begun by the Spirit, are you now being perfected by the flesh? So then, does He who provides you with the Spirit and works miracles among you, do it by the works of the Law, or by hearing with faith?"* [14] The Holy Spirit used Paul's letter as an influence or activity of the Kingdom of God in the lives of the Galatians, to chasten them, in order to see if they would respond to it in faith or resist it.

---

[14] Galatians 3:1-5 (emphasis mine)

It doesn't have to be religious ritual and legalism that sets us on the path of reprobating. It can be anything that we willingly or naively allow to turn our affections, passion and focus away from responding in faith to the influences and activities of God's Kingdom in our life. Paul referred to the Galatians' embrace of Jewish legalism and ritual as "a work of the flesh", or that which is opposed to the work of the Spirit. Anything, if it turns our affections, passion and focus away from responding to the activities of the Kingdom of God in our life, is a "work of the flesh". The "flesh" (our unbridled physical and soulish desires) and the Spirit are in opposition to each other in our life.[15] God bought us with a price; the life of His dear Son.[16] As a result, He doesn't want anything or anyone to draw our hearts, affections and passions away from intimate fellowship with Him and the influence of His Kingdom activities. He doesn't want us to give it or them a higher priority and place of prominence in our life. Our God is a jealous God.[17]

Yes, there are many reasons why we may not always respond to God's influence in our life. It could be that we are unaware of the methods by which God influences us, or our inexperience with recognizing when God is influencing us, or our unwillingness to respond because of a fear of failing, or we may have willingly resisted His influence, previously, and therefore have become more resistant to Him influencing our life in this area in the future. Regardless, we willingly choose our response to the influences we receive.

As followers of Jesus we can engage in reprobating and be deceived into doing so; being unwilling to respond to what God is endeavoring to do in our life. We can hinder Him and the activity of His Kingdom in our life through our unawareness, deception, or through attitudes and misconceptions we develop. Through the process of reprobating we can find ourselves suffering from a growing lack of desire, passion, and experiential knowledge and authenticity when it comes to our relationship with God and the workings of His Kingdom in and through our life. He still loves us and desires to work in our life but He will not violate our free will.

God is a patient and loving Father who helps us in our weakness. He understands that we are weak and need His grace and ability in our lives. This is true with developing an intimate relationship with the Holy Spirit and responding to the influences and activities of the Kingdom of God in

---

[15] Galatians 5:16-17
[16] 1Corinthians 6:17, 20
[17] Exodus 34:11-14

our life. He knows that before we became His Kingdom people, we were so accustomed to the ways of this world and living our life according to our five physical senses and our untamed physical and soulish desires.

Now that we are citizens of His Kingdom, we don't just flip a switch and have an established relationship and fellowship with the Holy Spirit, and are able to respond effectively to all of the influences and activities of the Kingdom of God that take place in our life. He knows it takes time for us to train our spiritual senses in order to move from simply responding to the desires of our bodies and souls to responding to the influences of the Holy Spirit and the activities of the Kingdom of God. This is all part of the "purifying" or sanctifying process. It begins when we are born again by the Spirit of God and is completed when we receive our new, glorified bodies at the end of the age.

In the meantime, the Spirit of God teaches, trains and mentors us as we make the transition from living by the "flesh" (our soulish and physical desires and passions) to walking in the Spirit (responding in faith to the influences of the Holy Spirit and the activities of the Kingdom of God). This is the purpose and work of the Holy Spirit in our life in this age. It is those who are being led by the Spirit of God who are sons of God.[18] God knows we will make mistakes along the way as we learn to respond in faith to the Spirit of God and His Kingdom activities in our life. We can't be afraid of failure or making mistakes. It is a completely different orientation for us; living for what God wants for us instead of what we want for ourselves.

Yet, He hasn't left us alone, powerless, and without resources to make this transition. He has given us His Spirit and Kingdom resources to successfully make this transition in our life. The influences and activities of the Kingdom of God are prophetic in their nature and operation in this age and we must be taught and trained to prophetically recognize and respond to His influences as we make this transition. We can't do this if we continue to be dominated by our physical and soulish desires, while being unaware of or resisting the influence and activities of the Spirit.

God looks at our heart and gives us His grace, forgiveness, and ability to make this transition to living as His Kingdom people, when we make mistakes and experience failures. As long as we don't give up and keep our eyes and hearts focused on "the prize", He will work with us and help us grow and mature spiritually (making the transition from walking in the flesh to walking in the Spirit; seeking to know Him and living our lives for Him).

---

[18] Romans 8:12-14

This is a life-long process and endeavor and we won't reach completeness or full maturity in this life. But, we can make great strides in our fellowship and relationship with the Holy Spirit and responding to the influences and activities of the Kingdom of God in this life. These influences and activities are prophetic in nature, in this age but we are prophetic people and we can learn to recognize and respond in faith if we set our hearts to learn and grow.

Now, we not only need intellectual knowledge about God and His Kingdom, which comes through reading the scriptures. We also need revealed knowledge that comes through the revelatory influence of and personal experience with the Holy Spirit. We cannot rely on intellectual, sense-based knowledge and understanding of God, alone, if we are to establish an intimate relationship with the Spirit of God, experience the activities of the Kingdom of God, and resist the deceptions of our spiritual enemy, Satan. There are many people who know what the Bible says but have no experience with the presence and activities of the Holy Spirit and the Kingdom of God.

It is the difference between knowing *about* someone from a book and knowing someone *experientially* through personal relationship and interaction. We need to pursue the intellectual knowledge and understanding of God and His Kingdom but we also need to pursue the revelatory knowledge and understanding of God and the activities of His Kingdom. It is our engaging with the living and active Word of God and experiencing God's Kingdom activities in our life that gives life to and transforms our spirit, soul, and body. Again, Paul tells us, *"…all who are being led by the Spirit of God, these are sons of God."* [19]

Throughout His life and ministry, Jesus recognized and acknowledged that the Kingdom of God was the foundational truth and reality for all that He thought, said and did. How can we expect to effectively understand and experience the truth of the scriptures if we don't comprehend, embrace and experience the reality of God and His Kingdom, on which the scriptures are based? How can we expect to accomplish the plan of God for our lives if we have no understanding and personal experience with God and the present realities and activities of His Kingdom?

"And it was reported to Him, "Your mother and Your brothers are standing outside, wishing to see You." But He answered and said to them, "My mother and My brothers are these ***who hear the word of God and do it,****"".*[20] The word *hear* in this

[19] Rom. 8:14
[20] Luke 8:20-21 (emphasis mine)

verse means *to actively hear*, as opposed to passively hear. To *actively hear* is to hear with the intent to immediately respond and act on what is heard. Jesus tells us that it is these who *actively hear* – who hear and immediately respond and act who are truly His family.

As a result, the Kingdom of God and our relationship with the Holy Spirit is the foundation on which everything else is built, especially as it involves our life as a follower of Jesus. It has been this way from the beginning and it will be this way for all eternity. Even Jesus' mission on earth, including His redemptive death, burial and resurrection, finds its purpose in the Kingdom of God and His reliance upon the Holy Spirit in His life. We must comprehend, embrace and experience the realities of the Kingdom of God and of the Holy Spirit in this life, if we are to effectively proclaim the good news of this same reality as a witness to the nations.

"My people are destroyed because of a lack of knowledge." [21] This is a true statement made by God to His people and it has been true throughout the history of humanity. This word *destroyed* can also be translated *cut-off* or *silenced*. The enemy of God and His people, Satan, is always at work to minimize, confuse and deceive (*silence*) God's people in an effort to distract us and keep us (*cut us off*) from the foundational truth and reality of the Kingdom of God. Yet, God is at work to restore the truth of His Kingdom to the lives of His people. This Kingdom reality will engage the passion of His people, confront the onslaught of evil, and bring forth a Church that is *"a mature man…the measure of the stature which belongs to the fullness of Christ"*.[22]

This book focuses on the Kingdom of God; its nature, presence, and activities in the lives of God's people in this age. We will discover the nature and presence of the Kingdom, how it engages and confronts each of us, and how we can see and experience the activities of the Kingdom in our life and the lives of those around us, as we bear witness to the good news of the Kingdom of God to all nations. Only then will Jesus return to establish the complete manifestation of the Kingdom of God when He comes back to rule the earth.

---

[21] Hosea 4:6a
[22] Ephesians 4:13

Chapter Questions & Notes

Talk It Over....

1) Have you ever thought about why you find it difficult to pray sometimes? Is it difficult to get motivated to pray? Have you thought about the reason(s) behind your lack of motivation to pray?
    a. Take a minute or so and think about why you lack motivation to pray, list 2-3 reasons for your lack of motivation, and talk about them with those in your group:

    b. What did you discover about your difficulties in prayer? Did you discover any commonalities between you and those in your group? Did you gain any insights while talking about these within your group? List those insights here, for future consideration and discussion:

2) As a believer in and follower of Jesus Christ, do you consider yourself a witness of the presence and reality of the Kingdom of God on the earth? If so, what have you witnessed and experienced concerning the Kingdom of God? What do you have and what have you experienced that you can confidently share with other people, that would entice them to become followers of Jesus, themselves? List three Kingdom experiences that you can confidently share with others:

3) When you read the Bible and discover things that God says about Himself, His desire and plans for humanity, and the activities that He wants to engage in with us as human beings; how do you respond to them? Do you always accept them at face value or do they sometimes rub you the wrong way? Do you ever ask God questions about the things that He says in the Bible? When things

happen in your life and the lives of people around you, do these experiences ever make you question what you have read in the Bible about God? If so, how do you respond to them and Him? Do they impact your perception and opinion of God, positively or negatively?

Leaders: Pray with the group and ask the Holy Spirit to lead them in these individual and group activities so He is able to lead them and influence them, as they engage with one another in these thought-provoking questions. The Holy Spirit has something He wants to communicate and accomplish in each of our lives through this exercise and we don't want to rush Him. Therefore, allow enough time for people to engage with the Holy Spirit and for Him to significantly influence their lives, through this activity.

(2)

The Hidden Treasure

"What is the kingdom of God like and to what shall I compare it?" Luke 13:18

Whatever our pursuit in life, it is critical to our success that we possess a central purpose and committed allegiance that directs us, keeps us focused, is worthy of our affections and passion, and deeply influences our every thought, word and deed. As followers of Jesus, there can be only one such allegiance and purpose - the Kingdom of God. As children of God and citizens of His Kingdom we must comprehend, embrace, and passionately pursue the Kingdom of God in our lives - its nature, character, purpose and activities.

There are a number of opinions and perceptions of what the Kingdom of God is. Some believe the Kingdom of God is heaven because this is where His throne is currently located. Others believe it is the nation of Israel because He chose them out of all the nations of the earth to be His people. Others believe the Kingdom of God is the Church, the Body of Christ because they are His New Covenant people. Still others believe the Kingdom of God is the earth and all things that inhabit it because it has been His focus from the beginning. Even though all of these statements accurately express an aspect of the Kingdom of God, none quite captures what it actually is.

A clear understanding of what the Scriptures tell us about the Kingdom of God is fundamentally important to our active involvement in the plan and activities of God. Therefore, I will give you a basic, scriptural definition of the Kingdom of God followed by what the Bible actually says about it. Simply stated, *the Kingdom of God is the rule of God; the sovereignty and authority God possesses enabling Him to rule.* As a result, the Kingdom of God is not limited to heaven, or the Church, or the earth.

Throughout the Scriptures, God's sovereignty and authority to rule is central to His purpose, plans and activities. Righteousness and justice must rule if peace and prosperity are to be the result. Mercy and truth must rule if love and life are to be the fruit. Only God is worthy of such dominion and capable of administrating such a government. It is an absolute blessing when God rules because the foundation of His sovereignty and authority

(His throne) are righteousness, justice, mercy, and truth…they flow from His nature, as He rules.[23] His government has ruled from eternity and it will continue to rule in the ages to come.

God's Kingdom is inclusive, not exclusive, as He desires all of His creation to experience the depth of His eternal love and the purity of His eternal life. The Kingdom of God encompasses the vast heavens, where galaxies, stars and planets continue to be created and expand even today. The Kingdom of God includes humanity and the other creatures of this present earth (Genesis 1), as well as creatures from God's previous creative activities; angels, cherubim, and seraphim.[24] Some reside with God in heaven and some will experience eternal separation from God,[25] having rejected the rule of God. God's Kingdom rule is sovereign and this sovereignty is communicated and exhibited through His revealed nature, purposes, plans and activities within His creation.

When we say God is sovereign, we mean He possesses the absolute right and privilege to do all things as He chooses, for His own good pleasure. What we must understand about God's sovereignty is how He has chosen to apply that sovereignty to His Kingdom purposes, plans and activities involving humanity and throughout His dominion. Nothing or no one can rise above or go beyond His sovereignty or exercise privilege and authority over Him because He is the creator of all things and His sovereign authority is over all things. When we understand this we will better comprehend how His Kingdom rule influences and affects us in our daily lives.

The only limiting factor upon God's influence and actions is what God in His sovereignty chooses to establish, Himself. In His sovereign authority, God can willingly choose to limit His influence and activities, even subjecting them to the will of another, if it accomplishes His purposes and produces the results He ultimately desires. Yet, we know that any limitations God may choose to place upon Himself and His actions are wise and faultless because His nature, character and wisdom are absolutely faultless. No one may bring a charge against God's sovereign will, purposes and activities because He rules in all wisdom and acts according to His complete authority and unquestioned character. The question is not whether God is sovereign but how He chooses to apply His sovereignty in order to accomplish His ultimate purpose, for His own glory and good pleasure.

---

[23] Psalm 85:10; Psalm 89:14

[24] Gen. 19:1; Gen. 28:12; Ps. 91:11; Ps. 103:20; Matt. 4:11; Luke 2:9-15; John 1:51; Heb. 13:2; Rev. 7:1

[25] Ezekiel 28:12-19 ; Isaiah 14:3-15 ; Ephesians 6:12 ; 2Peter 2:4; Jude 1:6

As we will see, the purpose, plans and activities of the Kingdom of God in this present age are focused on the relationship between God and humanity. The Kingdom of God has encountered and engaged humanity from the very beginning and throughout human history. All of God's creations, past and present, are integrated into His present purpose and are engaged in this endeavor.

From the beginning, God delegated His ruling authority to human beings - declaring that we should rule as His Kingdom representatives (regents) over all that He created to inhabit the earth. As a result, when the creatures of the earth experienced the ruling activities of human beings, it was as if they experienced God, Himself, making the decisions and initiating the various activities. To experience the rule of humanity was to experience God's rule with the same character, integrity, justice and righteousness in which God Himself would act.

This "Regency Rule" of humanity was God's plan from the beginning and nothing has changed that plan.[26] We were to establish the Kingdom of God and the environment and culture of the rule of God on the earth as if God was here on the earth ruling it, Himself. This is truly "good news" for humanity. God, in His unquestioned sovereignty, determined and established this as a Kingdom reality.

After Adam and Eve surrendered their regency rule of the earth to Satan, when they chose to obey Satan in the Garden rather than God, Satan established his "domain of darkness" upon the earth and exercised considerable influence over the lives and affairs of the human race. Yet, God did not give up on us and did not give up the earth to the rule of the domain of darkness. God had a plan in place to bring humanity back into His Kingdom and to bring the rule of the earth back under the Kingdom of God. He accomplished this when He sent His Son, Jesus, the God/Man to the earth. When Jesus came, He brought the Kingdom of God and the "good news" message of the Kingdom with Him.

When Jesus came, He came as the Evangelist of this "good news" of the return of the Kingdom of God to the Earth. He also came as the Prophet, Apostle, Pastor and Teacher of this same Kingdom reality. He was sent by the Father to proclaim the mysteries of the Kingdom that had been hidden from ages past and have now been revealed (prophet); to reestablish this "Regency Rule" and the Kingdom foundation and culture upon the earth (apostle); to teach us of the nature of the Father and the operation of His

---

[26] Gen. 1:26; Ps. 8:4-6; Ps. 115:16

Kingdom (teacher); and to lead and guide His Kingdom disciples – watching over them and protecting them from the activities of the enemy (pastor).

When Jesus began His earthly ministry, He went about proclaiming the Kingdom of God everywhere He went. When asked by His disciples what would be the sign of His coming and of the end of the present age, Jesus told them that this good news of the Kingdom of God would be preached throughout the whole world as a witness to the nations and then the end of this present age and the time for His return would come.

At the end of the book of Revelation, we are told that the restoration and completion of all things involving this present purpose and plan of God will be completed when the actual throne of God descends from heaven and is established on the new earth. Earth, is where the rule of His Kingdom will be centered and where He will dwell with His people forever.[27]

God's purpose and plan for humanity in this present age is beyond comprehension and it has eternal ramifications for each and every one of us. This is why we must make every effort to understand the nature, character and activities of the Kingdom of God and set ourselves to experience it in our lives. There is much that He has revealed to us and that we will discover as we encounter His Kingdom activity in and through the lives of people in Bible times, as well as what He is doing up to and including our present time. Experiencing Him and the current activities of His Kingdom will alter our understanding of Christianity and how we live our lives as citizens of His Kingdom from this day forward.

In Matthew 13, Jesus uses seven parables to teach His followers about the Kingdom of God. These seven parables are: 1) *Parable of the Sower*; 2) *Parable of the Tares/Weeds*; 3) *Parable of the Mustard Seed*; 4) *Parable of the Yeast*; 5) *Parable of the Hidden Treasure*; 6) *Parable of the Pearl*; and 7) *Parable of the Net.*[28] Each one of these parables describes the Kingdom of God in relation to the earth and the people of the earth, as a result of the ministry, death, burial and resurrection of Jesus. Each parable describes from a different perspective the gospel or "good news" of the Rule of God coming to the earth. These parables describe the dynamics involved with the rule of God coming to the earth, "invading" the domain of darkness, confronting the people of the earth, and the demands this "invasion" places upon us.

Following is a summary of what Jesus is saying through each parable so we can understand what the "good news" message of the Kingdom of God

[27] Revelation 21:1-9
[28] Matthew 13:1-52

consists of and realize the demands that the Reign of God places upon us as a result of its presence with us.

1. *Parable of the Sower*

This parable compares the message of the Kingdom of God to a seed that is sown. The Kingdom message will encounter four different types of hearts (soil) when it is proclaimed (sown): A) these people don't understand the message of the Reign of God (the seed that falls on the path), so it has no impact upon their hearts or lives; B) these people receive the message of the Reign of God with initial gladness but, subsequently, they allow peer pressure and resistance to the Kingdom message by others to hinder the reality of the message from sinking in and bringing effective change to their lives (seed falling on rocky ground); C) these people receive the message of the Kingdom but the difficulties of life and the pursuit of wealth and riches robs them of the reality of the Kingdom, so the message lies dormant in their hearts and is unable to affect real change in their lives (seed falling among thorns); D) these people receive the message of the Kingdom and understand and embrace it; the message is able to impact and bring effective change and the faith that is produced from this change empowers them to trust in and experience the activities of the Kingdom of God in their lives (seed falling on good soil).

Jesus describes the four different types of people who hear the message of the Reign of God and how it impacts their lives, based on their attitude and lifestyle choices when and after they hear it. How the message impacts their lives is determined by the receptivity of their hearts.

2. *Parable of the Weeds/Tares*

Again, the message of the Kingdom of God is compared to a seed sown on the ground. Yet, there is another seed that is sown, the seed of the domain of darkness and sin. There are two spiritual kingdoms at work on the earth and both are vying for the hearts of men and women. One is the true Kingdom, the reign of God. The other is not a legitimate kingdom (it has been defeated by Jesus) but it is, nevertheless, present on the earth at this time.

At the time God created human beings, His Kingdom ruled on the earth and we were his Regents - His resident rulers. When Adam and Eve sinned against God, Satan took the control given to him by Adam and sowed sin and darkness on the earth. Jesus came to bring the Kingdom of God with Him (wheat) and to defeat the powers of darkness. Now, the Kingdom people of God are going into the domain of darkness throughout this present age to proclaim the good news of the Kingdom and to turn the hearts of people back to God. As a result, Jesus hasn't yet returned to the earth to remove darkness (tares) and to establish His complete reign. He is waiting as long as possible because He desires that none should perish but that all would come to repentance.[29] Jesus is allowing the two kingdoms to exist together until He returns to forcibly remove the domain of darkness and to establish the Kingdom of God on the earth, in its fullness.

3. Parable of the Mustard Seed

The Kingdom of God is compared to a mustard seed which is one of the smallest seeds. When Jesus brought the Kingdom of God with Him, it was not the complete manifestation of the Rule of God. It came in a reduced form, as a seed, in the person of Jesus. Jesus defeated the domain of darkness and ascended to the Father, sending the Holy Spirit into the hearts of His disciples. As a result, the Kingdom of God (the seed) grew and has been growing throughout the last 2000 years. The Kingdom of God is not completely visible but when Jesus returns, it will reign over the entire earth.

4. Parable of the Yeast

The Reign of God is compared to yeast. God took a reduced measure of His Kingdom rule, in the person of Jesus, and mixed it into the makeup and environment of this world through His life, death and resurrection. It began to expand when the Holy Spirit was sent into the hearts and lives of His Kingdom people on the day of Pentecost. This yeast of the Kingdom of God has been mixing and expanding in this world for 2000 years and will be completely mixed in when Jesus returns at the end of the age to establish the fullness of His Kingdom rule on the earth.

5. Parable of the Hidden Treasure

[29] 2Peter 3:9

The Kingdom of God is compared to hidden treasure. It is the most valuable thing on the earth, yet it is difficult to see and experience because it is "hidden" – it is not here in its complete manifestation. When a person discovers the reality and value of the Reign of God, he or she grasps it and embraces it, doing whatever he or she must to have it and to experience it in his or her life as a precious prize.[30]

6. *Parable of the Pearl*

The Rule of God is compared to a priceless pearl. When a person is looking for life's answers and discovers the message and truth of the Reign of God, that person makes whatever personal decisions and lifestyle choices necessary for he/she to embrace, pursue, and experience the Kingdom of God in his/her life.

7. *Parable of the Net*

The Kingdom of God is compared to a net. When Jesus returns to the earth with the full manifestation of the Reign of God, He will forcibly remove the domain of darkness and its disciples in order to establish His complete reign over all the earth. Those who chose to serve the domain of darkness will be separated from those who serve the Kingdom of God.

The Kingdom of God is present and is the most valuable thing on the earth, even though it is not here in its complete manifestation. Yet, even though it is not completely manifest in this age, it is valuable beyond anything else and should be pursued by those who hear and embrace the message of its reality, as a precious prize. We need to understand what the Kingdom of God is if we are to embrace it and pursue it with all of our energy and resources.

[30] Matthew 11:12

Chapter Questions & Notes

Talk It Over....

1) God rules the universe according to His personality and nature, as a person. His nature and character are on display throughout His creation and we can observe creation and get a glimpse of what God is like. What are different aspects of creation and how we can observe the nature and character of God in them?

2) God is sovereign and does all things according to His divine will and for His good pleasure. Identify three things God has sovereignly established that demonstrate His desire and willingness to minimize or share His sovereignty in order to accomplish something He set out to do:

3) Read the parables of the Kingdom of God, in Matthew 13, and identify four ways the Kingdom of God influences our lives as individuals, and how we can embrace and interact with the Kingdom of God in our daily lives:

(3)

"Kingdom" - The Definition

"A nobleman went to a distant country to receive a kingdom for himself, and then return." Luke 19:12

Herod was born in 73 B.C. and became a soldier for Rome as a young man, rising to the rank of General. After the assassinations of Julius Caesar (in Rome) and Herod's father Antipater (Rome's regent in Judaea) in 44 BC, Herod became tetrarch of Galilee, one of several tetrarchs in the region of Judea. When war broke out between Rome and the Parthians in 40 BC, Herod went to Rome and petitioned the Roman emperor Octavian and the Roman Senate to declare him to be the *basileus* – the ruler of Judea. At that time, by decree of Octavian and the Roman Senate, Herod received the governmental authority and sovereignty to rule over all of Judea, while remaining subject to Octavian as ruler of the entire Roman Empire. In 37 BC, Herod, accompanied by the armies of Rome, went back to subdue Judea, his domain, by removing the remaining tetrarchs in the region, by force if necessary, and to establish himself as king. [31]

In 40 B.C., the empire of Rome was well on its way to ruling much of the known world. As a result, it was necessary for the emperor of Rome to share his ruling authority and sovereignty with others, who would then exercise this limited rule in the more remote places of the empire. Rome saw the value of doing this because these designated and delegated rulers would be *on the ground*, closer to the action, and be able to govern with a more *hands-on* approach than Caesar would be able to do from Rome. Therefore, men like Herod were given a level of Caesar's sovereignty and authority in order to effectively rule the domain (people and land) they were commissioned to govern for Rome. These men had no inherent sovereignty and authority of their own with which to rule. They could only rule with what they were given and they had to receive this authority from those who possessed it and were authorized to give it to them.

The sovereignty and authority one possesses, which enables him or her to rule is the basic definition of *kingdom*. It is also the Biblical definition.

---

[31] LIVIUS – Articles on Ancient History (www.livius.org/he-hg/herodians/herod_the_great01.html)

Today, we often confuse kingdom with domain. We often say that a person's kingdom is the people and land they rule or govern. In a very broad sense, this is true. Yet, in order to have a domain over which you rule or govern, you must possess the sovereignty and authority to rule it in the first place. In addition, you must receive this sovereignty and authority from those who possess it and have the authority and ability to give it to you. This is called *receiving the kingdom* or receiving the authority and sovereignty to rule. The domain is determined by the scope of the sovereignty and authority that a person receives. The domain is the people and land over which a person exercises their sovereignty and authority to rule.

It is important to make the distinction between the sovereignty and authority one possesses to rule and the domain over which one rules, when defining "kingdom" because a person can receive the sovereignty and authority to rule (the kingdom) and not be actively ruling over a domain. Throughout human history, kings have been over-thrown and/or gone into exile. They remain kings but they do not actively rule a domain. The exercise of their kingdom has been delayed or suspended.

Those who gave them the sovereignty and authority to rule did not necessarily retract it from them. Yet, the domain over which they rule may require time and/or preparation before their rule begins. If they have already ruled, the domain could have been ceased maliciously by someone else, or the king could have left the domain in order to return to rule it at a later time. Therefore, it is important for us to separate the sovereignty and authority one possesses to rule from the domain over which one rules if we are to understand the Biblical view of kingdom and the reality and dynamic operation of the Kingdom of God.

The Bible and "Kingdom"

"The Lord has established His throne in the heavens, and ***His sovereignty* (kingdom)** ***rules over all****. Bless the Lord, all you works of His,* ***in all places of His dominion;"*** Psalm 103:19, 22 (emphasis mine)

The Bible reinforces this definition of *kingdom* in several places. One reference is in a parable where Jesus speaks to the people following Him, who were expecting the Kingdom of God to come immediately. We find the parable in Luke 19:11-27.

"While they were listening to these things, Jesus went on to tell a parable because He was near Jerusalem and they supposed that the kingdom of God was going to appear immediately. So He said, 'A nobleman went to a distant country to receive a kingdom for

himself and then return. And he called ten of his slaves and gave them ten minas and said to them, 'Do business with this until I come back.' But his citizens hated him and sent a delegation after him, saying, 'We do not want this man to reign over us.'"

"When he returned, after receiving the kingdom, he ordered that these slaves, to whom he had given the money, be called to him so that he might know what business they had done. The first appeared, saying, 'Master, your mina has made ten minas more.' And he said to him, 'Well done, good slave, because you have been faithful in a very little thing, you are to be in authority over ten cities.' The second came, saying, 'Your mina, master, has made five minas.' And he said to him also, 'And you are to be over five cities.' Another came, saying, 'Master, here is your mina, which I put away in a handkerchief; for I was afraid of you, because you are an exacting man; you take up what you did not lay down and reap what you did not sow.'"

"He said to him, 'By your own words I will judge you, you worthless slave. Did you know that I am an exacting man, taking up what I did not lay down and reaping what I did not sow? 'Then why did you not put my money in the bank, and having come, I would have collected it with interest?' Then he said to the bystanders, 'Take the mina away from him and give it to the one who has the ten minas.' And they said to him, 'Master, he has ten minas already.' I tell you that to everyone who has, more shall be given, but from the one who does not have, even what he does have shall be taken away. But these enemies of mine, who did not want me to reign over them, bring them here and slay them in my presence."

Here, Jesus gives us the process by which a person receives the kingdom. In this parable, a nobleman leaves the geographic location where he resides in order to go to a distant country to receive the kingdom from those who both possess it and can give him the sovereignty and authority to rule it. Once he is with these distant sovereigns, in spite of and over the objections of the delegation of people from the nobleman's homeland, the sovereigns give this nobleman the kingdom and they designate his homeland as the specific domain over which he will rule; much like Octavian and the Roman Senate gave Herod the kingdom over Judaea, in the previous example. Once the nobleman receives the kingdom, he returns to the geographic location of his domain, possessing the kingdom, and he begins to rule and subdue it.

A ruler must, either, possess the sovereignty and authority inherently, or he/she must make petition to receive it from those who actually possess this sovereignty and authority. This kingdom can be given unconditionally or with conditions attached to it, based on appropriate performance or satisfying specific requirements.

Another reference for the Biblical definition of *kingdom* is located in 1Samuel, where we find God working in the life of a young man named David.

"Now the Lord said to Samuel, "How long will you grieve over Saul, since I have rejected him from being king over Israel? Fill your horn with oil and go; I will send you to Jesse the Bethlehemite, for I have selected a king for Myself among his sons." "So Samuel did what the Lord said, and came to Bethlehem…Jesse made seven of his sons pass before Samuel. But Samuel said to Jesse, "The Lord has not chosen these." And Samuel said to Jesse, "Are these all the children?" And he said, "There remains yet the youngest, and behold, he is tending the sheep." Then Samuel said to Jesse, "Send and bring him; for we will not sit down until he comes here." So he sent and brought him in. Now he was ruddy, with beautiful eyes and a handsome appearance. And the Lord said, "Arise, anoint him; for this is he." Then Samuel took the horn of oil and anointed him in the midst of his brothers; and the Spirit of the Lord came mightily upon David from that day forward." 1Samual 16:1,4,10-13

In this scripture we see an individual (David) receiving a kingdom (sovereignty and authority to rule). But, we see a different form of the kingdom process taking place. In this example, we see the one who possesses the sovereignty and authority to rule (the kingdom) go to a particular person and give that person the kingdom in order to rule over a particular domain – in this case the people and geographic area of Israel. God, the absolute possessor of the sovereignty and authority over the entire earth, goes to the home of Jesse, through His Kingdom representative Samuel, to give David the sovereignty and authority to rule over the domain of Israel.

God gave Samuel authority to act as His human agent in this Kingdom transaction, but it was God giving David the kingdom of Israel. David did not go to God to request it from Him. God went to David to give it to him. Even though another man, Saul, was ruling Israel at the time and David did not begin ruling the domain of Israel for years, the kingdom (the sovereignty and authority to rule Israel) had been given to David by God.

Sovereignty & Authority

Sovereignty is the status, dominion, power, and authority belonging to a sovereign. It is the supreme and independent power and authority in government as possessed or claimed by a person, state or community.[32] In

[32] Dictionary.com

Biblical terms, *Sovereignty* (Heb: *Mamlakah*) means kingdom, dominion, or reign.[33] Sovereignty is the ability to self-determine and exercise supreme influence or control, while being free from external accountability or counter-controls. A sovereign entity exercises supreme influence and self-determined control over the activities and affairs of its domain.

In terms of all creation, God is all-sovereign. His Kingdom is over all and unchallenged. He self-determines everything pertaining to all of His creation, which includes all created things in Heaven, throughout the universe, and on the earth. He exercises supreme influence and control over all aspects of His creation, and He is free from any external accountability or counter-controls. No one can bring a charge against His authority and sovereignty, nor can they act as His counselor regarding His actions, thoughts and words.[34] God subjects Himself to no one for permission to act - all of His actions are established after the counsel of His will.[35]

The Biblical definition of *authority* (Gr: *exousia*) is the power of influence and privilege. A person possesses the *right* and *ability* to act, in order to fulfill, accomplish or enforce. The sovereign of a nation or of any other community of people possesses authority over all matters involving and affecting that community, no matter how large or small the community is. This authority is part of the *kingdom* this sovereign possesses. The sovereign may not be an individual at all but may be the community itself. The community would choose a group of people or an individual from within the community to exercise governing authority for the entire community and to answer to the community for the manner in which they govern. The kingdom belongs to the community and is delegated by the community to the representative group or person so they can execute the day-to-day plans and activities of the community government. In all cases there is a sovereign who possesses the kingdom. Without it, there would be anarchy and rampant lawlessness.

God possesses all authority in the universe. He possesses all power of influence and of privilege. He possesses the unchallenged right and ability to act in order to fulfill, accomplish and enforce His will and purposes throughout His dominion. Who among us can legitimately say to God, "What are you doing? By what authority do you do these things?"[36] God's authority gives Him the right and privilege to determine and execute anything and everything He chooses to do, according to His own will, by

[33] StudyLight.org
[34] Isaiah 40:13
[35] Ephesians 1:11
[36] Ecclesiastes 8:4-5

His limitless ability, and for His own good pleasure. In His complete sovereignty and authority, God has established times, seasons, and the entire process by which the universe exists and operates.

It is not for us to stand in the face of God and demand to know why he has established creation the way He has. It is for us to seek to know Him and to understand the ways in which He has chosen to establish His creation. We do this so we can cooperate with Him and experience the joy and blessings of working with Him and not to resist Him and work against Him.

If possessing the kingdom is possessing the sovereignty and authority to rule, and the manner in which a sovereign exercises his sovereignty and authority has such a tremendous impact upon the domain he rules over, then it is important for the citizens of that domain to understand who it is who rules over them and what they can expect from this sovereign's rule.

<u>Chapter Questions & Notes</u>

Talk It Over....

1) *Kingdom* is the sovereignty and authority one possesses in order to rule a domain. The kingdom may belong to an individual or to a community of people. Looking at the different forms of government present on the earth, list a few of the different kinds of kingdoms and describe how the *kingdom process* works within each form of government:

2) As the absolute sovereign in the universe, God, as the creator and sustainer of all things, enjoys the right and privilege of ruling the universe as He sees fit and for His own good pleasure. Identify 5 things God has chosen to establish within creation that contributes to His rule over the earth and that affects us all on a daily basis:

Leaders: It is important that we understand what *kingdom* means and how sovereignty and authority are foundational to the effective rule of a sovereign within his or her domain. Encourage those in your groups to spend adequate time discussing the nature and characteristics of *kingdom* because this foundational understanding is critical to our ability to grasp the Kingdom of God and what we will be studying about the Kingdom of God throughout the rest of this book.

(4)

The Foundation of His Throne

The Character of the Kingdom

"The Lord reigns, let the earth rejoice; let the many islands be glad. Clouds and thick darkness surround Him; ***righteousness and justice are the foundation of His throne.****"* Psalm 97:2 (emphasis mine)

"Thus says the Lord, "Let not a wise man boast of his wisdom, and let not the mighty man boast of his might, let not a rich man boast of his riches; but let him who boasts boast of this, that he understands and knows Me, ***that I am the Lord who exercises lovingkindness, justice and righteousness on earth****; for I delight in these things," declares the Lord."* Jeremiah 9:23-24 (emphasis mine)

In the movie, "*Gladiator*"[37], the Roman emperor Marcus Aurelius is ill and very near death. Knowing that he will soon die, the emperor begins to "set his house in order" by taking the steps to set in place and announce his successor. The emperor calls for his trusted general, General Maximus, and proceeds to tell Maximus that he wants to establish him as the next emperor of Rome. He tells Maximus that the reason he wants him to be the next emperor is so Maximus can return the rule of Rome back to the Senate, making it a republic again.

When Maximus asks the emperor why he is not establishing his son, Commodus, as the next emperor, he is told that Commodus lacks the necessary character qualities or virtues to be emperor. Marcus Aurelius tells Maximus that Commodus must not rule. Later, when the emperor meets with his son, Commodus, to inform him of his decision to name Maximus as the next emperor, Commodus responds, in this dialogue:

Marcus Aurelius: "*Are you ready to do your duty for Rome?*"

[37] "Gladiator"; 2000 – DreamWorks Pictures

Commodus: *"Yes, father."*

Marcus Aurelius: *"You will not be emperor."*

Commodus: *"Which wiser, older man is to take my place?"*

Marcus Aurelius: *"My powers will pass to Maximus, to hold in trust until the Senate is ready to rule once more. Rome is to be a republic again."*

Commodus: *"Maximus?"*

Marcus Aurelius: *"Yes. My decision disappoints you?"*

Commodus: *"You wrote to me once, listing the four chief virtues: Wisdom, justice, fortitude and temperance. As I read the list, I knew I had none of them. But I have other virtues, father. Ambition. That can be a virtue when it drives us to excel. Resourcefulness, courage, perhaps not on the battlefield, but... there are many forms of courage. Devotion, to my family and to you. But none of my virtues were on your list. Even then it was as if you didn't want me for your son."*

Marcus Aurelius: *"Oh, Commodus. You go too far."*

Commodus: *"I search the faces of the gods...for ways to please you, to make you proud. One kind word, one full hug...where you pressed me to your chest and held me tight, would have been like the sun on my heart for a thousand years. What is it in me that you hate so much?"*

Marcus Aurelius: *"Shh, Commodus."*

Commodus: *"All I've ever wanted was to live up to you, Caesar. Father."*

Marcus Aurelius: [*Marcus Aurelius gets down on his knees*] *"Commodus. Your faults as a son, is my failure as a father. Come…"*
[*Gives Commodus a hug*]

Commodus: [*Commodus hugs Marcus and cries*] *"Father. I would have butchered the whole world... if you would only love me! "* [*Commodus begins to asphyxiate Marcus while they hug, Marcus grunts and dies*]

To rule legitimately, one must inherently possess the sovereignty and authority to rule or he/she must receive it from those who possess it and are willing to give it to him/her. In the example of Marcus Aurelius and Commodus, Commodus did not receive the kingdom legitimately from Marcus Aurelius. Marcus was unwilling to give the kingdom to Commodus.

Instead, Commodus ceased it by force - by murder; usurping the throne and ruling as an illegitimate emperor until his death.

In contrast, when Jesus taught His disciples about the Kingdom of God, He used the parable of a nobleman who went away to a distant country to receive a kingdom and then returned.[38] He said that the nobleman left the land in which he was residing to go to a distant country to receive the authority and sovereignty to rule, and then returned to his land in order to rule and subdue it.

The Biblical explanation of *kingdom* now helps us understand the context and message of the following scripture located in the book of Isaiah. In this prophecy, we see the leadership style of God shining through. In this prophecy of the coming of the Kingdom of God to the earth in the person of Jesus Christ, we are told that the character of this King is the very character of God. In addition, God says He will accomplish this activity with great zeal and passion. The character and nature of God motivating and supporting His Kingdom rule is not passive. Therefore, the leadership style that accomplishes His Kingdom activity is passionately directed.

"The people who walk in darkness will see a great light; those who live in a dark land, the light will shine on them. You shall multiply the nation, you shall increase their gladness; they will be glad in Your presence as with the gladness of harvest, as men rejoice when they divide the spoil. For You shall break the yoke of their burden and the staff on their shoulders, the rod of their oppressor…For a child will be born to us, a son will be given to us; and The government will rest on His shoulders; and His name will be called Wonderful Counselor, Mighty God, Eternal Father, Prince of Peace. There will be no end to the increase of His government or of peace, on the throne of David and over his kingdom, ***to establish it and to uphold it with justice and righteousness*** *from then on and forevermore. The zeal of the Lord of hosts will accomplish this.'"* Isaiah 9:2-4a,6,7 (emphasis mine)

In this scripture, we see that God recognizes the issues of the human race which need to be addressed with the installation of this King:

- People live and walk in spiritual darkness
- They carry an oppressive yoke that is burdensome

We also see in this scripture that God's Kingdom activity will come and affect the human race by:

- Shining the spiritual light of His Kingdom on them
- Increasing their gladness and rejoicing

[38] Luke 19:11-27

- Breaking their oppressive yoke

After He tells us what the effects of His Kingdom activities will be, He tells us what He is going to do to accomplish this:

- A son of Man, like ourselves, will come to us - given to us by God
- The presence and activity of the Kingdom and the destiny of the Kingdom of God regarding us will rest on Him
- He will be God in a human body, with the nature and character of God motivating and energizing the Father's Kingdom activities through him
- He will bring the light of truth of the Kingdom of God to us
- He will release us from our oppressive, burdensome yoke
- He will reestablish the rule of the Kingdom of God on the earth through us, and
- He will sit as its human King and Ruler when He returns to the earth, according to God's promise to David

How did God demonstrate His Kingdom leadership towards us? He demonstrated His godly character and nature by:

- Coming alongside of us to serve, deliver, and help us in the person of Jesus Christ
- He instructed us in His Kingdom's nature and character, through the person of Jesus Christ
- He bore the burden of bringing us and Himself together again in intimate fellowship, through the person of Jesus Christ
- He reestablished us as co-laborers and Kingdom rulers with Him forever, through the person of Jesus Christ
- He reestablished the Kingdom rule of the human race, according to the nature and character of God, through the person of Jesus Christ
- God was not passive; He was zealous and took the initiative.

When Jesus died on the cross and was resurrected, He went away to a far country (ascended into heaven) to receive a kingdom from the Father. He did not go to receive authority and sovereignty to rule in Heaven. He already possessed this as the second Person of the Trinity.[39] Every heavenly creature already bowed its knee to Him as God. Jesus went to Heaven to receive the authority and sovereignty from the Father to rule over the earth as a human being, as Adam was authorized to do, as one of us.[40] While on

[39] John 18:36-37

earth, Jesus had accomplished all that was required of Him to reestablish us to our relationship with God and as the rightful heirs to the regency rule of the Kingdom of God on earth – defeating the god of this world, Satan, and the domain of darkness.[41]

Therefore, God has given Him all authority - the name that is above every name in heaven and on earth.[42] Now, every creature in heaven, on earth, and in the domain of darkness will bow its knee to Him. Jesus now possesses all authority in heaven and on earth – as God and as a Human,[43] and we will rule with Him when He returns to the earth to rule over it and subdue it; as well as in the ages to come.[44]

We do not yet see all things subjected to Jesus and the Kingdom of God.[45] When Jesus does return, He must and will forcibly subdue and subject all earthly kingdoms and authorities to His rule. [46] He must and will eradicate the domain of darkness and its disciples from His Kingdom;[47] and He will rule the earth with a rod of iron.[48] Therefore, when we think that Jesus is slow to return and to setup His Kingdom on earth, we must understand that Jesus is not slow as some consider slowness but He is being patient to all because He does not want any to perish but for all to come to repentance.[49]

As a result, He is waiting as long as He can so that as many people as possible can repent and turn to His Kingdom before He must come back to rule. This is why He has placed us here as His Kingdom representatives in this age – to demonstrate the character of the King and the activities of His Kingdom to the people around us, as a witness; and to come alongside of them in order to serve them in an effort to reconcile them to God, through Jesus Christ.[50]

For this reason, the influence of the nature and character of God on His Kingdom rule is very important for us to understand because it affects and influences our Kingdom leadership and activities in this present age and in the ages to come. We can only develop the nature and character of God on

---

[40] Daniel 7:13-14
[41] 1Peter 3:21-22; 1John 3:8
[42] Philippians 2:5-11
[43] Matthew 28:17-20
[44] Daniel 7:18,26-27; 2Timothy 2:12; Revelation 2:26-27; Revelation 20:6
[45] Hebrews 2:8
[46] Revelation 11:15
[47] Isaiah 11:1-10; Revelation 20:1-3
[48] Psalm 2:8-10; Revelation 12:5; Revelation 19:14-16
[49] 2Peter 3:3-10
[50] 2Corinthians 5:18-19

the inside of us as we experience His nature and character first-hand – in intimate fellowship and relationship with Him through the Holy Spirit. Therefore, intimate relationship with the King is the foundation for Kingdom leadership and Kingdom ruling. Without it, we lead and rule through impersonal methods and principles with little Kingdom life, truth and experience motivating it. Leadership and ruling apart from Kingdom relationship and reality will only lead to oppression and legalism.

The will and purpose of God, then, is relationship – specifically, His establishment of an intimate personal relationship with each individual whom He has created and placed on this earth. Everything else is of secondary importance in this redemptive age in which we live. Therefore, projects, programs, activities and methods alone cannot accomplish the will of God in our lives, and are of secondary importance in regard to what we do and how we live.

We can deceive ourselves regarding the perceived value of these secondary priorities because they may seem to be extremely important to us. Yet, they are empty and powerless if they do not flow from God's presence within our own hearts, or do not draw our hearts and the hearts of others closer to Him. Conversely, the nature and character of God residing in and flowing from our hearts, developed in intimate relationship with Him, will accomplish the will of God with the life and power of God, in and through our lives. It brings the presence of the nature and character of God Himself to bear in all that we do – giving Kingdom life and purpose to all of our internal and external behavior and activities.

If we look at all the things God does and says in the scriptures, we can see the heart of a Person who wants to reveal and share Himself, and all that He is and has, with those He created. All of His words and all of His activities spring from that one motivation – the desire for intimate relationship and fellowship. If we do not see and comprehend this, we will completely miss the reason for what God has done, is doing, and will do. We will relegate the scriptures to a code of religious conduct and relegate God to a disinterested supreme being who lives in a far-away place, caring little and engaging in little interaction with the people He has created.

If what I have said about God and His Kingdom leadership style is true, then we should see evidence of His character qualities in the scriptures and in His words and activities toward humanity. We should not see a disinterested being who dictates terms, with little interest or desire to interact with His creation. We should see a Person who willingly and passionately engages His creation and comes alongside to help where His creatures lack understanding and ability and are unable to help themselves.

If this is what God is like, then we should live from His nature and character which resides in and motivates our own hearts.

The Holy Spirit, the Spirit of God, the Spirit of Christ, is the most important relationship we have in this world as the Kingdom people of God. We need to know, understand and embrace Him and the reasons why God gave Him to us. The Holy Spirit is the seal of our redemption and our inheritance,[51] and the one who reveals God's will, purposes and activities to us.[52] Knowing and living according to this truth will mean the difference between simply going through the motions of Christianity and dynamically experiencing the Kingdom of God in our lives as God intends. Let's find out how important the Holy Spirit is to us, as God's Kingdom people.

---

[51] 2Corinthiams 1:21-22; Ephesians 1:13-14
[52] John 16:13-14

Chapter Questions & Notes

Talk It Over….

1) Review Isaiah 9:2-7, referenced early in this chapter. As you read, ask yourself these questions; "Who is saying these words? Who is this person talking to? How does this person know these things, to be able to communicate them hundreds and thousands of years before they actually occur?" Based on your answers to these questions, what is your opinion of this person? Do they have any credibility with you? Why? If they were to say anything else, would you listen to them and have the confidence in them to take their words to heart and respond to what they say? Why? Write down your answers:

2) We know that God can do whatever He wants to do, whenever He wants to do it. We know that Satan and evil are no match for Jesus, so why does God seem to be so slow to put an end to Satan and evil? Why doesn't Jesus just get rid of Satan, now, once and for all time? If He did, how would that affect the human race? How would that affect God's plan to "fill His house" with His followers? How would that affect you and me, today? Write down your answers:

(5)

The Regency Rule Of The Human Race

"Then God said, 'Let Us make man in Our image, according to Our likeness; and ***let them rule'****...and God said to them, "Be fruitful and multiply, and fill the earth,* ***and subdue it;****"* Genesis 1:26, 28 (emphasis mine)

In Genesis 1 we have the Biblical account describing God's creation of the heavens and the earth. This account begins with the statement, *"In the beginning, God..."* [53] This simple statement establishes a very important truth which stands as the foundation for all other truths. It is a truth that defies all logic and intellectual comprehension. Yet, it is a truth that can and must be accepted through simple child-like faith or it will render us completely deaf, blind and powerless to understand the essential purpose for our existence. This foundational truth, which drives all others, is the existence and universal government of the Kingdom of God. If we do not establish this truth as the bedrock of our faith and our purpose for living, our past, present and future have no meaning or purpose. Or, as a wise man once said, "Vanity of vanities, all is vanity". [54]

God understands the importance of this truth to the human race and to all creation because He created us. Therefore, He established this truth within us from the very beginning.[55] According to His eternal purpose and plan, God established a purpose and destiny for His creation and provided complete ongoing support for it. As Creator, Owner and Ruler of all things, God and the administration of His Kingdom exercises complete dominion and jurisdiction over creation. Heaven, the current geographic location of the government and administration of God, is a real place. It is not a state of mind or a land born out of myth and imagination. It is eternal in its nature and characteristics but is more real than this planet on which we live.[56]

Genesis tells us that God created the earth, as well as the plants, sea creatures, and land animals that inhabit it. He then fashioned a unique species of being in His own image and according to His own likeness. Into this being God breathed the breath of life, His own life, depositing within

---

[53] Genesis 1:1
[54] Ecclesiastes 12:8
[55] Ecclesiastes 3:11
[56] Psalm 46:1-5

humanity, His own quality of life. This life, too, is eternal in its nature. It seems obvious that God had something very special in mind for this being when He created it. It was to have a purpose and destiny uniquely different from any other of God's created beings.

Then, in Genesis 1, God declared His purpose for this unique being, *"…let them rule over the fish of the sea and over the birds of the sky and over the cattle and over all the earth, and over every creeping thing that creeps on the earth…Be fruitful and multiply, and fill the earth, and subdue it…"* [57] Here we see an amazing thing. The God and King of the universe declared a being other than Himself to be ruler over part of His creation. God created this being in His own image and likeness and He declared that it should rule. Yet, not only did God declare it to be ruler, He commanded it to subdue the earth. This word translated *subdue* actually means; *"…to tread upon; to bring into subjection by assault or by force."*[58] The role and function God gave humanity within His creation is not to be taken lightly or approached passively. It is to be entered into with passion, energy, and commitment.

In order for us to be successful in what God commissioned us to do on His behalf, God gave us the necessary spiritual, physical and natural resources we needed. When God declared, *"…and let them rule over the earth…and subdue it,"* God both imparted and delegated to us His own nature, character, ability (power), and authority to rule and subdue the earth as if He was here to do it, Himself, while He maintained His throne in heaven. Humanity's rule on the earth was to be the next best thing to God ruling it, Himself.

As a result, God equipped us with everything we would need to carry out our assignment successfully, regardless of what confronted us in the course of those duties. God chose and equipped us to operate as His regents *over* His creation, as well as His agents *to* His creation. We were chosen to function as the Trinity's sole representative to the earth.

As with any relationship where a person or group represents the desires and interests of another, the most important element is an established personal and intimate relationship between them. Without this depth of relationship in place, our ability to effectively represent the Kingdom of God to this creation would be impossible. When God created us, He created us in perfect relationship to Himself. Yet, God did not create us as robots who have no choice but to be in this relationship with Him and to do His will. We were created free-will beings with, both, the ability and the opportunity to choose to be or not to be in this relationship with God.

---

[57] Genesis 1:26-28

[58] "Old Testament Word Studies" by William Wilson; 1978, Kregel Publications; Pg. 427

It doesn't matter if our relationship with God involves being a regent, an ambassador, a messenger, a mediator, a king, a priest, a prophet, an apostle, a son, a daughter, or any other representative relationship for the Kingdom of God. We must be engaged in the relationship and its associated activities of our own free will; not having it forced upon us.

In order for us to act or speak on behalf of God, we must be actively engaged with God in a personal, intimate relationship. This type of relationship is essential because we must be able to see what God is doing, hear what He is saying, and know how, when, and why God wants to do or say it. An individual or group must know His plans and purposes so that they are able to anticipate what He would do in any given situation. They must be able to respond accordingly, just as God would respond if He was present doing it Himself. How can we represent Him effectively if we don't know these things? What person would allow someone else to represent him or her, and their interests, in such important matters without having this intimate knowledge and relationship? The more personal or critically important the task, the more intimate the relationship must be between God and those who represent His Kingdom. Without this intimacy of relationship, there can be no effective representation of God and His Kingdom.

We see this level of relationship existing between God and Adam in the Garden of Eden. God manifested His presence and revealed His will to Adam, His regent, in the Garden when He made known to him His plans and purposes for creation.[59] Again, God manifested Himself to Adam when He brought the various birds and beasts of the earth to him in the Garden, and deferred to Adam in the naming of these creatures.[60] God and Adam established and built a strong, intimate relationship that served as the basis for humanity's role as the Regent and Administrator of the Kingdom of God on earth.

The nature and depth of intimacy God and Adam developed in the Garden is what God desires to develop with each one of His redeemed people. This same type of relationship existed and was developed between Jesus and the Father. God did not love Adam more than He loves us, and the Father does not love Jesus more than He loves us. In fact, Jesus tells us that the Father loves each of us just as much as the Father loves Him.[61] Consider the level of intimacy and relationship God developed with Abraham, Moses

---

[59] Genesis 1:28-31; 2:16-17
[60] Genesis 2:19-20
[61] John 17:23,26

and David and they were unredeemed men who were not yet born again and citizens of the Kingdom of God.[62] Jesus even said that there was no greater person born of a woman than John the Baptist, yet, the one who is least in the Kingdom of God is greater than John.[63]

God did not reveal and manifest Himself to Adam, to the degree He did, because He loved Adam more than He loves us. The Father did not reveal and manifest Himself to Jesus, to the degree He did, because Jesus was God or because God loves Jesus more than He loves us. God revealed and manifested Himself to Adam and Jesus to the degree He did because their top priority and activity was centered on establishing and building an intimate, personal relationship with God. They both knew and understood they could not accomplish God's purposes on the earth without an intimate, growing relationship with God. They knew their activities meant nothing and accomplished little apart from this relationship.

Granted, Adam and Jesus did not have the effects of sin in their bodies, minds and spirits to deal with, as we do. Yet, we have been born again by the Spirit of God and our spirits have been recreated by God. We have a much greater ability and capacity for developing a deep, vibrant and intimate relationship with God than we think. Look at what Moses, David, Elijah, Daniel and others under the Old Covenant did, and they were people who were not born again and did not have the Holy Spirit living inside of them. God will take us as far as we desire to go, in our relationship with Him. It all comes down to how much we want it and what we are willing to do to develop it.

It is not the amount of activity we conduct on God's behalf that makes us successful. It is the consistent development of our intimate relationship with Him that is key. Experiencing this consistent, intimate relationship produces the trust, faith and provision necessary for His Kingdom activities to be accomplished, no matter how great or small the task may be.

[62] James 2:22-23; Exodus 33:11; Acts 13:22
[63] Luke 7:28

Chapter Questions & Notes

Talk It Over....

1) God established someone other than Himself to rule within His universal domain. What kind of destiny does this create for this being? What sense of loyalty does this produce within this being? What level of honor does this bestow upon this being? What sort of response toward God should we expect to see from this being? Write down your answers:

2) If God provided everything humanity would require to represent the rule of God to the creatures of the earth, do you think that this provision still exists if God's purpose and commission for this being hasn't changed? What would keep humanity from fulfilling their divine destiny and exercising the loyalty toward God that you would expect to see from them? Write down your answers:

Leader: Encourage the members of the group to thoroughly discuss these questions before they write down their answers because they will find that these questions become highly personal when we realize that we must answer these questions about ourselves. It is important to make these questions personal.

(6)

When Earth Encounters The Kingdom Of God

"…according to the power of God, who has saved us and called us with a holy calling…according to His own purpose and grace which was granted us in Christ Jesus from all eternity, ***but now has been revealed*** *by the appearing of our Savior Christ Jesus."* II Timothy 1:8-9 (emphasis mine)

"Then I fell at his feet to worship him. But he said to me, "Do not do that! I am a fellow servant with you and with your brothers who rely on what Jesus is saying. Worship God because ***what Jesus is saying, is the spirit of prophecy.****""* Revelation 19:10 (emphasis mine)

The Church is comprised of God's Kingdom people on the earth. As His kingdom people, we are to communicate with and receive communication from God concerning His Kingdom activities taking place here on the earth. The question is; *"As His Kingdom people on earth, how do we, on earth, interact with a God whose geographic location is in heaven? How are we supposed to know and respond to what He wants us to do at any given time?"* How do we with physical bodies and senses communicate with someone who is spirit and not readily accessible to our physical bodies and senses? Yes, we have the Bible which is the written word of God but the Bible is black ink on white paper and doesn't give us "up to the minute" instructions as to what God may want us to do at any given time or in any given place.

God is always active and involved in His Kingdom, and the activities of His Kingdom, throughout the universe. He is not sitting idly by, disinterested and disengaged from His Kingdom rule, plans and activities. As Jesus tells us regarding His own earthly ministry, *"But He answered them, "My Father is working until now and I Myself am working,""*.[64] As we will discover, God and His Kingdom are very active on earth and in the lives of people, especially in the lives of His Kingdom people. Yet, He is not involved in a face-to-face manner as He was with Adam in the Garden. He is involved prophetically

[64] John 5:17

in the activities of earth through the work of the Holy Spirit and the agency of His Kingdom people, the Church.

For most of us, as followers of Jesus, we tend to equate anything *prophetic* with something a prophet does, especially as it relates to the prophets in the Old Testament. Upon reading the New Testament, we see that God continued His prophetic work in similar ways through individuals like Jesus, Paul, Peter, John and others.

The Apostle Paul, in his New Testament writings, tells us that all new covenant believers (*covenant* and *testament* mean the same thing) are endowed with grace gifts (impartations and manifestations of His grace) by the Holy Spirit for the sole purpose of communicating with God and engaging in the activities of the Kingdom of God with those around us.[65] These gifts are prophetic because they are spiritual in nature but they actively function within this natural world in order to accomplish what God wants to do or say. These spiritual manifestations and operations help to bridge the gap between the spiritual and the natural, between God and humanity, and are necessary to our being involved with the present day activities of the Kingdom of God in this world.

As followers of Jesus today, we still live under the authority and power of the New Covenant scriptures as they are written in the Bible. We don't live under a new New Covenant or an alternative New Covenant or an updated New Covenant. Therefore, all of the New Covenant instructions, resources, promises, gifts, ministries, manifestations, and endowments that appear in the Bible are still valid, available and necessary for us today. Nothing has been taken away from us and they still mean the same for us today as they did back in the first century and throughout church history. Likewise, the onset of our "advanced" culture, technology, medicine, knowledge, tools, and resources doesn't mean that we don't need all of the New Covenant instructions, resources, promises, gifts, ministries, manifestations, and endowments that God has given us and that appear in the Bible. We need all that Jesus gave us, as His followers; Jesus gave them to us for a reason.

God's word is timeless; His gifts and promises are timeless; the physical and spiritual needs of people are timeless; and the abilities and presence of the Holy Spirit are timeless and needed just as much today (if not more) as they were in the first century. To think otherwise is to ignore what the scriptures tell us about sin, the depravity of humanity, and the presence of demonic forces in this world bent on the destruction of humanity, regardless of how culturally "advanced" we may think we are. To entertain this mindset is to

---

[65] 1Cor. 12:7

let down our guard and to relinquish the arsenal of weapons and resources God saw fit to give us, and that He knows we need, regardless of when in the New Covenant time line we live. God gave us what He did for a reason so who are we to reason otherwise and second-guess Him and His provision?

The Nature Of The Kingdom Of God In This Present Age

To put it simply, a New Covenant Prophet is a person God has called, equipped and provided with a distinctive enablement to pursue, experience, and engage in the instructing, training and mentoring of other followers of Jesus in the scriptural teachings, communications and manifestations associated with the prophetic activities of the Kingdom of God.

We have the ministry designation and Kingdom purpose of the Prophet identified and explained to us in the New Covenant scriptures, along with the other ministry designations of Apostle, Evangelist, Pastor and Teacher. Jesus gave us the ministry of the Prophet (and the other Ascension gifts of Christ) for a distinct reason and for a specific purpose.[66] This hasn't changed over the centuries because the nature of the Kingdom of God and its activities, the mission of the Church, the activities of our enemy, and the spiritual needs of all of us in this present age haven't changed. The Church hasn't yet *"attained to the unity of the faith, to the knowledge of the Son of God, to a mature man, to the measure of the stature that belongs to the fullness of Christ."* [67] This is the condition that the followers of Jesus will find themselves, when these ascension gifts are no longer relevant and necessary for us. Until then, we need all of these gifts present and active in the lives of all followers of Jesus.

So, if we are the Kingdom people of God on earth, and we are to display and conduct the prophetic activities of God's Kingdom on the earth, and we are to get our communications and instructions prophetically from God, who is in heaven; it is important that we understand how this whole prophetic process works.

In his classic book, "*The Presence of the Future*", [68] George Eldon Ladd, former Professor of New Testament Theology & Exegesis at Fuller Theological Seminary in Pasadena, California discusses the subject of the Kingdom of God or sometimes referred to as the Reign of God. He discusses its

[66] Ephesians 4:7-13
[67] Eph. 4:11-13
[68] George Eldon Ladd, *"The Presence of the Future"*, Published by: Wm. B. Eerdmanns Publishing Company, Copyright 1974, reprint 1996

relevance to the Church and its mission in the world in this present age, as well as the Kingdom's complete manifestation in the age to come. The three prominent opinions regarding the nature of the Kingdom of God in the world today that Dr. Ladd raises and discusses are: 1) the *prophetic*: the Kingdom is present spiritually and is relevant in this age only; 2) the *apocalyptic*: the Kingdom is present physically and relevant only in the age to come; and 3) the *combined*: the Kingdom is prophetic - spiritually present and relevant now in this age; *and* the Kingdom is apocalyptic - it will be physically manifested and relevant in the age to come.

In order to better understand these three views of the Kingdom of God, let's take a brief look at what the basic belief is for each view. Our understanding of *prophetic* is critical to our ability and willingness to engage with the Kingdom of God's "mode of operation" in this age and how we must interact with Him if we are to accomplish our earthly commission. If we have a correct understanding of what is prophetic, we will be able to correctly and effectively interact with the Kingdom of God and His activities in this present age.

According to Dr. Ladd, the ***prophetic*** view of the Kingdom of God basically states: "*...the Kingdom of God is the personal relationship between man and God, the individual's experience of God's sovereignty over his life when he recognizes God's right to rule, and submits his will to God. The Kingdom comes when any man acknowledges God's sole sovereignty over his life, or when a group of men do the same, or when an ethically conditioned remnant, the church, acknowledges allegiance to God's sovereignty ... The Kingdom of God means the entrance of the eternal into time, the confrontation of the finite by the infinite, the intrusion of the transcendent into the natural. The Kingdom of God is timeless, eternal, and transcendent, and is therefore always near and always laying its demands upon men.*" [69]

This view of the Kingdom of God states that the Kingdom is spiritually present, completely, here and now. There is no future Kingdom to be manifested at a later time because the Kingdom is present through the work of the Church in this present age. In essence, "*The consummation of the Kingdom is nothing less than a world which has been brought into submission to God's rule through the Church's proclamation of the gospel.*" [70]

The ***apocalyptic*** view of the Kingdom of God basically states: "*The Kingdom is the new age, the purely supranatural state of affairs when God alone will rule over men.*

---

[69] George Eldon Ladd, *"The Presence of the Future"*, Published by: Wm. B. Eerdmanns Publishing Company, Copyright 1974, reprint 1996, Pg. 16, 17, 18.
[70] George Eldon Ladd, *"The Presence of the Future"*, Published by: Wm. B. Eerdmanns Publishing Company, Copyright 1974, reprint 1996, Pg. 17

When the Kingdom comes, history will end. The sayings about the presence of the Kingdom mean that the process of the coming of the Kingdom is already under way. God's initial act has been performed; and as soon as its consequences have been felt, the next act will follow and the Kingdom will come."[71]

This view of the Kingdom of God states that when Jesus fulfilled His earthly ministry, the process for bringing the Kingdom of God to earth began but the Kingdom itself is not and will not be present on the earth until He comes to the earth Himself to set up His Kingdom in the age to come. The Kingdom is imminent but it is not present. In essence, "*The Kingdom of God has not yet come, but is near, so near that it is already operative in advance…the certainty of the event is so overwhelming, the signs of its impendingness so sure, that it is said to have occurred, or to be occurring already…but to say that the Kingdom has come would overstate the case.*" [8]

The ***combined*** view of the Kingdom of God basically states: "*The ministry of Jesus is the Kingdom at work in the world. The Kingdom shows its power in the work of Jesus and his messengers by overcoming those forces of evil which degrade and destroy man. This act of God has created a new period in history which succeeds that of the law and the prophets: the period of the Kingdom of God. Thus the Kingdom is a state of affairs into which men may enter…and are to therefore experience… rather than a state of mind. The Kingdom is both present and future. Jesus set in motion supranatural forces which go on inevitably until they reach their consummation. The consummated Kingdom is now present in the world as really as the harvest is present in the sown field. How the growth takes place and when it will come to full fruition – these are questions which the sower cannot answer. They are God's affair. The Kingdom may be said to have come with Jesus, for with him occurred the first manifestation of the Kingdom in the world. That is, Jesus was the first to experience the full meaning of the reign of God; His mission was to lead other men into this same experience of the reign of God.*" [72]

This third view of the Kingdom of God states that the Kingdom was brought to earth through the person and ministry of Jesus and is therefore still present and active through the ongoing work and ministry of the Holy Spirit in and through the Church. Yet, the full manifestation of the Kingdom will not take place until He personally establishes and manifests His throne here on the earth in the age to come. In essence, "*The Kingdom of*

---

[71] George Eldon Ladd, *"The Presence of the Future"*, Published by: Wm. B. Eerdmanns Publishing Company, Copyright 1974, reprint 1996, Pg. 9
[8] George Eldon Ladd, *"The Presence of the Future"*, Published by: Wm. B. Eerdmanns Publishing Company, Copyright 1974, reprint 1996, Pg. 10
[72] George Eldon Ladd, *"The Presence of the Future"*, Published by: Wm. B. Eerdmanns Publishing Company, Copyright 1974, reprint 1996, Pgs. 28, 37, 12
[10] George Eldon Ladd, *"The Presence of the Future"*, Published by: Wm. B. Eerdmanns Publishing Company, Copyright 1974, reprint 1996, Pg. 13, 25

God is man's acceptance of God's gracious sovereignty which is essentially timeless, for it is the individual's compliance with God's will...The Kingdom is not the victory of God's irresistible royal power, but the willing personal acceptance of His fatherly rule by men...The Kingdom of God is the heavenly realm where God's will is done, the supra-historical sphere where God rules...and Jesus announced the coming of this miraculous supranatural realm. This event ...will mean the breaking off of history and the descent of the heavenly realm to earth. The Kingdom...will come down from above and effect a marvelous transformation of the world." [10]

My purpose for bringing the nature of the Kingdom of God into this book is to establish and promote the fact that the Kingdom of God is the single, over-arching, sovereign government in which all things find their existence and fulfill their purpose in the universe. We can no more approach the nature and purpose of what is *prophetic* apart from its place within the purpose and plan of God's Kingdom, than we can approach the nature and purpose of what is missional, evangelistic, intercessory, and pastoral apart from its purpose and plan within the Kingdom of God.

I will not go into an in-depth analysis of these three views of the Kingdom of God at this time. Of the three views of the Kingdom of God discussed by Dr. Ladd, I embrace the third view mentioned, the *combined* view, as being the true scriptural view of the Kingdom of God. I believe the Kingdom of God is *prophetic*; that it is present and active now in this present age. I also believe that it is *apocalyptic*; that the full consummation and complete manifestation of the Kingdom is yet to be seen and will take place at a later time, in the age to come.

As a result of the Kingdom of God being prophetically present in this age, the Church has experienced the prophetic activities of the Kingdom of God throughout its existence. I believe the Church today will continue to experience an increasingly greater awareness and manifestation of the Kingdom of God as we draw closer to the conclusion of this present age. I do not believe the Church will bring about the full manifestation of the Kingdom of God on the earth through our endeavors to confront and infiltrate this present earthly culture. The fullness of the Kingdom will come when Jesus returns to the earth to establish His throne.

The scriptures indicate that there will be a great conflict at the end of the age between the Kingdom of God and the domain of darkness. This conflict will still be raging and unsettled when Jesus returns to the earth to overcome and displace the kingdoms of this world and to establish his Kingdom on the earth. Jesus will establish His earthly reign, to rule over and subdue the earth for 1000 years, and then submit all things to the Father at its conclusion.[73]

Now, having said that, we have identified the nature of the relationship between the Kingdom of God (located in heaven) and the people of God (located on the earth) in this present age, as being *prophetic.* In order to effectively communicate the dynamic nature of this relationship between the Kingdom of God and those who reside on the earth, we will use the following definition of *prophetic* to describe the interaction between the two.

Prophetic - *The entrance of the eternal into time, the confrontation of the finite by the infinite, the intrusion of the supranatural into the natural. The spiritual activity by which God reveals and exhibits the operation of His Kingdom within the realm of our earthly, natural existence. In essence,* ***prophetic*** *is the revelation of God, His Kingdom and its activities, including His wisdom, knowledge, and will, into the realm of time and our present experience. It is the thoughts and activities of God finding their expression and manifestation within the present natural world in which people live and function.*

Revealing What Is Hidden

The *prophetic* is the invasion of the spiritual into the natural; it is revealing what is hidden. In Numbers 12, God speaks to the children of Israel in the wilderness concerning His relationship with Moses. God says to them, *"Hear now My words: If there is a prophet among you, I, the Lord, shall make Myself known to him in a vision. I shall speak with him in a dream. Not so, with My servant Moses, He is faithful in all My household; With him I speak mouth to mouth, Even openly, and not in dark sayings, And he beholds the form of the Lord."* [74] Here, God gives us a great example of His Kingdom interacting prophetically with His people on earth. Whether He communicates through dreams, visions, audible voice, revealing His form or some other manifestation of His Kingdom activities to someone on the earth, the nature of the interaction is prophetic.

From the beginning God has purposed, according to His boundless grace, to deliver complete salvation and an eternal purpose within His Kingdom for all of us through the redemptive work of Jesus Christ. This was an established fact long before God ever created Adam and placed him in the Garden. It was an established fact even during the years when Israel, God's chosen people, wandered from Him and were taken into exile. Even though God had often prophetically spoken to us regarding His plan to redeem us and to deliver us back into His Kingdom, the vehicle for our deliverance

---

[73] Rev. 20-21
[74] Numbers 12:6-8

and restoration was revealed in a single prophetic event; the life of Jesus Christ.

This event; the appearing, life, ministry, death, and resurrection of Jesus Christ was entirely prophetic in its nature and purpose. As a result of the prophetic life of Jesus, the lives of people are still being impacted today. When an individual's life is impacted by the prophetic life of Jesus, to the point of being born again, that individual's life is changed and their own nature becomes prophetic through the regeneration and indwelling presence of the Holy Spirit. They have been transferred from the domain of darkness into the Kingdom of God. Being prophetic is not a single act or event. It is a lifestyle of interacting with the Holy Spirit and the Kingdom of God as His prophetic people.

It is a commitment to this prophetic lifestyle; this daily interaction with God and the reality and revelation of the Kingdom of God that every believer should pursue in this present age. If we as followers of Jesus hold a belief that beyond our own personal salvation experience there is little or no practical interaction with the Kingdom of God, in this life, we relegate nearly all of God's Kingdom activities and promises to the future. By our actions, we say that all Jesus is doing now is sitting in heaven waiting for the world to get so bad that He has to come back in order to keep it from destroying itself. And, we as believers are simply trying to "hold on" until He comes to take us out of here.

Conversely, if we believe that the prophetically-present Kingdom of God is active, now, in this age, interacting with the lives of people on earth and that we as God's prophetic people have a defined role to play in the plans of the Kingdom, now, we must believe that God will prophetically reveal His plans and activities to us so we can be co-laborers with Him. If we honestly read the gospels, we will see that Jesus truly believed He was actively involved in the day-to-day activities of the Kingdom of God being restored to the earth. He believed that He and the Father were working together in order to bring about the reestablishment of the reign of God on the earth.[75] As a result of this knowledge and faith, Jesus committed Himself to seek the will of the Father, to hear what the Father was saying and to see what the Father was doing, to live a life based on that revelation from the Father, and to tell others what the Father had revealed to Him.[76]

The New Testament believers had this same mindset and spiritual orientation, as they turned the world upside down through their prophetic

[75] John 5:17
[76] John 5:19-20; John 13:50;

testimony and activities. We, today, must have this same mindset and orientation. To deny or ignore our prophetic nature and purpose as children of the Kingdom, is to deny or ignore the presence of the Kingdom itself and our vital role in its ongoing activities. Interacting with and acting on behalf of the Kingdom of God…this is what it means to be a prophetic person.

Chapter Questions & Notes

Talk It Over….

1) "Is the New Testament and what it says still valid and relevant to the followers of Jesus, like us, today? Is there anything in the New Testament that tells us that some of the words of Jesus or the writings of John, Paul, Peter and the rest of the New Testament writers are no longer relevant and meaningful to us, today? Did the New Testament believers have anything or were they expected to conduct themselves in a way that is no longer available to or expected of us, today? If so, can you give some examples and the scriptures to substantiate what these might be?"

2) If the relationship between the throne of God located in heaven and His Kingdom activities taking place on the earth is prophetic in nature, what impact does that have upon the Kingdom people of God on the earth (the Church) and our responsibility to represent God and His Kingdom to the people around us? What must we do to put ourselves in a position to effectively cooperate with Jesus and to allow the prophetic activities of His Kingdom to operate through us, to confront and engage with the people around us?

(7)

A Historical Testimony

"God, after He spoke long ago to the fathers in the prophets, in many portions and in many ways, ***in these last days has spoken to us in His Son****"* Hebrews 1:1-2a (emphasis mine)

"But I tell you the truth, it is to your advantage that I go away; for if I do not go away, the Helper will not come to you; but if I go, I will send Him to you…But when He, the Spirit of truth, comes, He will guide you into all the truth; for He will not speak on His own initiative, but ***whatever He hears, He will speak****; and* ***He will disclose to you what is to come****. He will glorify Me, for* ***He will take of Mine and will disclose it to you.****"* John 16:7,13-14 (emphasis mine)

I want to take some time and provide some examples of prophetic activities of the Kingdom of God that have taken place in Church history and are still taking place today. We all know that the prophetic activities of the Kingdom of God took place in the Old Testament and in the early Church believers because we can read about it in the Bible. What many believers have a difficult time seeing is that these same types of prophetic activities have taken place throughout Church history, since the death of the apostles, and that they are still taking place today. This is important because we need to realize that the Kingdom of God and its prophetic activities are just as real, present and active, now, as it has ever been.

Prophetic Kingdom Activities In Church History

The prophetic activity of the Kingdom of God has continued throughout the Church age and didn't end after the ministry and death of the original Apostles and the early church believers. Following are three examples from church history of the prophetic activities of the Kingdom of God being carried out by His Kingdom people. There are many more examples but due to space limitations we will highlight these three. The first account is in the life and ministry of Patrick of Ireland.

When Patrick began his ministry in about 430 A.D., Ireland was overrun by paganism. Druid priests performed human and animal sacrifices to appease the local gods. They practiced Spiritism and black magic through incantations and occult rituals. The Irish knew nothing of Jesus at that time. For the demonic power over Ireland to be broken, the power of the Kingdom of God had to be introduced and it had to prevail. Patrick challenged the powers of darkness at its stronghold --Tara—the seat of the high king Loegaire and his two evil druid priests, Lochru and Lucetmael.

Tara was filled with many local kings, generals, nobility, and druids who were attending the pagan feast of Beltine, which happened to coincide with Easter, that year. While Loegaire and his guests prepared to celebrate the feast of Beltine, Patrick was encamped in full view of the castle, in order to celebrate the resurrection of Jesus Christ.

On the day before the pagan festival, it was the custom, upon penalty of death, that the high king should light the first bonfire before any others in the land. Patrick, however, had kindled a great fire just outside his camp and it could be seen by the inhabitants of the whole area and by all those gathered in the hilltop castle. King Loegaire was livid and demanded that Patrick be put to death for lighting his bonfire before the king started his fire. But the druids replied, "O king, live forever. This fire will never be put out unless it is put out this night on which it has been lit. He who lit the fire and the coming kingdom by which it was lit will overcome us all." The king rejected the words of the druids. He prepared twenty-seven chariots for the druids, kings, and other guests, and drove for Patrick's fire.

When the king and his guests arrived at Patrick's fire, Patrick was summoned before the king. When Patrick came before Loegaire, only one man rose to honor Patrick; the rest sat in silence. The druid Lochru began to insult Patrick and to slander the Christian faith. Suddenly, a boldness took hold of Patrick. His eyes were locked with the eyes of the pagan priest. Sensing God's presence, Patrick shouted: "O Lord, who can do all things, who sent me here. May this wicked man who blasphemes Your name be carried up out of here and die straightaway!" Suddenly, the druid priest flipped into the air and crashed to the ground, and his skull was shattered when it landed on a rock.

Another king, one of Loegaire's many guests, shouted, "Seize him!" But Patrick stood and called out, "May God arise and His enemies be scattered!" Darkness suddenly fell on the camp. Confused guards began to attack one another. The ground shook and frightened horses galloped off, smashing the chariots. Suddenly, that terrified king approached and knelt before Patrick, though his eyes still burned in anger.

Easter morning Patrick and his five companions marched into the castle and entered King Loegaire's banquet hall. A confrontation with the remaining druid, Luctmael, ended in the magician's fiery death. Patrick then faced King Loegaire boldly, saying, "Unless you believe now, you will soon die, for God's wrath will come down upon your head." That day a broken king Loegaire knelt before God's servant, Patrick.

This confrontation between Patrick's God and demonic forces marked the beginning of a thirty-year mission to Ireland. Danger and hardship remained his constant companions. Many sought his life and twice he was imprisoned by those who were his enemies, but he was not to be intimidated. "Daily I expect murder, fraud, or captivity," he wrote, "but I fear none of these things because of the promises of heaven. I have cast myself into the hands of God Almighty who rules everywhere."[77]

In this prophetic event, God sought to further the influence of His Kingdom in Ireland. Many times, the prophetic activity of the Kingdom of God is intended to wage spiritual warfare against the powers of darkness. If these dark powers are to be confronted and overcome, it must be through the power of God as exhibited through His prophetic people, as they take their place as God's co-laborers on the earth. Without this prophetic activity of God, we are left to our own human wisdom and devices. If we must rely on our human abilities, we will not be able to stand against the forces of darkness that are destroying the lives of people today. We must embrace and pursue the Kingdom of God in our lives. Let's take a look at another prophetic event where the Kingdom of God manifested itself in the lives of His people in church history.

In the life of Benedict of Nursia, we see the prophetic activity of the Kingdom of God take place in order to preserve the truth of the gospel, frustrate the works of the powers of darkness, and to move the purposes of the Kingdom forward on the earth. In this event, Benedict, who was the leader of an order of monks, was saying his morning prayers when he received a prophetic communication from God that said, "Today Satan will pull one of his tricks." Upon hearing this, Benedict sent a word of warning to the others who were in the process of building the monastery. Soon after issuing this warning, the wall of the monastery where the others were

[77] "Will The Real St. Patrick Please Stand Up?", by Dr. Ralph F. Wilson, Christian Articles Archive 1999

working collapsed and a fellow monk working in that area was mangled and killed.

When Benedict heard of the wall collapsing and the monk being killed, he ordered the monk's body be brought to him. When the body was brought to him in his room, and those who had brought it were gone, Benedict began praying over the body. Suddenly the dead man arose from the floor and announced to Benedict that he was healed, and went back out to continue his work on the monastery.[78]

Benedict believed in the prophetic activity of the Kingdom and that he was an essential part of its success on the earth. He wasn't shocked or doubting when the prophetic word from God came to him. He had developed a personal history of communicating with and hearing from God. He simply obeyed what God said to him. Benedict made himself available to God and His kingdom, to cooperate with Him, and this is why God used him to further His purposes on the earth. Let's look at one more prophetic event from recent church history.

In the life of Charles Spurgeon (1834-92), we see several prophetic events take place, but I want to mention this one in particular. One Sunday, as Spurgeon was preaching his sermon to his congregation, he stopped in mid-sentence and pointed to a man in the congregation, saying, "Young man, those gloves you are wearing have not been paid for. You have stolen them from your employer." We are told that the man later came to Spurgeon and confessed that the gloves were indeed stolen, and that he would make restitution to his employer.[79]

In this prophetic event, God sought to bring His people to a place where they became more aware of His continual presence, that of His Kingdom, and the spiritual world around them. Until we learn that the Kingdom of God is active all around us, that He is working in this world through His Kingdom people, and that the activities of the Kingdom are "heard" and "seen" by us, prophetically, we will miss out on so much of what God wants to do in and though us as His prophetic people. We should start now to take the time every day to connect with the Spirit of God who lives inside of us so we can learn to experience His presence and distinguish His voice from all the other voices out there. This is the first step to experiencing the prophetic activity of the Kingdom of God in and through our lives. Now that we have seen several prophetic Kingdom events in church history, since

---

[78] Idlephonse Cardinal Schuster, *Saint Benedict and His Times* (London, England: B. Herder Book Co., 1951) pp. 186-187

[79] *C. H. Spurgeon: Autobiography*, Vol. 25, *The Full Harvest*, Banner of Truth Trust, 1973. page 60

the end of the first century, let's take a look at some prophetic Kingdom events that are taking place in the Church today.

Prophetic Kingdom Activities In The Church Today

I have experienced many prophetic Kingdom events and activities throughout my years as a follower of Jesus. What I want to do here is share several of these experiences with you and here is the reason why. It's important for you to see that I am writing this book from a position of personal and practical experience with the Kingdom of God and its prophetic activity and not as a "bystander" who can only offer a theoretical, theological or doctrinal account of the subject matter with little or no personal experience. I am a witness of the Kingdom of God and its activities in this present age and I am giving testimony to its reality and presence in this age.

Also, when we hear or read about prophetic experiences in the Bible or in church history, we tend to say to ourselves, *"That was Jesus, or, that was Paul, or, that was Moses, or that was one of the church fathers".* It's important that one of your contemporaries; someone who lives, works, eats, and sleeps just like you can and has experienced these Kingdom activities and can write about these experiences – encouraging you, as a fellow believer in Jesus and child of His Kingdom. The same Kingdom, the same Holy Spirit, and same prophetic activities of the Kingdom that I experience are also available to you. I'm a normal Christian just like you. That's who Jesus is looking for, normal Christians who will let Him demonstrate His prophetic Kingdom activities through them to touch the world around them. I desire the presence of God in my life and have left myself open to hearing from Him and doing what He tells me to do. I have kept myself open to the activity of the Kingdom of God, even though I didn't always understand what that meant or what it would entail.

I didn't always know what to do or how to do it. I did a lot of things wrong and still miss it more than I would like. But, I have found that God is very patient and wants to see you and me walk in these types of prophetic experiences, more than we want to see it. Why? Because He wants to work through all of us, as His Kingdom people, in order to impact others for His Kingdom. He engages in Kingdom activity through us because He wants to reveal Himself and the presence of His Kingdom to all humanity.

It's not about how much or how often or how dynamic the activities are, when it comes to our experience with the activities of God and His

Kingdom. It's about the experience of knowing that we are participating in something that God planned before the world was created and that Jesus came to re-establish. It's about experiencing what the Holy Spirit is here to do, in this present age, through the people of God. God doesn't want any of us to be left out of His plan and activities. But, it is up to each of us to decide whether we want to engage and pursue the Kingdom of God and His activities, or stand by and watch. As Jesus told us, *"From the days of John the Baptist until now, the Kingdom of heaven* (same as the Kingdom of God) *has been forcefully advancing, and violent men seize it by force, as a precious prize".*[80]

Now, here are several of the prophetic Kingdom events and activities that God has included me in, in order to establish the reality of His Kingdom in my life and to further the plans and purposes of His Kingdom in the lives of those around me. This first prophetic event involves the activities of the Kingdom of God in my life, as a baby. That may sound strange to you; that I would say this about an event that took place so early in my life but when my parents told me the story of these events when I was in my mid-30s, there was no doubt in my mind, or theirs, that God was at work in my life, and theirs, in this event.

I was a newborn, who was just brought home from the hospital. As the family settled into a new routine, everything seemed to be fine. I was given a clean bill of health from the doctors before coming home; for several months, life was routine. I was progressing normally – moving from milk to eating strained food. But shortly after beginning to eat strained food, my parents began to notice something unusual. I was not having regular bowel movements. When I did, they were not sufficient to account for the amount of food I was eating.

Over the next few weeks, my stomach became more bloated and distended. My mother took me to the family doctor on several occasions, only to be given a prescription for some medicine, told to not worry, and sent home. In the succeeding weeks, my mother took me, again, to the doctor because of my seemingly deteriorating condition, only to be sent home; again, being told that everything was fine and that she shouldn't worry – I'll eventually grow out of it. But, I didn't grow out of it. In fact, my stomach began to grow more and more distended. I began to lose more and more weight, and became increasingly gaunt in my appearance.

One day, my mother called the pharmacy to have my prescription medicine refilled. When the delivery boy arrived (the pharmacy used to deliver medicine to your home in those days), he knocked at the front door. When

[80] Matthew 11:12; Amplified Bible

my mother let him into the house to pay him, the delivery boy saw me lying on a blanket and said, "WHAT'S WRONG WITH THAT BABY?" Realizing that the delivery boy immediately noticed something was terribly wrong, and hearing the alarm in his voice, my mother immediately picked me up and took me to the doctor's office again. When she entered the office, she demanded to see the doctor right away. When the doctor came out to see her, she demanded that he thoroughly examine me again because something was very wrong. The doctor proceeded to tell my mother that I was fine; that they had run tests and there was nothing wrong and that she should take me home and try not to worry.

At that moment, hearing the commotion from the outer office, another doctor emerged from a back office. As this second doctor approached my mother and me, he saw my appearance and my distended stomach. He asked my mother how long I had been like this. When she told him that I had been like this for a few months, the second doctor told my mother to get me to the hospital as quickly as possible and he would meet her there.

When my mother, father, and the second doctor arrived at the hospital, more tests were run and it was determined that I had a congenital illness called Hirschsprung's Disease. I had been born with the disease but it didn't become evident until I began to eat semi-solid food. The second doctor, a surgeon, scheduled immediate surgery for me in order to remove the diseased part of the colon. In the coming year, I would experience three major surgeries in order to reconstruct and restore my colon to proper working condition. My parents could not afford to have the surgeon perform the emergency surgery, so a resident surgeon from the hospital performed the surgery while the second doctor assisted and guided his surgical cuts. The second doctor, commenting on the quality of the surgery performed by the resident, told my parents that he couldn't have performed the surgery any better himself.

After the emergency surgery, the surgeon told my parents that if I had remained in that diseased condition for another few weeks, without having the surgery, I would have died. The surgeon also told my parents that he was one of a handful of doctors in the entire country who could, both, properly diagnose and perform the surgery to correct Hirschsprung's Disease. He also told my parents that he was a medical school friend of their family doctor and that he just happened to be in their doctor's office that day, for a visit, when she arrived with me.

The surgeon also told my parents that due to the internal damage I had suffered as a result of Hirschsprung's Disease, the length of time I lived with it before it was diagnosed, and the effects of the three surgeries to repair it; I most likely would not be able to enjoy an active life. My insides just wouldn't be able to handle playing sports or other physically demanding activities. Yet, I went on to play football, baseball, run track, and play college basketball with no restrictions or repercussions from the Hirschsprung's Disease or the three major surgeries.

In my mind, and in theirs, there was only one explanation for all of this. God orchestrated these events and these people, bringing them all together at this one moment in time, to save my life and to influence my life, the lives of my parents, and the lives of the doctors and nurses involved. I knew I had this big scar on my stomach and that I was very ill as a baby but I didn't know the extent to which God so deeply impacted my life and the lives of others. The Kingdom of God was at work in my life that day, touching my life and the lives of others even though I had no way of realizing it at the time.

This next prophetic Kingdom event taught me a very valuable lesson regarding the prophetic activities of the Kingdom of God. This event emphasizes the importance of being attentive to God and aware of His presence and activities going on around us at all times. If we get sidetracked or begin to focus too much on ourselves and our own affairs, we may miss a prophetic Kingdom event God wants to work in or through us at any time.

This event took place when I was in my early twenties. I was working for an apartment complex as an outside maintenance person during the summer. One day I was cutting the grass outside the front of one of the apartment buildings. I was quite a distance from any of the other buildings or cars in the vicinity. As I was cutting the grass in this section of the complex, suddenly my mower stopped running. I checked the fuel, checked under the mower, checked the spark plug, checked the fuel line, and checked the oil. I checked everything I could think of and nothing seemed to be causing the problem.

Here I was, squatting down next to the mower, trying to figure out why it suddenly stopped, when I happened to look up and to my left; toward the street and the corner intersection. As I looked, I saw a man in his late twenties or so cross the street and begin walking down the sidewalk that passed in front of the apartment complex. He wore a hoodie sweatshirt and walked with his head down, in the direction of the building where I was mowing.

Just when I was about to turn my head back to look at my mower, this man, without looking up at all, changed his direction and began trotting off of the sidewalk and straight toward where I was kneeling over my mower. I watched him trot up the hill toward me. I quickly looked back toward my mower because I didn't feel like talking to anyone, especially a stranger, being frustrated about the mower not starting. As I was looking down at the mower, this man came up behind me, bent over me with his hands on his knees, and asked, "Have you heard any good news lately?"

When I heard this question, I thought to myself, "Are you kidding me? Here I am trying to get this stupid mower running and you come up here and ask me about the news." I turned my head to the side, in his direction, and said, "Nope". I looked back down at my mower for 2-3 seconds and then looked back toward him, but he was gone. I turned all the way around to see where he went and he wasn't there. I looked to my left, and then to my right, and then behind me. I got up from beside the mower, glanced all around the yard, I looked toward the building and toward the cars along the street, but he was nowhere to be seen.

I thought to myself, "There's no way he could have gone anywhere that fast. I only turned my head away for a few seconds." Then I started to think about the whole situation and the question he asked me, "Have you heard any good news lately?" The thought suddenly struck me, "Was that an angel?" No, it couldn't be. Yet, no one else could have possibly gotten away that fast. As I thought more about the possibility that he may have been an angel, I kept thinking about the question he asked me, "Have you heard any good news lately?" Could he have been prompting me with that question to see if I would respond by telling him about Jesus?

I collapsed to the ground, sitting next to the mower. I thought to myself again, "That had to be an angel, there's no other explanation for him getting away so quickly." He may have had a message for me from God but I didn't give him the time of day. If I had just responded to him the way I should have, what would he have said to me?

This event nagged me for several years. I believe it was an angelic visitation. What would have happened if I had just taken my eyes off of myself and my own concerns long enough to give this man a few minutes of my time, to respond to his question the way I should have? Who knows what kind of conversation we would have had? Who knows what kind of things he would have said to me? Since then God has helped me understand more about His grace, patience, and mercy. I didn't blow my entire life's purpose or take myself out of God's plan for me because I failed this particular prophetic opportunity. In fact, it has served as a good lesson for me to always try and maintain my connection and open line of communication with Him, just in case He wants to do something like this again sometime.

He hasn't stopped working in my life as a result of this failure. He has continued to engage me in His prophetic activity over the years. This was a prophetic Kingdom event that was intended to teach me more about the prophetic purpose and plans of God, and to bring me a little closer to participating with Him in His Kingdom activities taking place around me. Let's look at some more prophetic Kingdom events in my life.

These next prophetic events that I will relate to you took place within actual ministry situations; at a Saturday night youth meeting, in a street evangelism situation, and on a short-term mission trip. What I hope you take away, as a result of reading about these events in my life, is the fact that God wants to use all of us, as prophetic people, to impact the lives of the PEOPLE around us for His Kingdom. He wants to make us aware of His constant presence in our life and of all that is going on in and around our life. He will use His prophetic activities in all types of day-to-day occurrences and ministry situations. We need to be sensitive and attentive to Him, as much as possible, so we don't miss an opportunity where He wants to engage us in the prophetic activity of His Kingdom.

This next prophetic event took place at a youth meeting about three years after my encounter with the angel. A friend of mine was the youth pastor of a large church in a large city. One night he came to me and asked me to speak at the youth meeting that next Saturday night. The next day I sat down and started praying about what the Lord would have me speak on. I continued to pray and read the scriptures but nothing seemed to "bear witness" that this is what I should teach on. I continued to spend time with the Lord, praying about the message and reading the scriptures over the next few days but nothing seemed "right" in my heart. A few more days went by, and nothing. Finally, that Saturday morning came and I again went to the Lord about my message but nothing seemed right. I put a few notes together on a subject but I knew it wasn't what He wanted me to say.

Finally, Saturday night came and I still didn't have a message prepared. When it was time to leave for the church, I got up from the chair and said to myself, "Either God has something planned that I don't know about, or I am about to become the biggest fool in town." I went to the church and we started the meeting with praise and worship time. Another friend leaned over to me and asked me if I was ready. I told him, "Yep." The amazing thing about the whole situation was that I really wasn't nervous or alarmed. I had never been in this position before, not having a message prepared before I was to speak. Yet, I knew that I had done all I could to prepare, but God had not given me anything to say.

So, it was in His hands. I stood there with everyone else, worshipping the Lord, when suddenly, across my mind's eye, came the words, "Psalm 34". As soon as I saw that scripture in my mind, I knew this was what I was to speak on. The only problem was I wasn't sure what the scripture said. It had been awhile since I spent time in that Psalm. I got my Bible out and read the Psalm quickly so I knew what it said.

When the worship time was over, I was introduced. I walked up onto the platform, opened my Bible, and prayed that God would help me say what He wanted me to say that night and that people would be touched and helped. I opened my Bible to Psalm 34 and began to speak. Within a few moments after I started speaking, something happened that had never happened to me before. I will tell you what happened, the best I can, and then comment about it later.

As I was speaking, suddenly, I became very aware of the space around me on the platform. The air, itself, seemed to be electrically charged. At the same time, I had the physical sensation of an electric charge starting at the top of my head and going down my neck and into my back. Then, suddenly, I felt as if someone took a coat or a blanket and draped it over my shoulders. I could feel it on the back of my neck and across my shoulders, even though there was nothing there.

I continued to speak for the next twenty to twenty-five minutes. From one word to the next, I did not know what I was going to say until just before I said it. I had to get the tape after the meeting was over to know what I said. I talked about placing God as the focal point and centerpiece for our lives. That He would always be there, even when the times seemed desperate and hard. He would be there to walk us through it and bring us out on the other side, if we would trust in Him. He would be there for us as we spent time with Him, in His presence. Regardless of how difficult things get, God is bigger than those times and He will bring us through it. There were many people who came forward and the message seemed to help many who were there. I had a number of people come up to me afterward and tell me that God spoke to them.

What happened a week later, and that I didn't know anything about when I spoke the previous Saturday night, was that the pastor of the church had been involved in a personal sin and stood up that following Sunday morning to confess it to the church. Needless to say, the church went through some very difficult times over the next several months as a result of that event. During the first days of that difficult time in the church I had several young people come up to me and tell me that the message I gave that Saturday night had continued to help them in that current and difficult situation.

God's purpose for His prophetic Kingdom event that Saturday night was to personally encourage and equip the young people for what the church was about to experience. Many of them were of college/career age and did not have their families in the church with them to help them in this difficult time. The pastor was very popular and the situation affected the entire congregation very deeply. God wanted them to know that He was there with them and for them, and that He would bring them through this difficult time, if they trusted in Him. For me, this prophetic event taught me more about the purpose and plan of God for His people, and that He is always active and always on time and always has something He wants to communicate.

Now, regarding my description of what happened to me that night, after I started to speak. As I mentioned, the air around me on the platform seemed electrically charged and I felt something like an electric charge go down my head and neck, and into my back. Then, I felt something like a coat or blanket being draped over my back and shoulders. This was God's way of letting me know that He was with me that night and that He had something specific for me to say.

The prophetic activities of God manifest themselves in the manner He chooses. They are not subject to the ways, means, and opinions of this world (or ours) but in many cases, actually "cut against the grain" of the ways of this world. He often offends the mind in order to impact the heart. He seeks to impact the lives of people for the good, to bring people out of the clutches of this worlds system and to deliver them from the domain of darkness and into the Kingdom of God. What He does and how He does it is His decision and we need to "go with it" when He engages us in it.

We do not always understand these prophetic activities and cannot always explain them adequately to others. Therefore, we have to live with the fact that the prophetic activities of God will, at times, seem mysterious and unusual to us and to those around us. There is an orderly manner in which these prophetic activities can be conducted and administrated when they take place, without quenching the Spirit (the spirits of the prophets are subject to the prophets[81]). But, we must also remember that God is King and if He wants something done a certain way, we need to be obedient.[82] Thankfully, He has given us guidelines and leaders who will give guidance and oversight for these prophetic activities, so we are all instructed and trained, and God receives the glory for what He does through us. Let's look

[81] I Corinthians 14:32
[82] John 9:6-7; II Kings 5; Mark 7:32-35

at another prophetic Kingdom event from my personal experience that took place in a street evangelism situation.

This next prophetic event took place a couple of years after the previous event at the youth meeting. I was living in a large city at the time and was involved with a street-evangelism ministry. From time to time, several of us would go to the city's convention center to engage in conversations about Jesus with people attending concerts held at the convention center. One night, before one of these concerts, approximately eight of us met to pray for the Lord's presence and working in the lives of people that night. While we were praying, I had an unusual experience.

As I was praying with my eyes closed, I saw something like a ticker-tape message scroll across my mind's eye. It said, "Pray for backstage passes". Without even thinking, I prayed out loud, "Lord, I pray for backstage passes to the concert tonight." I opened my eyes and, needless to say, several in the group were looking at me like I was crazy. But, the group leader was wise enough to stay focused and actually agreed with my prayer…that backstage passes would be a great tool and opportunity.

Many times we can recognize the voice of the Spirit speaking to us by a thought that comes into our minds that is very gentle in its tone and yet will be totally unrelated to our current stream of thought. Many times we let these thoughts escape, dismissing them as frivolous. In some cases, they may be frivolous thoughts but in other cases it may be the voice of the Spirit speaking to us. The more we pray and respond to Him, the more we develop a communication history with Him, where we are better able to know His voice when He speaks to us.

Sometimes, when a prayer is prayed that we question or we don't quite know what to do with it, it is better to be still or remain in "neutral" concerning it and just see what happens. Many times we feel it is our obligation to respond to or give our personal commentary on "unusual" prayers that come up. By doing so, we can breed an atmosphere of unbelief and actually hinder the move of the Spirit in our midst.

Now, if the prayer spoken is obviously contrary to the scriptures or is otherwise out of line, it is the responsibility of the leadership to deal with the situation in a gentle and loving manner. This can be done in such a way that the person praying is taught correctly without condemnation, and the hearers are not offended and do not become afraid to pray out loud, for fear of making a mistake and being reprimanded. If you do not know what to do with an unusual prayer, just be still and wait to see what God does.

At the end of this prayer time together, we went to the concert and stood in the parking lot of the convention center, talking with people about Jesus as they were going in. Just before the concert was to begin, and as I was finishing a conversation with two individuals, a car pulled up next to me in the parking lot. The person in the front passenger seat rolled down his window and asked me, "Would you like two backstage passes to the concert?" After I picked my jaw up off the ground, I said, "Sure." He handed me two backstage passes and the two men drove off, out of the parking lot and down the street. I took the passes and walked to where several in our group were talking. I showed them the passes and, after they picked their jaws up off the ground, we prayed concerning who should use the tickets to go backstage, and for spiritual guidance once they got there.

It was decided that one of the ladies in the group and I should use the passes to go backstage. As we entered the auditorium and went backstage, we prayed and asked God to show us who He wanted us to talk to. We talked to several members of the road crew. Then the lady who was with me said that there were several young ladies sitting in chairs just off stage, probably the girlfriends of the band members, and they were staring at us. As we walked up to them, we introduced ourselves and asked if we could talk with them for a moment. We began to explain that we were there to talk with them about the love of God and salvation through Jesus Christ.

As we talked with them, one of the young ladies spoke up and said, "Oh, I've heard all that before, my father is a Baptist minister." Many times God makes His will fairly obvious, once we take the initial step of faith. We knew this young lady was the person God wanted us to talk to. I told this young lady that God had provided us with backstage passes just so we could tell her that God loves her and had not forgotten her. He sent us to tell her that He wants her to come back to Him and that He hasn't given up on her. Suddenly, her jaw dropped and her eyes got real wide.

After a few more minutes of speaking with them, we said goodbye and turned to leave. Just before we went through the door, we looked back at the one girl whose father was the Baptist minister and she was still staring at us. We knew God had gotten her attention and that we had delivered to her the message He wanted her to hear.

God doesn't send a messenger for the benefit of the messenger. He does so for the benefit of those who need to hear the message. God wanted to do something "unfathomable" to get that young lady's attention. He will often go to great lengths to get our attention when He wants to influence and communicate with us. Therefore, many times, the method He chooses to use will be unusual or in some instances almost shocking. He loves us and wants us to have every opportunity to hear what He is saying and see what he is doing. We need to develop ears to hear and eyes to see so we can be attentive to Him when He wants to speak or act.

God will use unusual methods to get our attention and to communicate with us. This method of communication may be unusual in appearance or in its method of delivery. We must remember that a person God uses to deliver a message for Him is an imperfect instrument. They have been affected by sin and its results and are therefore susceptible to carrying out God's communication in an imperfect way. It is these imperfections in the delivery of God's communications that have caused us, in many instances, to perceive the prophetic as "weird".

If we can separate the message from the imperfect messenger He chooses to deliver it, we can forgive the imperfections of the messenger, not be offended, and still receive the communication God wants us to hear. There are other times when God will communicate in such a way as to offend the mind in order to get to the heart, as in the case of Jesus' conversation with Nicodemus. Now, let's look at another prophetic Kingdom event that I have experienced in my life, and this one took place on a short-term mission trip.

This prophetic event took place during my seminary days. I had been praying about going on a short-term mission trip for several months. I contacted one of my seminary professors and he recommended the trip he was going to lead that next May, to a country in east Asia. We would be conducting Bible training with indigenous pastors in this country for two weeks.

After spending some time praying about the opportunity, I decided that this was the trip I wanted to go on so I contacted my professor and told him that I would like to be on the team. He told me that, as a student, I would not be doing any teaching but would observe what took place and then write a report on the trip. After that conversation, I went to the Lord and said that if this is the role I am supposed to fill on this trip then that is fine. But if He has something else in mind for me while I am there, and it is not in my professor's plans, then He will have to change the plans.

Several months later and about a month before we were to leave on the trip, I was eating lunch in my office at work, just thinking about the Lord. As I was eating, I started thinking about the book of Revelation, specifically the letters that were written to the seven churches. Over the next few minutes, God organized a teaching on a specific aspect of those letters, right there inside my heart. You could say it was a spiritual download. I got a pen and paper and wrote it down so I wouldn't forget it. As I prayed concerning that teaching, I sensed that I was supposed to teach this on the mission trip. The only problem was I was not in the plans to do any teaching.

I told the Lord that if I am to deliver this message to those pastors, He would have to change the current plans. Two days later I got a phone call from my professor's wife, asking me if I wanted to do any teaching on the trip. I told her that her husband had told me that I wasn't going to be teaching because I was a student. She told me that he had changed his mind and was going to let me teach if I wanted to. I told her that I would like to do that. When I got off the phone, I looked up at the ceiling and said, "I don't know what You have planned but I'm sure looking forward to seeing it."

Within a few days of this experience, I began having a recurring dream at night while I slept. Without going into the specifics, it occurred several different times in the space of two weeks. I wrote it down the first time, after I woke up, and just made notations in my notebook after the other occurrences. At the time of the dreams, I did not associate the dreams with the mission trip but I did associate them with our contacts in that country. In essence, the Lord told me in the dream that these contacts were very precious to Him and that He was going to protect them. He used very specific symbolism in the dream that conveyed this message very clearly. I was to be very careful while I was there because their lives were in extreme danger. I kept the dream to myself because I did not sense that I was to share it with anyone at that time.

The day came for us to leave on the trip. We all carried native language bibles in our bags to distribute to the indigenous pastors, when we saw them. As we were exiting airport customs, several from our group were told by the airport security team to run their bags through the x-ray machine. We all started praying because we knew if their bags were scanned, the bibles would be discovered and we'd be sent back home. As the bags were on the belt moving toward the scanner, suddenly the belt stopped. The security personnel ran to the x-ray machine and began talking among themselves. It seems the x-ray machine broke down. During the commotion, we all grabbed our bags and left the airport as quickly as we could. We got into our bus and left for our hotel.

That night, I had another dream that incorporated elements of that previous recurring dream. The dream was very vivid and very detailed. When I woke up from the dream, I wrote it down in my notebook, with the interpretation. That morning I went to one of the leaders of the trip (who I knew was open to these types of things) and I told him about my previous recurring dreams, the dream I had that previous night, as well as what I thought the interpretation of the dream was. He agreed, he thought it was from God and that the interpretation was correct. We went to my seminary professor and told him about the dreams and he agreed that we needed to tell the team because God was speaking to us about the situation we had entered into in this country. There were about twenty people in our group.

The essence of what God was telling us through the dreams was that we were not only being watched very closely but, also, being listened to on a regular basis. There were people all around us who were trying to find out why we were there, since we had gone into this country in the guise of tourists; authorities of this country don't allow people identifying themselves as missionaries into the country. If we were not careful, if we were slack in our speech and our actions, we could place our contacts and the indigenous pastors, as well as other Christian contacts and "secret" missionaries there, in danger. We had to walk and speak cautiously while we were there.

We Americans have tremendous freedoms and liberties in our country. Not that we take them for granted but sometimes we forget that Christians and missionaries in other countries do not enjoy these same liberties and freedoms. Talking publicly about God is commonplace here. In other countries it can have you put in prison or killed. We need to be sensitive to the environment of the country we are entering and remember that these people are very precious to God and He does not want their lives put in danger because of our negligence or insensitivity.

That morning at breakfast, the three of us made the rounds of the team, quietly explaining the situation, giving references to the dream, and encouraging everyone to be cautious in their deeds and words. Immediately after breakfast it became very clear why God warned us about the environment we had entered. We had to meet with the indigenous pastors secretly, two at a time, in a remote place. We had to drive around for thirty minutes before arriving at the location where the pastors were being taught, just in case we were being followed. The rest of the team acted like tourists so the authorities wouldn't suspect anything.

Immediately after breakfast that first morning, without our knowledge, the government-controlled television station had assigned a news team to follow us wherever we went, filming us and asking us questions, on camera, as to what we were doing there and what our plans were while we were in their country. Our tour guides (we had to have some or we would not have looked like tourists) were with the large group everywhere we went, always asking us what we were doing there. The second day we were there, one of the pastors in our group met with one of the secret missionaries in that country that his church supported.

After telling this missionary about the dream I had that first night, the missionary told the pastor that the hotel where we were staying may be "bugged"; that this hotel is one of several where the government puts visiting tourists from western countries. When the pastor relayed this information to our team, we knew we had to be careful about mentioning the names of our contacts or of missionaries in that country so that we would not put them in danger.

About five days into the trip, one of the team leaders and his wife had a startling incident take place in their hotel room one morning. That morning, the wife woke up and went into the bathroom and found water on the floor from where a faucet had been leaking. She went back into the bedroom and told her husband about it. A few minutes later there was a knock at their door. When the man opened the door, there was a maintenance person at the door, who said, "I understand you are having a water problem in your room. May I fix it?" He fixed it and then left. What is so startling about this incident is that neither the man nor his wife had said anything to any of us or anyone at the hotel about the water problem. When they told the team this, we knew we had to be very careful and that we could not speak openly about what we were doing, in our rooms or anywhere in or near the hotel.

God used this set of prophetic events to protect His people and resources in that country, and to teach us a valuable lesson regarding mission work. He also made all of us more aware of the fact that He knows everything that is going on and is never caught by surprise. I was open to being used prophetically and God used me to communicate the need for extreme caution in regard to our words and deeds on that particular trip. God used these prophetic events to teach us and to bring us all a little further along in our understanding of the Kingdom of God and His prophetic activities taking place all around us.

God and His Kingdom are continuously active all around us. He is never unaware or surprised by what is happening. We just need to develop the ability to hear what He is saying and to see what He is doing so we can recognize when He is speaking to us and acting on our behalf. We won't always "pick up on it" when it happens but the more we develop our ability to hear the Holy Spirit, the more we will see His hand in our everyday experiences.

God is not a respecter of persons. God wants all of us, as His Kingdom people, to operate in the prophetic activity of the Kingdom. We will experience it at different levels and in varying frequency. Some will experience it in different ways than others. Much of what we experience has to do with what God has placed us in the Body of Christ to do, and the prophetic activity taking place through our life is tied to our function in the Body. Likewise, a person's spiritual maturity is not tied to the level and frequency of the prophetic activities of God operating through his/her life.

Paul told the Corinthians that they were immature, babes in Christ, even though they were not lacking in any spiritual gift and were experiencing the prophetic activity of God at a high level.[83] Spiritual maturity is tied to the level of the fruit of the Spirit being exhibited through a person's life.[84] Let God use us however and whenever He wants to, and He will take care of the frequency and level at which we experience these prophetic activities. All we have to do is have an attentive mind and heart, spend time with God getting to know Him and letting Him reveal Himself to us, and over time we will begin to experience these activities in and through our lives.

[83] 1Corinthians 3:1-3; 1Corinthians 1:4-7
[84] Galatians 5:22-23

Chapter Questions & Notes

Talk It Over….

1) God desires to build a prophetic history with each of us where He establishes His spiritual communications and Kingdom activities in and through our lives, over time. He has, most likely, begun this Kingdom activity in our lives but we may not be aware of it. Can you remember a time when you believe God spoke to you or you experienced God working in or through you to in a prophetic manner?

Leader: Encourage your group to begin keeping a personal journal where they can write down experiences where they believe God worked prophetically in and through their lives, as well as when they believe God spoke to them. Have them capture what He said to them and the situation in which He worked in their lives, and any results that came from these activities. If they had a prophetic dream or vision, have them write down the specifics of it, in as much detail as possible, including prominent colors, people, words that were spoken, imagery, and movements. As they keep a log of these activities, they may find that God is speaking to and acting through them more often than they think.

(8)

Prayer & Music:
Catalysts For The Prophetic Activity of God

"When I remember You on my bed, ***I meditate on You*** *in the night watches."* Psalm 63:6 (emphasis mine)

"'But now bring me a minstrel.' And ***it came about, when the minstrel played, that the hand of the Lord came upon him.*** *And he said, 'Thus says the Lord…'."* I Kings 3:15-16 (emphasis mine)

"And when He had taken the book, the four living creatures and the twenty-four elders fell down before the Lamb, ***having each one a harp*** *and* ***golden bowls full of incense, which are the prayers of the saints.****"* Revelation 5:8 (emphasis mine)

If we look closely at the prophetic events that have taken place throughout human history, we can see two specific spiritual activities that seem to go hand-in-hand with or act as spiritual catalysts for the prophetic activity of the Kingdom of God. These two spiritual activities or catalysts are music and prayer. We know that after the fall of the human race in the garden, the hearts of men and women drifted away from God, and as a result, we no longer knew how to seek after or approach God, nor did we know how to place ourselves in a position to hear from God and to effectively communicate with Him. Therefore, God established models or examples that we can observe and learn from in order to place ourselves in a position to connect with, receive from, and engage with the person and ministry of the Holy Spirit and the prophetic activities of the Kingdom of God in our lives.

One of these models or examples that God established for us is the spiritual life of Moses. Moses is the man God used to establish the model or example for the prophetic catalyst we call prayer. There are examples of many types of prayer in the life of Moses. The type of prayer that God specifically introduced to His people through Moses is what we now call *contemplative prayer* or prayer that contemplates or ponders the person and presence of God. If we recognize this aspect of his life and embrace, learn from and consistently engage in this contemplative prayer, we too can begin to grow in our experience of the presence and spiritual communication with God and the prophetic activities of the Kingdom of God.

As we follow the life of Moses, we see that this contemplative prayer often leads to Moses engaging in intercessory prayer because the prophetic nature of contemplative prayer prepared Moses to receive direction and insight from God for engaging in prayer for the children of Israel. Intercessory prayer (placing oneself between another and God in order to request, on their behalf, the benevolence or provision of God) can take place for situations, individuals, groups of people, and nations. The prophetic nature of contemplative prayer is an opportunity for direction and insight to be communicated by God for the purpose of intercessory prayer. There isn't enough room in this book to dwell on the prophetic catalyst of prayer to any great extent but I believe we can gain a tremendous amount of insight in regard to this activity by looking at two key events in the life of Moses.

The Prophetic Catalyst Of Prayer

The first key event takes place in Exodus 33:7-11.

"Now Moses used to take the tent and pitch it outside the camp, a good distance from the camp, and he called it the tent of meeting. And it came about, that everyone who sought the Lord would go out to the tent of meeting which was outside the camp. And it came about, whenever Moses went out to the tent that all the people would arise and stand, each at the entrance of his tent, and gaze after Moses until he entered the tent. And it came about, whenever Moses entered the tent, the pillar of cloud would descend and stand at the entrance of the tent; and the Lord would speak with Moses. When all the people saw the pillar of cloud standing at the entrance of the tent, all the people would arise and worship, each at the entrance of his tent. Thus the Lord used to speak to Moses face to face, just as a man speaks to his friend. When Moses returned to the camp, his servant Joshua, the son of Nun, a young man, would not depart from the tent."

When God used Moses to lead the children of Israel out of Egypt and through the wilderness for forty years, God often met with Moses to speak with him. As a meeting place for these times of prayer and communication with God, Moses set up a tent outside the camp of the people, which he called the Tent of Meeting, set apart specifically for the purpose of meeting with God. God used these times of communication with Moses to instruct Him and the children of Israel on how to dwell with and cooperate with Him as their God. Moses would spend time in the tent contemplating, pondering and communicating with God. God would also speak to Moses regarding His purpose and plans for His people. As a result of these intimate times of prayer between God and Moses, Moses and God developed an intimate, spiritual connection and relationship to the point where God called Moses His friend because they would speak to one another face to face.

We are told in Psalm 103:7 that God *"made known His ways to Moses, His acts to the sons of Israel."* God exhibited His mighty deeds and miraculous acts in the presence of the children of Israel but He revealed Himself and His ways, as a person, to Moses. This is the result of a heart that was fascinated with God and engaged Him in personal, intimate, contemplative prayer. Moses didn't simply know about God, he knew God, Himself, on an intimate, personal level.

When we pursue and relate to God in such a way, as His son or daughter, He will meet with us and reveal Himself to us. We will, over time, develop an intimacy of relationship with God where He will call us "friend". He will reveal to us what He is thinking, doing and saying. We will develop a loyalty and trust with Him, where He will reveal things to us, not for us to go around telling everyone but as a friend who reveals secrets and personal information to a close friend.

We will see a greater frequency and level of prophetic Kingdom activity in our lives because we will be so attentive to Him and be so aware of His immediate presence in our lives that He will guide us in what He wants us to pray for and how we can help someone who needs an encouraging word from Him, that only He can deliver to them. He will be able to speak the softest words or give us the slightest impression of His will and we will "hear" or "see" it and be able to respond to Him or act for Him. Contemplative Prayer is a significant key or catalyst for experiencing the intimate presence of God and the prophetic activity of God in our lives.

A second event in the life of Moses that teaches us about contemplative prayer is in the same chapter of Exodus 33, verses 13-19. Here, Moses speaks with God, saying, *"Now therefore, I ask You, if I have found favor in Your sight, let me know Your ways, that I may know You, so that I may find favor in Your sight"...And He said, "My presence shall go with you, and I will give you rest"...And the Lord said to Moses, "I will also do this thing of which you have spoken; for you have found favor in My sight, and I have known you by name"...Then Moses said, "I pray You, show me Your glory!" And He said, "I Myself will make all My goodness pass before you, and will proclaim the name of the Lord before you..."*

After all of these years of developing a personal history of contemplative prayer, communication, and fellowship with God, face to face, Moses still wasn't satisfied. He wanted as much of God as he could get. He went before God and asked God to show him His glory - His brilliance and His beauty. Because of the intimacy of the relationship that had developed over the many years between Moses and God, God told Moses that he had found favor in His sight and that He knew him by name – considered Moses His friend.

Therefore, when Moses came to God and requested to see God's glory, God did not turn him away. Even though God could not allow Moses to see His face because it would kill him, God did place Moses in a position where he could catch a glimpse of God when He passed by him. The more time we spend in contemplative prayer before God and allow Him to reveal Himself to us and speak to us, the more we will become dissatisfied with a superficial intellectual knowledge about Him. We will want to know and experience the Person of God; who He is, as one knows an intimate friend. This is when we begin to see God manifest Himself in and through our lives because God is a revealer of mysteries and a rewarder of those who diligently seek Him.[85]

Prayer is a key catalyst for the prophetic activities of God. Contemplative prayer will enhance the effectiveness of our other kinds of prayer because contemplative prayer builds our personal intimate experience and history with God, in His presence. Contemplative prayer is where God reveals Himself to us on a personal level. We begin to "hear" the still small voice of the Spirit of God as He speaks to us in our spirit. He illuminates our mind and gives us revelation of His divine nature, as well as His plans and purposes. The reason is because this type of prayer focuses completely on God and on spending large amounts of time simply pondering the person of God.

This type of prayer requires time alone, free from distractions and other activity. It requires "a place to meet" because you will want to spend

[85] Daniel 2:47; 1Corinthians 2:10-13; Hebrews 11:6

extended amounts of time with God, meeting with Him in His presence. The mind and body must be quiet in order to focus our attention and thoughts on God and God alone. Only then will we be able to see what God is doing and hear what He is saying. This is when we see the prophetic activity of the Kingdom of God really become active in our lives. Not because God is finally deciding to reveal Himself and His Kingdom to us but because we are finally putting ourselves in a position to be able to hear and see what He is already saying and doing, allowing Him to work through our lives just as He has worked and continues to work in and through the lives of others.

The Prophetic Catalyst Of Music

Another significant prophetic catalyst is music. There are many forms of music and they all appeal to us and affect us in different ways. Music is a spiritual communication and it affects us within the deepest recesses of our being. It affects our bodies, souls and spirits. As a result, music has been used throughout the history of the human race to bless the hearts of people, as well as to manipulate the hearts of people. Music is used by the god of this world and the domain of darkness to communicate the messages, values, and activities of this world's system; and music is used by God to communicate the message, values, and activities of His Kingdom. Music influences the human heart. Therefore, we must guard our hearts with all diligence, for from it flows the springs of life.[86]

Now, the music I am referring to as a prophetic catalyst is not the "popular", entertainment-based music we predominantly hear in the world around us. The music that can be a catalyst for the prophetic activities of the Kingdom of God in our lives is music that is most often "born" in times of "quietness before the Lord", where the Spirit of God imparts "a bit of heaven" into the heart of a person and that impartation is set to music.

It is when a person's spirit responds to the presence of God through a musical instrument and/or their voice. This music is another form of "spiritual communication" between God and an individual, which communicates the heart of God to an individual, prompting a response from the individual back to Him. This music truly has a dimension to it that is "other worldly" and impacts the human heart in a way that no other music can. It is more than a nice tune with meaningful words. A person

---

[86] Proverbs 4:23

who engages in this type of spiritual music, born in the presence of God, is often called a psalmist.

There is a dimension of music where the Spirit of God inhabits the music; where the Spirit manifests His power and presence through the music. It is a form of music that produces a response of praise and/or worship to God from those who engage with it. When this prophetic music is in the heart and on the lips of God's people, the scriptures tell us that "He inhabits the praises of His people." [87] This music is often referred to as "prophetic music" because of the spiritual interaction that takes place between heaven and earth in and through the music. It may be instrumental only, lyrics only, or may include instruments and lyrics together. Like other things that defy adequate description, it can be said of prophetic music, "I know it when I hear it." It has a divine quality that cuts through the distractions, noise, and the "clutter" of life in order to connect the human heart with the heart of God.

As I mentioned before, God establishes models or examples of the significant truths and activities He wants us to understand and engage with. Just as God used Moses as a model and example for the prophetic catalyst of Contemplative Prayer, God has established models and examples for us in the area of Prophetic Music. One of these examples is King David, who the scriptures refer to as "the sweet psalmist of Israel".[88] Let me explain how God has established David as a model for His people regarding the exercise and ministry of prophetic music in our personal and corporate lives.

In the New Testament, David is one of the most often referred to and quoted individuals from the Old Testament. Many places throughout scripture, we see it written, "David says"[89], "David speaks"[90], or "saying through David".[91] We are all aware of the many prophecies that God spoke through David when he was alive, especially through his psalms. From the time he was anointed by Samuel as a young boy, God's calling and purpose for David was that of a king over His people. Yet, he was such a prophetic person and God revealed so much to him prophetically. The simple reason God did this is because David had discovered, learned, and applied the catalysts for the prophetic in his personal experience and life with God: Contemplative Prayer and Prophetic Music.

---

[87] Psalm 22:3

[88] 2Samuel 23:1

[89] Acts 2:25 Romans 11:9 Acts 4:25 Luke 20:42

[90] Romans 4:6 Mark 12:36

[91] Hebrews 4:7 Acts 1:16

David is called, in scripture, "a man after God's heart," [92] and God used David as a model for us to observe and understand how we can experience the prophetic activity of God in our day-to-day lives through an intimate relationship with God. We too can experience and grow in the prophetic activities of the Kingdom as we commit ourselves to be "people after God's heart" and as we discover, learn, and apply the truths regarding Contemplative Prayer and Prophetic Music to our own personal experience with God. We don't have to be great musicians or singers. It's not the quality of our voice that God is after. It's the humility, sincerity and desire of our heart.

Even though we are not told explicitly in the scriptures that David practiced Contemplative Prayer and Prophetic Music, we can see the results of what Contemplative Prayer and Prophetic Music will have on a person's life, in the life of David. Even while he was a shepherd boy guarding his father's sheep in the fields, there are scriptures that strongly imply that he engaged in these spiritual activities. In 1Samuel 16 we see the prophetic event where God sends the Prophet Samuel to the home of Jesse in order to anoint the person who would replace Saul as the next king of Israel.

As Jesse had his sons pass before Samuel, one at a time, God instructs Samuel about one of Jesse's older sons by saying, *"...Do not look at his appearance or at the height of his stature because I have rejected him; for God sees not as man sees, for man looks at the outward appearance but the Lord looks at the heart."*[93] It is soon after God said this to Samuel that David is brought before him. As David comes before Samuel, God says to him, *""Arise, anoint him; for this is he." Then Samuel took the horn of oil and anointed him in the midst of his brothers; and the Spirit of the Lord came mightily upon David from that day forward."*[94]

We can see from this first mention of David in the scriptures that he has been engaged in some sort of spiritual activity that is having a profound effect upon his personal experience and relationship with God. God already knows David, as a young boy, and chooses him as the next king of Israel as a result of his tender and devotional heart before God, not as a result of his intellectual, personality, or physical attributes.

Again, in 1Samuel 16, after the anointing of David as the next king of Israel, we are told that an evil spirit comes upon King Saul as a result of his

---

[92] 1Samuel 13:14 Acts 13:22
[93] 1Samuel 16:7
[94] vs. 13

rebellion against the will and word of God. Saul's servants suggest that they find *"a man who is a skillful player on the harp; and it shall come about when the evil spirit from God is on you, that he shall play the harp with his hand, and you will be well."* Then one of the other servants of Saul speaks up saying, *"Behold,* ***I have seen a son of Jesse*** *the Bethlehemite* ***who is a skillful musician,*** *a mighty man of valor, a warrior, one prudent in speech, and a handsome man;* ***and the Lord is with him,"*** [95] (emphasis mine).

We are given three points here regarding Prophetic Music and David's skill and ability to engage in the ministry of Prophetic Music: *1)* The servants of Saul know that Saul is experiencing the effects of an evil spirit tormenting him and they know that if they can find a musician to play for him, who is skilled on the instrument, he can be relieved of the torment; *2)* David is recognized as one who is, not only skilled in playing the harp, but one of the servants of Saul has actually observed David engaged in playing the harp skillfully; *3)* This servant has also observed and acknowledges that the presence of God is with David when he plays the harp skillfully.

We are told in the first point that music influenced and directed by the Spirit of God can have a tremendous effect upon the influence and activity of evil spirits in the lives of people. We also know that if the Holy Spirit is present to manifest His activity through the life of an individual, then He is working prophetically in and through that individual. If the Holy Spirit is working in the life of Saul to rid him of the tormenting effects of an evil spirit and He is doing so through the skillful harp playing of David, then David's music created on the harp is prophetic in nature. In this instance, David can be said to be a prophetic musician. David is not just skillfully playing music that is pleasing to hear; he is spontaneously and skillfully playing music that is being used by the Holy Spirit to manifest the activities of the Kingdom of God in Saul's life.

These few scriptures help us to understand that David was actively pursuing the prophetic activities of the Kingdom of God in his life, at an early age, through Contemplative Prayer and Prophetic Music, even when he was alone in the fields tending to his father's sheep. He developed the skill of playing the harp but he also set his heart to know God. By setting his heart to know God, he was able to spend those days and nights alone with his father's sheep developing an intimacy and personal history with God through Contemplative Prayer.

---

[95] 1Samuel 16:16-18

As David spent more and more time contemplating and pondering the person of God, God began to unite his Contemplative Prayer with his musical skills. The thoughts and words that David expressed to God during his times of Contemplative Prayer with God were spontaneously put to music. He would simply play the tunes that arose from his heart and whatever words came into his heart, he would sing them to God as he played the tune. It was also at these times that God spoke to David, revealing more and more of who He is to him.[96]

David didn't stop pursuing this prophetic activity in his life when he left the fields and his father's sheep to run from the hand of Saul and, then, to be king over Israel. He continued engaging in it and growing in it for the rest of his life. As he grew and matured as a prophetic musician, the spontaneous prayers he prayed to God became prophetic songs he began to write down after he prayed them to God. These prophetic songs became part of what we now call the Book of Psalms in the Old Testament. They are David's prayers to God put to music at the time he first expressed them to God. As David matured as a prophetic musician, not only did he put his own prayers to music as he prayed them to God, but God's own words spoken to David during these times of Contemplative Prayer were also put to music. This is why we see so many prophecies in David's music.

As David engaged in Contemplative Prayer with God, he truly began to see what God was doing and hearing what God was saying. God began revealing His purposes and plans to David in their times together and David would put these thoughts from God to music. That is why we see such powerful prophetic songs such as Psalm 2, Psalm 22, Psalm 24, and Psalm 40.

In David, God combined the prophetic catalysts of Contemplative Prayer and skillful music in order to establish a new wineskin called Prophetic Music. God established David as a forerunner for this new wineskin and placed him in a prominent leadership position, as king of God's chosen people, in order to promote its practice and to establish its operation within the worship activities of Israel after he became king. We see where David engaged the prophetic singers and musicians to lead the procession to bring the Ark of the Covenant back to Jerusalem,[97] and where he established the regular, ongoing ministry of the prophetic singers and prophetic musicians within the house of God in Jerusalem.[98]

---

[96] Psalm 63:6
[97] 1Chronicles 15

David also instructed his son Solomon in regard to the ministry of Prophetic Music in the house of God. After David died, we see that Solomon, the new king of Israel, continues this ministry to the Lord in the new temple that he builds for the presence of the Lord and the Ark of the Covenant. In 2Chronicles 5, we are given the account of this event where they bring the Ark of the Covenant from the temporary tent into the new Temple of Solomon. Solomon gathers all of the priests, singers, and musicians into the temple. Then we are told:

"And when the priests came forth from the holy place (for all the priests who were present had sanctified themselves, without regard to divisions), and all the Levitical singers, Asaph, Heman, Jeduthun, and their sons and kinsmen, clothed in fine linen, with cymbals, harps, and lyres, standing east of the altar, and with them one hundred and twenty priests blowing trumpets in unison when the trumpeters and the singers were to make themselves heard with one voice to praise and to glorify the Lord, and when they lifted up their voice accompanied by trumpets and cymbals and instruments of music, and when they praised the Lord saying, "He indeed is good for His lovingkindness is everlasting," ***then the house, the house of the Lord, was filled with a cloud, so that the priests could not stand to minister because of the cloud, for the glory of the Lord filled the house of God.*** *"*

This is the result of embracing, introducing, and integrating the prophetic activity of God into the life of God's people. God introduced and established this model or wineskin among His people in and through the life of David, until they turned away from God and let these things slip during the later reign of Solomon. David, as a forerunner of this Kingdom model, established it in the corporate life of God's people. Solomon took this model and incorporated it into the new Temple of Solomon.

As a result of their obedience and the established operation of Prophetic Music and its ministry before God, the manifest presence and power of God so filled the Temple of Solomon that the priests could not stand to minister. God, truly, inhabits the praises of His people. They were physically unable to stand and continue their ministry before God that day. The manifest presence of God filled the Temple. Years later, during the ministry of the prophet Elisha, we see that Elisha understood the nature and ability of prophetic music, and was still engaging prophetic music in his ministry, in 2Kings 3:15-16. Prophetic music is a catalyst for the prophetic activity of God.

---

[98] 1Chronicles 16

We also see Contemplative Prayer and Prophetic Music in the New Testament. We often see Jesus removing Himself from the crowds, and even from His own disciples, in order to retreat to a place of solitude where He can be alone with the Father. Jesus had to contemplate and ponder the Father, just as we do, in order to see what the Father was doing and to hear what He was saying.[99] We also see in the life of the Apostle Paul, where he and Silas were being held in a Philippian jail. As Paul and Silas prayed and sang songs of praise to God, a prophetic event took place that shook the jail where they were being held. The chains that were holding them fell from their wrists, and the doors of their jail cell swung open. Contemplative Prayer and Prophetic Music establishes an environment where the prophetic activity of God can take place to further the purpose of God on the earth.

Paul also teaches us regarding Contemplative Prayer and Prophetic Music, in 1Corinthians, when he instructs the believers in Corinth regarding the prophetic activity of God in their personal lives, *"For if I pray in a tongue, my spirit prays, but my mind is unfruitful. What is the outcome then? I shall pray with the spirit and I shall pray with the mind also; I shall sing with the spirit and I shall sing with the mind also."*[100] Paul was not addressing Prophets only in this letter, he was addressing all of God's people when he said, *"For you can all prophesy one by one, so that all may learn and all may be exhorted."*[101] Paul goes on to instruct us to, "*...not get drunk with wine, for that is dissipation, but be filled with the Spirit, speaking to one another in psalms and hymns and spiritual songs, singing and making melody with your heart to the Lord; always giving thanks for all things in the name of our Lord Jesus Christ to God, even the Father.*"[102]

These songs and prayers are intended to be spontaneous, from our hearts, to the Lord. In recent years we have seen the tremendous impact that contemporary worship music has had upon the Body of Christ. We have experienced a greater reality of the presence God in our personal lives and in the lives of our churches as a result of these "new" songs. Yet, we need to understand that God is continually moving forward with the purposes of His Kingdom. There will be new "moves" of the Spirit in the area of music and worship. We must be "in tune" with the Spirit when the "new wine" of spontaneous worship, prophetic music and intercessory prayer breaks out in our midst.

---

[99] Matthew 14:13 Mark 1:35 Luke 4:42
[100] 1Corinthians 14:14-15
[101] 1Corinthians 14:26-33
[102] Ephesians 5:18-20 Colossians 3:16

In this scripture in Revelation, we are told, *"And when He had taken the book, the four living creatures and the twenty-four elders fell down before the Lamb,* ***having each one a harp, and golden bowls full of incense, which are the prayers of the saints.*** *And* ***they sang a new song,*** *saying, "Worthy are You to take the book, and to break its seals; for You were slain, and did purchase for God with Your blood, men from every tribe and tongue and people and nation. "And You have made them to be a kingdom and priests to our God; and they will reign upon the earth."* "

The harp that each creature and elder holds, in heaven, represents the prophetic music of the Kingdom of God. Music is not "just music" in heaven. It is alive, active, and powerful. The bowls that each one holds represents the prayers of the saints, including Contemplative Prayers. Prophetic Music and Prayer (including Contemplative Prayer) are continually before the throne of God, even today. They are, both, very important to Him. He places these things in the possession of the creatures and the elders in order that they may continually bring them before the Lord day and night. Just as Prophetic Music and Prayer affect us as God's people, they also affect God, Himself.[103]

It is important for us as leaders and as those who have chosen to embrace and integrate the prophetic activities of the Kingdom of God, to make a place for Prayer (including Contemplative Prayer) and Prophetic Music within our personal lives and our congregations. We must begin with our own personal lives and let God use us to bring about the change within the lives of those in our congregations. These catalysts for the prophetic activities of God must begin in the individual lives of God's people, especially the leaders, before they can be expected to expand corporately.

God started it in the personal lives of Moses and of David, in the back-side of the wilderness, and then brought it to His people when He made both of them leaders over His people. We as His leaders must allow God to do the same with us. We must develop these things in our personal life with God, and then allow God to use us to establish them in the corporate life of our churches.

---

[103] Zephaniah 3:17 Exodus 32:9-14

Chapter Questions & Notes

1) Contemplative prayer, or prayer that ponders or contemplates the person and presence of God, is an experiential prayer activity. We aren't actively making requests of God as much as we are being quiet before Him in order to allow the Holy Spirit to engage our spirit in fellowship and communication. It is in these times, when we are quiet before Him, that God reveals Himself and connects with our hearts in fellowship and prophetic experience.

   If we haven't engaged in this contemplative prayer before or don't have much experience with it, there is only one place to start....at the beginning. At times when you are in your group and, more often when you are alone, be quiet and still (perhaps having some quiet music playing in the background, and your eyes closed). Focus your attention on a scripture from the Bible or on a particular attribute of God. As you do this, simply speak to God, in your heart, telling Him how much you love Him and appreciate Him for who He is. Don't be in any hurry because He isn't. Allow your mind and emotions to become quiet and still. This may take some time, at first. As you contemplate God, you will find that the Holy Spirit begins to connect with you, in your heart. You may get an impression about something, perhaps Him telling you how much He loves you.

   Stay with these impressions by responding to them with your own thoughts. Don't do all the talking. Listen for the voice of the Spirit inside of you. Enjoy just being in His presence and allowing Him to respond to you as you respond to Him. You may not experience very much the first time or two of praying like this but keep at it. Don't be in a hurry and don't get frustrated with it. God loves that you are taking the time to be with Him and He will train you to hear His voice and to respond to Him, over time. Set aside time every day to be with Him and to engage with Him in this way. You will grow in this contemplative prayer and He will expand your capacity to respond to Him and to engage with Him in other types of prayer.

Keep a journal of these times of contemplative prayer. Write down what you experience; what you say to Him and any impressions you get, that seem to be a response from Him. If you believe God says something to you, write it down. If you see something in your mind's eye, write down what you see. Keep these experiences in your journal and review them from time to time. You will find that, over time, you will hear the voice of the Spirit and will experience the prophetic presence and activities of the Spirit more and more in your life, over time.

These times and experiences may ebb and flow, over time but stay with it. You will find that God trains you and establishes with you a prophetic communication history. You will find that He establishes a pattern or modes of communication with you that is His "signature" communications with you. Enjoy it and allow Him to teach and train you in this prophetic fellowship and communication. It will change and impact your life.

Leaders: Have your groups spend time together, in contemplative prayer, where you can be available to answer questions and give guidance and encouragement to them, especially in the beginning stages of their prayer experience with Him. Encourage them to be patient and not in a hurry. Provide an environment where they can be quiet and still before God. Play soft, instrumental music in the background that will not be a distraction to them but will assist them in focusing their hearts and minds on God.

(9)

The Beauty Of God: The Only Wonder Worthy Of Our Fascination

"One thing I have asked from the Lord that I shall seek, that I may dwell in the house of the Lord all the days of my life; ***to behold the beauty of the Lord*** *and to meditate in His temple."* Psalm 27:4 (emphasis mine)

"...he will dwell on the heights, his refuge will be the impregnable rock, his bread will be given him, and his water will be sure. ***Your eyes will see the King in His beauty****, they will behold a far-distant land."* Isaiah 33:16-17 (emphasis mine)

We were created to be fascinated! God created us with tremendous spiritual, mental, emotional and physical prowess so that we could experience, respond to, and interact with Him and His creation at the highest possible level. Our physical senses and soulish desires were in perfect harmony with and in subjection to our spirits, which was in intimate fellowship and communication with God. When we experienced God and His creation, we experienced them as God intended for us to experience them and to receive the best possible benefit from them, as He intended it to be. When God completed His creation, He said that it was "very good".[104] When God says something is "very good", it is awesome!

When God created human beings, He created us with our entire being aligned perfectly with the will and purpose that God had intended for us – nothing was out of place or "misaligned". God created us to enjoy, rule over and subdue the earth as His regents but God created us to be fascinated with Him and Him alone.[105] We were fascinated with God until we turned our eyes from the beauty of God and onto ourselves. We thought that we could be just like God.[106] In one sinful act, we became fascinated with ourselves and turned our eyes from the only person we could ever, truly, be fascinated with - God.

[104] Genesis 1:31
[105] Deuteronomy 6:5
[106] Genesis 3:5

Since the sin of Adam and Eve in the Garden, we have been trying to discover something or someone who could, once again, fascinate us. As much as we have endeavored to maintain our fascination with ourselves and our achievements, we always seem to come up short of our expectations. We believed a lie to begin with. We believed that we could fascinate ourselves but we were wrong…we are, still, wrong. Some of us have come to the stark realization that we will never be able to fascinate ourselves but the great majority of us still believe the lie and are going to great lengths in an effort to fascinate ourselves with our own devices.

God never intended for us to be fascinated with anyone or anything but Him. We were created to gaze upon Him with fascination and amazement. He created us with such advanced attributes and capabilities, nothing was to amaze us and fascinate us like only God can. He was to be the only wonder worthy of our fascination. The fact is, He still is…that hasn't changed. As much as we endeavor to discover other creatures or manufacture other things to fascinate us, everything else comes up short. We keep inventing and authoring and developing new things, hoping that they will bring us the fascination we so deeply desire and long for. Yet, nothing seems to satisfy that longing.

In 1977, the original "Star Wars" movie was released. It has been said that in that moment, in the opening scene of the movie when the large space ship slowly entered the screen from overhead and seemed to fill the entire room with its presence and sounds as it pursued the much smaller ship in front of it, moviemaking and the movie "experience" changed forever. People seemed to finally experience what we had all hoped for - we were finally fascinated and amazed, or so we thought.

Even though we thought we were fascinated, we kept clamoring for more; better cinematography, better sound, and a better physical interaction with the movie. This desire to be even more fascinated brought the Dolby Surround Sound experience. Yet, that wasn't enough. Next came the 3-D experience, where the characters and action seemed to leap off the screen and include the audience in the action.

When that didn't seem to satisfy us, we were given the IMAX experience, which brought the video quality and size to a new level. And, again, when this didn't quite fascinate us enough, we rigged the seats in the theater so we could experience the movements and "shaking" associated with what was going on in the movie. Now, we didn't have to be satisfied with simply seeing the explosion happen in the movie, we could hear it, feel it, and experience the effects of it while sitting in our seats. The plot of the movie doesn't really matter as long as we can shake, rattle and roll with what we are watching.

Do not think that I am against the proliferation of technology or doing what we can with technology to be more efficient and effective on the job or at home. On the contrary, I have been involved with developing and introducing new and emerging technology for over thirty years. Our lives have been greatly enriched and aided by technology development over the centuries. What I'm bringing to our attention is that we, as the human race, have often looked to technology, people, and other "things" as a means to satisfy our deep longing to be fascinated but these things have never filled the void. God created us to be enthralled with Him and we will continue to be unsuccessful in our efforts to be fascinated in any other way but with Him.

Even as God's people, we tend to look to "the created rather than the creator" to be fascinated.[107] The creature and the created were never intended to fascinate us and to be the focus of our amazement. We are to appreciate the created and be thankful for how it positively impacts our lives but we were never intended to be fascinated by it. We were created to appreciate and be thankful for the created while being fascinated and amazed by the creator.

Even the prophetic activities of the Kingdom of God (signs, miracles, visions, dreams, angelic visitations, etc.) are not and have never been intended to do anything but to seize our attention, supply a solution to a need, communicate information, or provide validation or proof. In the scriptures, when angels appeared to individuals; when the individuals responded by expressing more honor and recognition to them then they should have, the angels responded by encouraging the individuals to worship or be enthralled with God, not them.[108]

Later in this book I will talk about the need to cast vision for the prophetic activities of God in the local church. Throughout this book I talk about the need for God's Kingdom people to "lust for" the gifts, operations and manifestations of the Spirit – the prophetic activities of the Kingdom of God.[109] God, Himself, encourages us to lust after them and He is the one who performs them in and through our lives. He talks about the need to cast vision[110] and He casts vision for what He will do on the earth using the

[107] Romans 1:25
[108] Daniel 10:4-12; Revelation 19:10; Revelation 19:10
[109] 1Corinthians 12:31; 1Corinthians 14:1,39
[110] Proverbs 29:18

prophetic activities of His Kingdom through His Kingdom people. Yet, He never tells us to be fascinated or enthralled with these activities, to where they take our focus and attention away from being fascinated with Him.

We can't really appreciate the value and purpose of the prophetic activities of the Kingdom of God and their place in our lives without having a deep fascination and amazement with God, Himself, through an intimate relationship and fellowship with Him. Without it, we will give too much value, time and attention to the "created", which undermines its value and purpose. The prophetic activities of God are good and necessary but without our relationship with God and realizing that He is the one who gives these activities meaning, purpose, and context, the misuse of these activities can actually contribute to us doing spiritual harm to ourselves.

Let me give you an example of what I mean from personal experience. For a time, during the 1990s, I was the communications manager for the IBM Personal Computing Division's Chief Technology Officer. His job was to see the technologies the IBM scientists and developers were inventing and developing and understand where these technologies could be incorporated and brought to market within IBM PC products. My job was to help and support him by understanding the benefits of these technologies, identifying the needs these technologies would satisfy, recognizing who would benefit from these technologies, developing the messaging for these technologies, determining the best forms of communication to use to reach those who need these technologies, and reaching out to the best communication channels for communicating these messages to those who needed to hear them.

Most of all, I was to promote the CTO as the person who knew the technology landscape, recognized the needs in the marketplace, and had the technology solutions and technology roadmap for satisfying these needs. It wasn't about the technology itself but how to implement the technology that provided the solution. I needed to make sure that the CTO was recognized as the "expert" in the PC-related technology solutions that mattered most to the marketplace. I needed to help him "cast the vision" for PC-related technology solutions by putting him in front of the people who had the need so they could see him, know who he was, and hear what he had to say. The "wow" of technology isn't enough. It is the person behind the technology, who determines how best to implement it, who gives the technology value and context.

As the CTO's communications manager, one of the communications activities I conducted was to arrange for a technology press and media tour in a handful of cities in Europe. The purpose was to give the CTO exposure to the press, media, influencers and "opinion leaders" in the European geography so he could present some of IBM's emerging technology concepts, as well as give them a roadmap for how to get from point A to point B, implementing these and other technology tools being developed by IBM. The "showcase" technology we used for the tour was what we called the "Wearable PC", which was developed by IBM-Japan. The manager of the group that developed the technology actually came with us on the tour to demonstrate the technology to those attending.

Of the five European cities where we held this emerging technology briefing, everyone was "oohing and ahhing" about the technology in this Wearable PC. Yet, when the fascination with the technology settled down, the first questions asked in every city were, "What do you do with it? Who will want to buy this?" Of course, the CTO had already done his research and had identified some of the needs that this technology could satisfy, as well as who would be a customer for this technology. That is when "the lights went on" in the minds of the press, media, influencers, and "opinion leaders" who attended. The technology was great but it didn't mean much until the CTO gave it a purpose and context – he gave it value. Without the CTO, the technology would have made a splash in the trade magazines, television programs, and newspapers but it would have faded away pretty quickly. Those in attendance appreciated the technology but they applauded the CTO for the purpose, context, and value he gave the technology.

The prophetic activities of the Kingdom of God are good and we can appreciate them for what they are able to do but they need God to give them purpose, context, and value. He knows what He wants to do and why He wants to do it. He sees the heart and life of every person and is able to impact their life and get their attention through the use of these prophetic activities. It is God, Himself, who is the real focus and wonder of the Kingdom and the only wonder who is worthy of our fascination.

Being Fascinated With The Beauty Of God

Okay, if we want to be truly fascinated with God, how does that happen? What do we have to do? The main vehicles through which we "behold the beauty of the Lord" [111] and experience the reality of His beauty in our lives is through prayer and life's experiences. As I mentioned earlier, prayer is a catalyst for the prophetic activities of the Kingdom of God. Yet, we will find that most of the prophetic activity in our lives will take place when no

[111] Psalm 27:4

one else is around; when we are alone with God, simply being with Him and enjoying fellowship and talking with Him. God speaks to us; reveals Himself to us.

We receive "glimpses" of who He is and experience His presence with us in prayer and in our life's experiences. We begin to see and appreciate His beauty - His attributes, His character, and His personality, as He makes them known to us in our daily activities. We don't necessarily see His beauty with our physical eyes but we can see it with our spiritual eyes, as He reveals Himself and makes Himself known to us. This is what prayer, contemplative prayer, and recognizing the activities of God in our lives are all about. All other forms of prayer flow from this "gazing" on the beauty of God.

When we look at the scriptures, we see some of the most astounding prophetic experiences taking place when God reveals Himself to people. When God revealed Himself to Abram, when He made His covenant with him, God revealed Himself to Abram as a flaming lamp and a smoking furnace.[112] God used these common symbols to communicate two of His divine attributes to Abram that would be meaningful to Abram at that moment. God revealed that He is light (flaming lamp), 1John 1:5, and He revealed that He is righteous (smoking furnace), Hebrews 12:29. Is God a lamp or is God a furnace? No but He chose to reveal two of His divine attributes to Abram in this way because that is what Abram needed to experience and understand about God at that moment in his life. These are only two attributes of the multi-faceted beauty of God.

When God revealed Himself to Moses, He actually revealed Himself progressively, over a number of years. He first revealed Himself to Moses as fire burning in the bush, revealing to Moses His justice and righteousness. Later, He revealed Himself to Moses in a cloud, which led and shepherded Moses and the children of Israel in the wilderness, and stood at the door of the Tent of Meeting when Moses entered to fellowship and communicate with God. Later, God revealed Himself to Moses in physical form, when Moses asked God to show him His glory or beauty but Moses could only see Him from behind.

This is when Moses had grown in his relationship with God to where he and God were friends and spoke face to face. God did not have to reveal Himself and His beauty to Moses through object representation, as He and Moses now related to each other person to person. Is God fire or is God a

[112] Genesis 15:17-18

cloud? No but God chose to reveal aspects of Himself, His beauty, to Moses in this way.

When God revealed Himself to Isaiah, He actually gave Isaiah a vision of Himself seated on His throne in the temple of God in heaven.[113] God revealed Himself to Isaiah in His exalted position as King of the universe, in His glory and beauty because Isaiah needed to see this aspect of God's beauty in order to have the courage and confidence to speak what God would have Him say, do what God would have him do, and successfully carry out the assignment God was giving Him to accomplish. As God's prophet and spokesman to His people, Isaiah would confront them and speak to them on God's behalf.

When God revealed Himself to David, He did so in many ways. God revealed Himself as a shepherd who leads David beside still waters, restoring his soul.[114] God also revealed Himself as an avenger who personally came to David's rescue to deliver him, when he was in deep distress and anguish because of his enemies.

When God revealed Himself, David saw what God was doing and says, *"Then the earth shook and quaked; and the foundations of the mountains were trembling and were shaken, because He was angry. Smoke went up out of His nostrils, and fire from His mouth devoured; coals were kindled by it. He bowed the heavens also, and came down with thick darkness under His feet. He rode upon a cherub and flew; and He sped upon the wings of the wind. He made darkness His hiding place, His canopy around Him, darkness of waters, and thick clouds of the skies. From the brightness before Him passed His thick clouds, hailstones and coals of fire. The Lord also thundered in the heavens, and the Most High uttered His voice, hailstones and coals of fire. He sent out His arrows, and scattered them, and lightning flashes in abundance, and routed them. Then the channels of water appeared, and the foundations of the world were laid bare at Your rebuke, O Lord, at the blast of the breath of Your nostrils. He sent from on high, He took me; He drew me out of many waters. He delivered me from my strong enemy, and from those who hated me, for they were too mighty for me."* [115]

Did God really get on the back of a cherub and fly to David's defense? That is how God revealed Himself to David in that situation. David saw another aspect of God's beauty and this is the way God chose to reveal this aspect of who He is, to David. God reveals Himself in ways that we are able to understand and relate to. He speaks to us in our native language; He speaks to us in visual references that we are able to recognize and

[113] Isaiah 6:1-6
[114] Psalm 23
[115] Psalm 18:7-17

understand what He is saying to us; and He speaks to us in written form where He is able to express to us who He is in word-pictures so we can visualize what it is He wants us to know about Him. He uses all of these methods of communication, and more, in order to effectively communicate with us about who He is and so we can, truly, see Him and gaze upon His beauty.

When God revealed Himself to Elijah, He told Elijah to stand on the mountain and He would pass by him. When God came to pass by Elijah, there was a great wind but God was not in the great wind. Then, an earthquake came by but God was not in the earthquake. After the earthquake, a fire came by but God was not in the fire. Then a gentle breeze came by and when Elijah heard the gentle breeze, he went out of the cave because he knew God was there to speak to Him. God came to David in a strong wind on the back of a cherub but He didn't come to Elijah that way. God came to Moses in fire but He didn't come to Elijah that way. God came to Moses and the children of Israel in an earthquake[116] but He didn't come to Elijah that way. God came to Elijah in the gentle breeze because that is the aspect of the beauty of God that Elijah needed to see and experience from God at that moment in his life.

God doesn't come to all of us and reveal Himself to all of us in the same way all of the time. He doesn't even come to each of us or reveal Himself to each of us in the same way all of the time. He comes and He reveals Himself in the way He wants to and the way we need for Him to at different times in our lives. He reveals the different attributes of who He is - His beauty, not only so we can experience what that aspect of Him can do for us but so we can see, experience and "gaze" upon that aspect of His beauty. If all we do is look for the activity of God, we will miss the opportunity to gaze upon that aspect of His beauty that He is revealing to us at that moment. Let me give you an example from my own life.

This experience happened on a particular business trip I took to New York. I arrived at my hotel the night before a meeting I was scheduled to attend. In my hotel room, I unpacked, changed my clothes, went to the hotel restaurant for dinner, and then came back to my room to watch the acceptance speech being given, on television, by the presidential nominee of the political party whose convention was going on at that time, as it was an election year. Then I went to sleep.

The next day I went to my New York office for the meeting. When the meeting was over, I left for the airport to catch my flight back home. In

[116] Numbers 16:28-35

order to get from the New York office to the airport, I had to cross a busy, major toll bridge. When I got close to the toll booth, I reached into my pocket to get my cash to pay the toll. When I reached into my pocket I realized that my cash was missing. I scrambled, trying to figure out what had happened to my cash. The only thing I could think of was that I had accidentally pulled the cash out of my pocket at the same time I pulled my car keys out of my pocket, in the parking lot at the office. I knew I had cash the night before, at the hotel.

When I got to the toll booth, I explained to the attendant that I had lost my cash and had just realized it. He told me that I could go through the toll gate and get off at the first exit in order to go to the local bank and get cash to come back and pay the toll. He told me he would have to hold onto my driver's license to ensure that I returned to pay the toll. So, I got off the toll bridge and found the bank. I didn't have my ATM card so I asked if I could get an advance on my company credit card. They told me I could but they would have to see my driver's license first as identification. I explained my situation and that the toll booth operator kept my license until I could pay the toll but they told me they couldn't give me any cash without seeing my license.

I turned around, walked out of the bank, and just stood in the building's lobby. As I stood there, all I could say was, "Okay God, what do I do now?" Suddenly, it was as if a black and white movie started playing right in front of my eyes. I can only describe it as something like a day dream but I was fully aware of where I was, what I was doing and what I was watching. As I watched this vision, I saw myself the night before, changing my clothes in my hotel room. I watched myself take the cash out of my suit pants and put it in the pants I wore to eat dinner. The vision then skipped forward to when I came back to my room from dinner. I saw that when I took those pants off to get ready for bed, I didn't take the cash out of my pocket. I watched myself pack those pants in my suitcase with the money still in the pocket. Suddenly, the vision ended and it disappeared.

I immediately left the lobby of the bank, went to my car, unzipped my suitcase, reached my hand into the pocket of those pants, and out came the cash I had left in there the night before. It was just as the vision had depicted. Due to some similar experiences I have had over the years, I wasn't as shocked at what had happened, as you would expect. Yet, I was ecstatic at what the Lord had done and I was extremely thankful that He prophetically broke into my situation to help me, as only He could. I thanked the Lord for showing me what had happened and for helping me find the cash. I went back to the bridge, paid my toll, and still made my flight home.

God broke into this particular situation in my life to, simply, help me. It wasn't related to a ministry opportunity or some other experience He wanted to use to impact the life of someone else within my sphere of influence. He simply wanted to show me that He loves me very much and wanted to help me in a personal situation that seemed impossible to me. He came to me in this unique way and revealed more of Himself to me, in this unique attribute of His beauty. He didn't do this because I deserved it or earned it but, simply, because He loves me.

God desires to connect with each of us and, over time, to develop a "spiritual communication history" with each of us. He wants us to discover and experience more of who He is, recognize when He is communicating and interacting with us, and when He is endeavoring to act on our behalf. We won't always "pick up on it" when it happens but the more we develop that communication history with Him, the more we will recognize and see Him, and experience His prophetic activity taking place in and through our lives.

We need to recognize when He is working in our lives and what He is revealing to us about His beauty in those moments. We also need to spend time pondering Him and who He is because that is when He not only reveals the different aspects of His beauty to us but we can take the time to gaze upon that beauty, ask Him questions about that aspect of who He is, and develop a history with Him where we know that we will continue to see Him work in our lives and continue to experience Him revealing His beauty to us, in these activities. Prayer doesn't have to be boring. It is fascinating because we are being enthralled by the only One who is worthy of our fascination.

Chapter Questions & Notes

Talk It Over….

1) There are so many things in our lives that vye for our affections and passions. There is nothing wrong with enjoying what God has given us and the people God has placed within our lives. Yet, we need to keep Him as the most important person in our lives, and He should be the object of our affections and passions more than anything or anyone else in our lives. We can appreciate and enjoy many people and things in our lives but we should be fascinated with God, alone, and who He is in our lives.

   Identify people, things and activities that you find great enjoyment and satisfaction with. List them and think about how much time, effort and resources you spend engaging in and with these people, things and activities. Discuss the place they hold in your life, especially as it relates to the time, effort and resources you expend to pursue your relationship with God.

2) Think about times in your life, where God seemed to help you in a situation or worked in your life to accomplish something you needed His help with. What did He do? How did He do it? Was God gentle and caring in His activity toward you or did He exhibit strength, passion and energy in His activity toward you? How did you see God during those times? Did He seem to "show up" as a different person or expressing a different attribute of Himself, each time?

(10)

The Mystery of God's Eternal Purpose Revealed

"He made known to us the mystery of His will, according to His kind intention which He purposed in Him ***with a view to an administration*** *suitable to the fullness of the times, that is,* ***the summing up of all things in Christ****, things in the heavens and things on the earth."* Ephesians 1:9-10 (emphasis mine)

When it comes to our own lives and how we live from day to day while still thinking about and planning for the future; sometimes we find ourselves thinking something like, "If I only knew what was going to happen in the future, it would be a lot easier to understand and put into perspective the things that are happening right now." We think that if we can catch a glimpse of "the big picture" of what God is doing; a basic knowledge and understanding of what is going to take place in the future, it will give us a point of reference for focusing our activities right now, as well as a hope that we can somehow be actively involved in the Kingdom activities that will bring these future events to pass. It is the desire of each one of us to be actively involved in something that is bigger than we are.

In regard to what is going to take place upon the earth as it relates to God's Kingdom, His people, and all of humanity; God has made much of His will and His purposes known to us. He has told us, *"Do two men walk together unless they have agreed to do so? Does a lion roar in the forest when he has no prey? Does a young lion growl from his den unless he has captured something? Does a bird fall into a trap on the ground when there is no bait in it? Does a trap spring up from the earth when it captures nothing at all? If a trumpet is blown in a city, will not the people tremble? If a calamity occurs in a city, has not the Lord done it? Surely the Lord God does nothing unless He reveals His secret counsel to His servants the prophets. A lion has roared! Who will not fear? The Lord God has spoken! Who can but prophesy?"* [117]

In this scripture from the book of the prophet Amos, God is telling us that there are principles that govern natural behavior in creation and there are principles that govern spiritual behavior, including the behavior and activities of the Kingdom of God. One principle regarding His own

[117] Amos 3:3-8

behavior that God Himself has established and chosen to reveal to us is that of communicating His current and future purposes, plans, and activities to His people. Not that God tells us every detail of what He is doing and will do, but He does speak to us about those things that He considers significant to His purposes for us and for the rest of His creation.[118]

More than just His activities and plans; through the scriptures God reveals Himself to us - His very nature and character. God tells us that He is, by nature, generous. He is a giver and not a withholder. He reveals Himself to those who seek after Him. Therefore, in accordance with His revealed nature and character, He does not shrink back from establishing and building relationships with people. In fact, God desires and actively pursues relationships with all of us. If this were not true of Him, why would He take the initiative to communicate with us about Himself, His purposes, and His activities in the first place?

As His Kingdom people, God wants us to know Him and what He is doing because He wants us to recognize and understand how the experiences of our individual lives and our corporate lives together contribute to the success and fulfillment of His overall purposes and plans…the "big picture". He wants us to know that we are significant to Him, to what He is doing now, and to what He will be doing in the ages to come. We, as followers of Christ and His Kingdom people, will be a vital part of His governmental administration when He returns to the earth to establish the Reign of God at the end of this present age, and beyond.[119] As His Kingdom people, now, we are vital to the growth and expansion of His Kingdom on the earth, in this age.[120]

You could say that our lives are made up of experiences that resemble individual pieces of a puzzle. These seemingly random, disjointed pieces of our Christian experience, which often do not seem to make much sense to us at the time, actually do fit together to compose a picture of what God is doing in and through our lives to accomplish His eternal purposes. Yet, this "picture" of our own individual life is but a small puzzle piece of a much larger picture – the expansion of the Kingdom of God. Our own "puzzle piece" must be joined together with the "puzzle pieces" belonging to the rest of God's people if we are to truly see the "big picture" of God's eternal purposes and plans coming to pass. This is why the community of believers and the building of relationships with one another are so important to God

[118] John 16:13
[119] 2Timothy 2:11-13; Revelation 20:4-6; Daniel 7:15-18; Revelation 3:20-21
[120] Luke 19:12-26; Acts 1:6-8; Acts 28:30-31; Daniel 12:3

and His purposes. We not only see the purpose and activities of God in our own life, we see it in the lives of others.

In Genesis 1:1, we are told that in the beginning there was God. God is the King who rules in eternity. His kingdom has always been and it always will be. Therefore, if we are to understand the eternal strategies, plans, and purposes of God, we must understand that they all revolve around Him and the unending supremacy of His eternal Kingdom. The increase of this eternal Kingdom of God is the focal point of all that God says and does. As a result, all of God's activities take place for His glory and after the counsel of His will. With this in mind, let's examine some of what God has already revealed about His eternal strategies, plans, and purposes.

In Ephesians 1:1-14, the apostle Paul gives us a glimpse of the "big picture" of God's eternal purposes and plans for His Kingdom. We are told that, before the foundation of the world, God determined that He would have a people *"who would be holy and blameless before Him."* [121] God, in His foreknowledge, saw that humanity would fall from grace and relationship with Him through sin. Yet, *"He predestined us to adoption as sons through Jesus Christ to Himself, according to the kind intention of His will."* [122] Through the cost of Christ's blood, God forgave us our sins and redeemed us or "bought us back" for Himself, "according to the riches of His grace which He lavished on us." [123] This predestined plan of God made room for fallen humanity to be reconciled to Him, by God's own will and choosing, and according to His loving, sacrificial initiative.

This predestined, eternal plan also includes a reward for Christ, in that, as a result of His personal, selfless sacrifice for the redemption of humanity, He would hold the preeminent position in God's eternal Kingdom, *"with a view to an administration suitable to the fullness of the times, that is, the summing up of all things in Christ, things in the heavens and things on the earth."* [124] All authority in heaven and on earth would be given to Jesus.[125] We too, who have trusted in Christ, hold a prominent position in God's eternal Kingdom, *"an inheritance, having been predestined according to His purpose, who works all things after the counsel of His will."* [126] We can be confident in our position in God's eternal Kingdom (our inheritance) because He has sealed it with the Holy Spirit, *"who is given as a pledge of our inheritance, with a view to the redemption of God's own possession."* [127]

---

[121] Ephesians 1:4
[122] Ephesians 1:5
[123] Ephesians 1:7
[124] Ephesians 1:10
[125] Matthew 28:18-20
[126] Ephesians 1:11

God's purpose in our redemption is to accomplish what He originally set out to do – to have us rule with Him over His creation. God will accomplish it through the Christ Jesus and His redeemed human brethren. We are to rule with Christ and share in the inheritance that God has for us as adopted sons. The reign of the Kingdom of God extends to, and will manifest itself once again on the earth through the God-Man, Christ Jesus, with redeemed human beings reigning with Him. This is the administration that Paul is talking about. It is the administration (or stewardship) of the Kingdom of God extended to include the earth, with Jesus Christ as the Ruler of all of God's creation. God's predestined, eternal plan and purpose for us on the earth will be manifested and fulfilled when Christ returns to rule on the earth and subdue it.

Just as the newly-elected President of the United States, who is chosen and placed into office by the American people, establishes a governmental administration (stewardship) that functions as a steward and manager of the authority and responsibilities bestowed upon him/her by the citizens of America; so Jesus Christ has been chosen by God and established in the position as Ruler, Steward, and Manager of all of God's creation, with us ruling with Him at His side. We do not yet see this King and His administration completely manifested on the earth at this time but we do see this King and His administration operating prophetically on the earth, now, through His redeemed people, His Body, the Church, according to the power and presence of the Holy Spirit.

The Body of Christ on the earth, the Church, represents to the people of the earth the current administration of Jesus Christ which is located, right now, in heaven. The Church is the present day ministry and rule of Jesus Christ on the earth. As His redeemed people, Jesus has given us the authority and power of His heavenly administration through the agency of the Holy Spirit, to carry out the activities of the Kingdom of God on earth in this present age.[128] The main focus of these activities involving His Kingdom people is to engage in the prophetic activities of the Kingdom of God in order to reconcile unredeemed humanity back to God through faith in the redemptive work of Jesus Christ, and to make disciples of Jesus Christ from these redeemed people. The authority, power, and resources of heaven are behind us in order to engage in and conduct the necessary activities to accomplish this task.

---

[127] Ephesians 1:14

[128] Matthew 28:18-20; John 20:21; Matthew 10:5-8

We are representatives of Jesus' government to this world. We are ambassadors for Christ to this present age. We are agents for Christ to unredeemed people on the earth until the appropriate time when Jesus, Himself, will come and manifest His government and administration completely on the earth. Until then, we as representatives of Jesus' heavenly administration operate on behalf of His government as it prophetically relates to and interacts with this world and the people of this world. We are prophetic intermediaries who receive our instructions from our King, prophetically, through the agency of the Holy Spirit and who allow the Kingdom of God to work through us, prophetically, to carry out its activities on the earth. We are not here to simply do good things and to be nice to people. We are here to represent the King of the universe and His Kingdom to a lost world in need of Him, as if He was here conducting these activities, Himself.

Paul tells us in 1Corinthians 13:8-10, *"Love never fails; but if there are gifts of prophecy, they will be done away; if there are tongues, they will cease; if there is knowledge, it will be done away. For we know in part, and we prophesy in part; but when the perfect comes, the partial will be done away."* Here Paul is speaking of the present prophetic activity of the Kingdom of God, in regard to the earth, as being temporary. He says that these prophetic activities take place now in an incomplete or temporary fashion. It is not the complete manifestation of the Kingdom of God and the administration of Jesus; it is the limited, incomplete manifestation. Yet, Paul tells us that when the perfect or complete manifestation of the Kingdom administration of Jesus comes to the earth at the end of this present age the limited, incomplete activities will stop. There will be no more need for them; the complete manifestation and communication will be present.

In order to accomplish these eternal purposes of God and completely manifest the Kingdom of God on the earth, there are preliminary activities that must take place and be accomplished first within this natural world. These activities involve the redemptive plan of God for us. During this redemptive phase of God's plan, the Kingdom of God and the chosen King of creation, Jesus Christ, are geographically located in heaven but spiritually present within His redeemed people on the earth through the Holy Spirit. This Kingdom will manifest itself here on the earth in order to accomplish specific Kingdom purposes. We must recognize and understand the plans and purposes of God and His Kingdom during this redemptive phase if we are to see the pieces of the puzzle in our lives come together.

Therefore, we are going to look at specific activities of God and His Kingdom as they have manifested on the earth during this redemptive history in order to see the nature and character of God. We are also going to see the prophetic nature of the activities of the New Covenant administration of Jesus Christ as well as how we can expect to see and experience these activities throughout the rest of this redemptive age. Jesus lived according to the Kingdom of God while on the earth as He was taught it by His Father. Before Jesus left the earth to return to His Father in heaven, He taught the same thing to us; how to recognize, interact, and cooperate with the prophetic activities of the Kingdom of God already active on the earth.

Chapter Questions & Notes

Talk It Over….

1) God, who is located in heaven, carries out His Kingdom activities on the earth, prophetically, through His Kingdom people, the Church, by the presence and ability of the Holy Spirit, the presence of God on the earth. What does that mean to each of us, as followers of Christ, and how important it is to each of us to develop and experience an actual relationship with the Holy Spirit. How practical does this relationship have to be if we are to cooperate with Him to accomplish the will of God on the earth? Write down your answers:

2) In 1Corinthians 12-14, Paul talks about the different spiritual manifestations that the Holy Spirit will manifest and conduct through His Kingdom people in order to carry out His desires and activities toward mankind, in this present age. What are these activities? How much of this activity is based on our own capabilities and how much is based on the grace God gives to us in order for us to carry out these activities? Are these natural capabilities or supernatural capabilities? Do they just happen or is there something we must do in order to see them operate in and through our lives?

Leaders: Focus the group conversation on the fact that this is God's Kingdom activity taking place through us, His Kingdom people, and He has provided the ability for us to conduct His Kingdom activities in an effective manner and to accomplish what He wants to accomplish. We shouldn't think that we can accomplish God's activities through our own abilities because, as His Kingdom representatives, we are here to carry out His purposes and activities as if He was here doing it Himself. We can't conduct God's activities through our own abilities because, if God was here conducting these activities Himself, He would be conducting them through

His abilities, not ours. We need to carry out God's Kingdom activities with the spiritual abilities He has given us through the Holy Spirit. Otherwise, we will fall short of what God intends for us to do, on His behalf.

(11)

The Yoke Of Jesus Is The Kingdom Of God

"...no one knows the Son except the Father; nor does anyone know the Father except the Son, and anyone to whom the Son wills to reveal Him. Come to Me, all who are weary and heavy-laden, and I will give you rest. ***Take My yoke upon you and learn from Me,*** *for I am gentle and humble in heart, and You will find rest for your souls.* ***For My yoke is easy and My burden is light."*** Matthew 11:27-30 (emphasis mine)

In Matthew 11:1-19, John the Baptist sends his disciples to Jesus in order to ask Him if He is the promised Messiah or if they should watch for another who would come. Jesus replied by telling them to consider the nature of the words and works they witnessed in Him and His ministry. According to the scriptures, these are the Kingdom words and works the Messiah was to display when He came.[129] He then warned them not to be offended by Him as the Jewish leaders were because He, and the words and activities He spoke and conducted, may not be what they had expected to see and hear in the coming Messiah.

After John's disciples left Jesus to return to John, Jesus spoke to His own disciples about the wisdom and plan of God being exhibited and conducted through John's ministry and His own ministry. Jesus tells His disciples that if some of the evilest cities and peoples of ancient times had seen and heard what this generation was seeing and hearing from John and Jesus, they would have repented from their wickedness. Jesus uses this teaching on the nature and character of God and His Kingdom activities, to prepare His disciples for what He was going to say to them, next.

Jesus goes on to say to His disciples in Matthew 11:27; *"All things have been handed over to Me by My Father; and no one knows the Son except the Father; nor does anyone know the Father except the Son, and anyone to whom the Son wills to reveal Him."* The Father had revealed Himself to Jesus and Jesus had come to know and understand the nature, character and activities of the Father, before Jesus entered into His ministry. The words Jesus spoke throughout

[129] Isaiah 58:6-10; Isaiah 61:1-3; Matthew 11:4-5

His ministry were given to Him by the Father[130] and the works Jesus performed throughout His ministry were the Father's works, empowered by the Holy Spirit.[131] Jesus knew the Father – His nature, character, purposes and Kingdom activities. One of the reasons Jesus was sent to the earth was to reveal the nature, character and purposes of the Father to us and to reveal and demonstrate God's Kingdom activities to us.

Today, since Jesus is not physically on the earth with us, He gives direct revelation of Himself and the Father to us through the prophetic activity of the Holy Spirit.[132] We can know some things about God through what He has made[133] but we cannot know Him and His true nature, character, purposes and activities unless they are directly revealed to us through the Spirit of Christ – the Holy Spirit. This raises the question, *"How does the Spirit of Christ – the Holy Spirit, directly reveal Jesus and the Father to us 2000 years after Jesus left the earth to return to heaven?"* Jesus goes on to answer that question in Matthew 11, where He tells us; 1) God and His Kingdom are continually and dynamically moving forward, and those who wish to take hold of Him and His Kingdom must do so, passionately, as a precious prize;[134] 2) Jesus is calling all of humanity to come to Him and in so doing, we WILL find rest for our souls; 3) we are to take upon ourselves the yoke of Christ and learn from Him.

This third point is very unfamiliar to us in today's western culture. When we think of a yoke, today, we generally think of a wooden pole with two leather harnesses attached that, when worn, allow two oxen or other large animals to pull a load together, much easier than they could if they were not "yoked together" – pulling separately and not in unity. Even though there is a good lesson we can learn using this interpretation of a yoke, it is not what Jesus was communicating to His disciples. This interpretation does not fit the context in which Jesus was speaking and it does not take into account what He had previously said to His disciples about knowing and understanding the Kingdom of God.

What is the yoke of Jesus and how do we take it upon ourselves? We are told that by taking His yoke upon ourselves we will learn from Him. Jesus used this occasion of having John's disciples and His disciples present to conduct a discipleship lesson. In order to make His point to His disciples, about them learning of God and His Kingdom through their Teacher (Jesus), Jesus used a discipleship term of the day, a yoke.

---

[130] John 17:8
[131] Luke 4:14
[132] John 16:13-15
[133] Romans 1:19-20
[134] Matthew 11:12 (Amplified Bible)

At that time in Jewish culture, when a young Jewish man wanted to enter into religious service he would first complete his study of the Jewish scriptures and the Traditions of the Elders. Once he completed these initial studies the young man was obligated to come under the tutelage of an experienced rabbi (master, teacher). The young man would identify the rabbi who he believed would best help him achieve his purposes in becoming a rabbi. Once the young man identified which teacher was best suited for him, that rabbi would require the young man to enter into a very close, mentoring relationship with him by becoming the rabbi's disciple and taking upon himself his rabbi's "yoke".

By taking his rabbi's yoke upon himself, the young disciple would completely give himself to his rabbi's teaching, training, and oversight. Whatever his rabbi did, the disciple would do. Wherever his teacher went, the disciple would go. The disciple's life belonged to his rabbi from that moment on, until the disciple's training was completed. The training was established in such a way that when the tutelage was completed, the disciple would have become just like his master. No matter how difficult the rabbi's "yoke" was, the disciple had to completely submit himself to his teacher's training - trusting that his relationship with his master would transform him into what he wanted to be and to learn what he needed to know.

This is what Jesus asked His disciples to do and this is what He has asked us to do. He wants us to take His yoke upon ourselves, as His disciples, to learn from Him - who He is, what He knows, what He does, what He says and where He goes. He wants us to willingly submit ourselves to Him as our teacher and master. This should be a simple decision for us if we realize who Jesus' teacher was when He was learning about the Kingdom of God as a young boy. Yes, Jesus had to learn. Yes, Jesus was someone's disciple. Yes, Jesus had a teacher and Jesus took His teacher's yoke upon Himself to learn from him. Who was Jesus' teacher?

The yoke of Jesus is the yoke of the Father because everything Jesus said and did while on earth He learned from the Father. Jesus only spoke what He heard the Father saying and only did what He saw the Father doing. Everything Jesus said and did He received from the Father.[135] When we take the yoke of Jesus upon ourselves we are taking the yoke of the Father. What better way to know and learn about the Father and His Kingdom than to learn from the Father's prized disciple, Jesus.

---

[135] John 17:1-10

The Yoke Of The Father In The Life Of Jesus

Throughout the centuries, since the resurrection of Jesus, Satan has sought to undermine the truth of the gospel of the Kingdom of God by attacking the deity of Jesus; by saying that Jesus was not God when he lived on the earth. Satan is still attacking the deity of Jesus today through false teaching, cults and false religions. The Church has been and remains vigilant in order to expose the activities of the enemy in this area and to preserve the integrity and truth of the deity of Jesus.

Yet, in all of our vigilance to preserve the truth of the deity of Jesus, we have lost sight of the humanity of Jesus while He was on earth. We have been so focused on the deity of Jesus that we have been lax in preserving the humanity of Jesus and all that this means to our faith. We must rediscover the humanity of Jesus and what it means to the gospel and to our life of faith. Otherwise, we will be in danger of misinterpreting what the scriptures tell us about His life and ministry, what He accomplished for us through the cross and His resurrection, and we will be in danger of missing out on much of what God wants us to experience of His Kingdom, now, in this age.

We must embrace, both, the deity and humanity of Jesus while He was on the earth. He was fully God and fully human. He possessed the very nature of God and the very nature of humanity. We must understand how He lived on the earth as God and as a human being if we want to understand how we are to live as His disciples and citizens of the Kingdom of God in this age.

We need to embrace the humanity of Jesus as He was enabled by the power of the Holy Spirit; when He spoke and acted as the Kingdom of God's representative to a fallen and needy world. Over the centuries, the Church has associated Jesus' works on the earth with His deity and as a result, we have become intimidated by His works (miracles, signs, wonders) and have disassociated ourselves from them. In so doing, we have developed erroneous doctrinal positions that give us an "out" when it comes to obeying and experiencing the commands of Jesus pertaining to our ministry activities here on the earth as His "Body" – His Kingdom representatives on the earth in this age. By doing so, we are saying, "How can we, being human, do the same works (signs, wonders and miracles) that Jesus did as God?"

It's difficult to come to terms with the commands that Jesus obviously gave us; to go into the world and do the same works that He did, and greater works, as His disciples and representatives of the Kingdom of God, if we have this perception of ourselves and Him.[136] We readily admit to ourselves that we are not deity, as Jesus is, and are therefore incapable of performing the works that only deity can perform.

With this theological orientation and belief system concerning the works of Jesus, we as the current representatives of the Kingdom of God on the earth have little or no hope of performing the same works of the Kingdom that Jesus did unless God were to do so completely apart from any faith or initiative on our part. We even put the early Church believers on a pedestal, as being somehow more needful of these Kingdom activities than we are, or more special and therefore better equipped to be powerful Kingdom witnesses to their generation than we can or need to be to our own generation. As a result, we have developed doctrines and teachings such as Dispensation Theology to intellectually explain away what we have little faith in or hope to ever experience.

In order to free ourselves from this theological "straightjacket" we have wrapped ourselves in over the centuries, we must see that it is in Jesus' humanity, empowered by the Holy Spirit, that we have our example and hope for the life and ministry that Jesus commissioned us to engage in and accomplish as His Kingdom representatives. We cannot allow the fear of heresy and the Church's over-reaction to it to rob us of the truth that Jesus came to model for us, provide to us, and instill within us through the Holy Spirit. To do so is to substitute one heresy for another.

We must recognize and embrace the humanity of Jesus and the example He gives to us in His humanity, if we are to accomplish all that He desires for us as His representatives on the earth. We are told that this gospel of the Kingdom will be preached to the whole world *as a witness to all the nations*, and then the end shall come.[137] This word *witness* carries with it the idea that the message proclaiming this Kingdom is to be accompanied by the signs and demonstrations depicting and authenticating the reality and presence of the Kingdom of God. We are not preaching and representing a Kingdom that comes in word only but in demonstration of the Holy Spirit and the power of the Kingdom of God.[138]

[136] Mark 16:17-18; Matt. 10:7-8; John 14:10-12
[137] Matthew 24:14
[138] 1Corinthians 2:4-5

Jesus is coming again to establish the Kingdom of God, in its fullness, on the earth. He is coming as God and as *the Son of David*, which speaks of His humanity which He still possesses. It is in this humanity that Jesus is seated at the right hand of the Father, right now, and it is in this humanity that His governmental administration will rule the earth upon His return.

So there is no question in your mind about what I am saying, I want to reiterate that Jesus, while on earth, was both fully God and fully human. The scriptures are very clear regarding Jesus' deity.[139] In fact, many of the same scriptures that testify of His deity also testify of His humanity.[140] The writer of Hebrews clearly declares, both, the deity and humanity of Jesus while showing how both natures were completely integrated within His being during His earthly life.

The writer also shows us that not only were these two natures completely integrated within Jesus during His earthly life, they are, even now, completely integrated within His being as He is seated at the right hand of the Father in heaven. What we must recognize is that there was a difference between how these two natures functioned within Jesus while on earth and how they function within Him now in heaven. The difference is the priority of function that His humanity was given over His deity while He was on the earth. To better understand this truth and how it affects us as the Body of Christ today, we must look at what Paul tells us about this truth in Philippians 2:5-8.

Paul tells us that Jesus possessed and was fully functional in all of the divine attributes and privileges that belonged to Him as God, when He lived in heaven, in eternity before the foundation of the world. As the Godhead established its eternal purpose for the human race; seeing that we would willingly sin and would have to be redeemed in order to fulfill our eternal purpose, Jesus, the second Person of the Godhead, willingly chose to take upon Himself the humanity of those He would come to redeem.

He clothed Himself in this humanity without giving up His deity, His divine nature. Even though He did not give up His deity to become a human, He did empty Himself or "laid aside" for a time, His privilege and ability to function in the non-communicable attributes He possessed as God (those attributes of God that cannot be bestowed upon His creatures, such as being all-knowing, all-powerful, ever-present, etc.). Jesus, the second Person of the Godhead, "emptied Himself" of these divine attributes in order to become fully human.

---

[139] John 1:1-3; John 8:56-59; Hebrews 1:2-3,6; Hebrews 1:8-12; Hebrews 2:9,14
[140] Hebrews 1:2-5,9,13; Hebrews 2:9-18

While on the earth, Jesus was fully human and fully God, yet He chose to lay aside the divine attributes and privileges He had previously exercised as God. During His earthly life, the humanity of Jesus had the functional priority over the deity of Jesus. During His earthly life, Jesus was no longer all-knowing, ever-present, and all-powerful.[141] Jesus was fully human in His function, in that He only spoke what the Father revealed to Him and only did what He saw the Father doing. [142] Jesus was a man who was led by and empowered by the Holy Spirit.

The writer of Hebrews illustrates this point by telling us in Hebrews 2:10 how God the Father used the element of suffering in Jesus' life to bring about a necessary maturity. Through suffering, this maturing process in Jesus' life was made perfect or complete so He could bring about through His atoning work on the cross, the redemption of the human race. The Father had to bring Jesus to a place of maturity where nothing He experienced or suffered would tempt Him beyond His ability to overcome and thus fail the Father, bringing forth sin. Just like Adam, Jesus (the Last Adam[143]) was a free-will being who possessed the capability to sin as well as to not sin. Even though Jesus is both God and human, Jesus the human was tempted just as we are tempted, yet He did not sin.[144]

This truth is reinforced in Hebrews 5:8, where we are told, *"Although He was a Son, He learned obedience from the things which He suffered."* This may be difficult for us to comprehend but Jesus had to learn obedience. Jesus, the human, had to learn obedience to the Father through the spiritual maturation process which included the element of suffering. This suffering Jesus experienced was in regard to choosing obedience to the Father's will over the temptations of Satan and the difficulties of life that came against Him.

This continual, internal decision-making, to choose the Father's will over the temptations of Satan, brought about the external suffering we see in the verbal abuse He experienced at the hands of the religious leaders as well as the physical abuse He experienced at the hands of the Romans. Jesus' internal suffering, which we do not see, brought about His external suffering, which we do see.[145] This is true because the internal decisions He made to be obedient to the Father brought about His corresponding words and actions. As a result, these corresponding words and actions carried the

[141] Luke 2:51-52; Mark 13:32
[142] John 5:19-20,30
[143] 1Corinthians 15:45
[144] Hebrews 4:15
[145] Isaiah 53:3

power and authority of the Spirit of God, producing within those who heard and witnessed them, either, "life leading to life" or "death leading to death."[146] Those in whom they produced life, followed Him but those in whom they produced death, persecuted and killed Him.

If Jesus had functioned in His life on the earth according to His attributes and privileges as God instead of in His nature and attributes as a human, there would have been no need to grow and mature. There would have been no need to suffer because He would have already been completely mature and obedient at the time He was born. James tells us that God is not tempted by evil,[147] yet we know Jesus was tempted by evil, to sin, on several occasions.[148] It was not the deity of Jesus that was tempted, it was His humanity that was tempted. In order to be fully human and to be the perfect redemptive sacrifice for the sins of humanity, it was necessary for Jesus to possess the same capacity to be tempted and to sin, as Adam.

Jesus could not receive preferential treatment when it came to experiencing the evil strategies and tactics of the powers of darkness. Jesus could possess no greater ability to resist Satan and his temptations than Adam did. Jesus was not "off limits" to Satan. The temptations that Jesus experienced were legitimate temptations and were very real in His life. Jesus could have sinned and fallen from fellowship with the Father just as Adam had.

Since Jesus functioned on a day-to-day basis according to His humanity, His power and other divine privileges as God were not available to Him. As a result, He lived His life according to the power and ability that was provided to Him by the Father. This power and ability was made available to Jesus through the Holy Spirit.[149] Therefore, Jesus' ability to withstand and overcome the strategies, tactics, and temptations of Satan and the powers of darkness were a result of His submission and obedience to the Holy Spirit and the will of the Father. Jesus did not live a sinless life while on the earth because He was God or because of the power and ability He possessed as God. He did so by obedience and submission to the Father's will and to the operation of the Holy Spirit in His life.

As a result of the Holy Spirit's activity taking place in His life, Jesus was a prophetic person. The Rule of God, which is located in heaven, operated in Jesus' life through the Holy Spirit in order to reveal the Father's word to Him, reveal the Father's will to Him, and to manifest the Kingdom's

---

[146] 2Corinthians 2:15-16
[147] James 1:13
[148] Luke 4:1-13; Matthew 16:23
[149] Matthew 3:16-4:1; Luke 4:13-14

activities to this world through Him. Jesus, the son of David and the Son of God,[150] was submitted to the will of the Father and was led by the Holy Spirit in His life while on the earth. Jesus, in His humanity, set the spiritual precedence for all of us as future sons of God when He lived His life in the power of the Holy Spirit. Through His life, Jesus established the proof and Kingdom truth that a person is a son of God because he/she is being led by the Spirit of God.[151]

Jesus was able to do what Adam was unable to do…maintain His unbroken relationship and fellowship with the Father through all of the temptations and attacks of Satan against Him. Jesus clung to the Father and His word when the temptations and storms came. This is why He was counted worthy by the Father to present Himself as a sacrifice for our sins and to bear our judgment, and why the Father was able to accept it and place His judgment for us all, on Him.

If Jesus lived His life, withstood the temptations of Satan, and sacrificed himself for the sins of humanity as a human then He also gained His training and instruction, and conducted His earthly ministry as a human, not as God. He couldn't withstand temptation and die as a human while acquiring His knowledge and training and conducting His ministry as God. He either lived His entire life in the abilities of God or He lived His entire life in His abilities as a human. The Bible also gives us insight into this aspect of Jesus' life.

"Now it came about when all the people were baptized, that Jesus also was baptized, and while He was praying, heaven was opened, and the Holy Spirit descended upon Him in bodily form like a dove…And ***Jesus, full of the Holy Spirit, returned from the Jordan*** *and* ***was led about by the Spirit*** *in the wilderness for forty days, being tempted by the devil... And* ***Jesus returned to Galilee in the power of the Spirit;*** *and news about Him spread through all the surrounding district."*[152] In this scripture, Luke gives us insight into the life and ministry of Jesus. Jesus lived the greatest life and exhibited the greatest manifestations of the Kingdom of God of anyone who has ever walked the earth.

Jesus, Himself, tells us that the miracles He did and the life He lived, He did by the power of the Holy Spirit. He says, *"If I by Beelzebul cast out demons, by whom do your sons cast them out? For this reason they will be your judges. But,* ***if I cast***

---

[150] Luke 1:35; Romans 1:3-4

[151] Romans 8:14

[152] Luke 3:21-22; 4:1-2,14 (emphasis mine)

***out demons by the Spirit of God, then the kingdom of God** has come upon you."*[153] There are many other scriptures where Jesus tells us that He did not acquire His knowledge or conduct his ministry activities by His ability as God.[154]

Even Peter, who spent three years living with Jesus, witnessing His entire earthly ministry, testifies to the power behind Jesus' ministry. Peter tells us in Acts, *"Men of Israel, listen to these words: Jesus the Nazarene, a man attested to you by God with miracles and wonders and signs* ***which God performed through Him*** *in your midst, just as you yourselves know,"* Acts 2:22. And again, *"You know of Jesus of Nazareth,* ***how God anointed Him with the Holy Spirit and with power,*** *and* ***how He went about doing good and healing all who were oppressed by the devil, for God was with Him***".[155]

Therefore, as a result of living a sin-free life as a human and providing redemption for all of humanity through His sacrificial death (according to Paul's word to us in Philippians 2:9-11), God highly exalted the man, Jesus, giving Him the name that is above every other name in all of creation. It is Jesus the God/Man who has been given all authority in heaven and on earth. It is Jesus the God/Man who sits at the right hand of the Father in heaven. It is Jesus the God/Man who will return to the earth and establish His administration in Jerusalem as the Son of God and the Son of David. It is Jesus the God/Man who will sit on His throne beside the Father for all of eternity.[156] It is Jesus the God/Man who gave us His authority to go and make disciples of all nations, engaging in the same prophetic activity of the Kingdom of God as He did when He was here.[157]

As adopted sons of God, we are to prophetically demonstrate the reality and presence of the Kingdom of God to the world and to this generation, just as Jesus did when He was here. The early Church understood this truth and operated in it. The Church today, for the most part, does not understand this truth and is, therefore, not operating in it. We are not living in a different dispensation from the believers in the early church. They simply believed this to be true and operated in faith in this area, while we do not believe this to be true and we operate in unbelief in this area. God honors faith not unbelief.

---

[153] Matt. 12:27-28 (emphasis mine)
[154] Luke 4:18-21; John 5:30; John 8:28; John 12:49; John 14:10
[155] Acts 10:38
[156] Revelation 21
[157] Mark 16:17-18; John 14:12-13

When we surrender ourselves to God, live by the power of the Holy Spirit, believe the word of God given to us, and operate in faith as His Kingdom representatives on the earth, we will experience these same Kingdom activities. We can't simply say, "If God wants me to experience these prophetic activities, I will", any more than we can say, "If God wants me to experience the New Birth, I will." It requires an active faith to receive from the Lord.[158] It is by grace through faith…it is **ALL** by grace through faith.

In addition, we must realize that when Jesus returned to the Father after His death, burial, and resurrection, His divine attributes and privileges as God were once again restored to Him and given their priority. We see this in John 17 when Jesus is about to go to the cross and He prays to the Father on behalf of those He was leaving behind.[159] He asks the Father to restore to Him the glory He had with Him before the world began. He asked the Father to restore to Him, upon His return to heaven, the non-communicable divine attributes and privileges He laid aside when He came to the earth as a human.

As a result, Jesus is once again all-knowing, all-powerful, and all-present. Yet, Jesus did not stop being a human when He ascended to the right hand of the Father. The divine attributes and privileges He laid aside in order to become a human on the earth were restored and became fully integrated and functional again with His humanity. As Jesus is sitting at the right hand of the Father in heaven right now, both His human nature and attributes and His divine nature and attributes are fully integrated and functional. This is a mystery but, nevertheless, true.

We must recapture the truth of the humanity of Jesus. We must recognize and accept the truth that Jesus lived His life, suffered temptations, conducted His ministry, performed miracles, and suffered and died a sacrificial death for us as a human, not as God. It completely changes the way we approach our faith, how we live our lives as believers in Jesus Christ, and it totally changes how we approach our ministry to the world around us and to the gospel of the Kingdom we are to proclaim to them. Yes, we should continue to fight for the truth of the deity of Jesus but we should, equally, fight for the truth of the humanity of Jesus.

Jesus tells us that He wants us to take His yoke upon ourselves and learn from Him. If Jesus lived His life as a human and in the abilities of a human, how did Jesus learn the truths that He learned, gain His understanding, and grow in His relationship with the Father? How did He learn all of this? We

[158] James 1:5-7; Hebrews 11:6
[159] John 17:4-5

can see that Jesus, even at a very young age, was demonstrating wisdom and understanding of the scriptures and the activities of God and His Kingdom far beyond even the most learned Jewish teachers and scholars of His day.

Luke tells us, *"And when He became twelve, they went up there* (Jerusalem) *according to the custom of the Feast…Then, after three days they found Him in the temple, sitting in the midst of the teachers, both listening to them and asking them questions. And all who heard Him were amazed at His understanding and His answers…And He said to them, "Why is it that you were looking for Me? Did you not know that I had to be in My Father's house?""* [160] How is it that the most learned Jewish teachers and scholars in Jerusalem were amazed at what Jesus knew and the answers He gave to the questions they asked Him? If these Jewish scholars and teachers were asking questions and learning from Jesus, who taught Jesus what He knew?

We know that Jesus did not live His life exercising the attributes of God and, therefore, possessing all knowledge because He lived His life as a human and with the attributes of a human. Luke tells us that Jesus had to grow in wisdom, physical abilities, and favor with God and people. He had to learn it and grow in it as a human.[161] If Jesus didn't possess and operate in these things as God but had to acquire and grow in them as a human, then there is only one place for Him to get this knowledge and wisdom...God the Father, Himself. In fact, Jesus tells us this several times.

In John's gospel, Jesus says, *"When you lift up the Son of Man, then you will know that I am He, and I do nothing on My own initiative,* ***but I speak these things as the Father taught Me****".* [162] Jesus tells us that He was taught what He knew, what He said, and what He did by the Father.

In John 17, when Jesus is about to go to the cross and, then, return to heaven; He is praying to the Father on behalf of His disciples who would remain behind. He acknowledges to the Father, *"Now they have come to know that everything You have given Me is from You;* ***for the words which You gave Me I have given to them;****"* [163] Jesus acknowledges that the words He had spoken throughout His ministry, He had received from the Father and He had delivered them to His disciples and the people. Jesus was dependent on His relationship with the Father and the activity of the Holy Spirit in His life to complete the work the Father had sent Him to do. Yet, the question remains, *"How did the Father teach Jesus what He knew, said, and did?"*

---

[160] Luke 2:42-49
[161] Luke 2:40,52
[162] John 8:28
[163] John 17:7-8a (emphasis mine)

Jesus tells us that He was taught what He knew and given the words that He spoke by the Father. How did the Father do this? He is in heaven and Jesus is on the earth. Jesus tells us how the Father taught Him and discipled Him, in John 3. It is the account of Jesus' conversation with Nicodemus, THE teacher of Israel at the time.

In John 3, we find Nicodemus coming to Jesus at night to find out more about Him. Jesus immediately "cut to the chase" and offended Nicodemus' mind in order to get to his heart. After telling (and confusing) Nicodemus about his need to be born again, Jesus says to Nicodemus, *"Are you the teacher of Israel and do not understand these things? Truly, truly, I say to you,* ***we speak of what we know and testify of what we have seen, and you do not accept our testimony****. If I told you earthly things and you do not believe, how will you believe if I tell you heavenly things?"* [164]

Here, Jesus states His surprise that Nicodemus doesn't grasp a thing that He is telling him and Nicodemus is supposed to be THE teacher of Israel. Then, Jesus identified Himself to Nicodemus as a prophet[165] and proceeded to include what He had been saying throughout His ministry, with what the prophets of the Old Testament had said, and with what John the Baptist had said throughout his ministry as a prophet. Jesus told Nicodemus that He, the Old Covenant prophets, and John the Baptist had testified of what they had seen, yet, the Jewish leaders (past and present) had not received what the prophets had told them.

Jesus goes on to tell Nicodemus that if he can't receive what he was being told by Jesus, concerning matters pertaining to the earth (in this case, the new birth), how can Nicodemus expect to receive information from Jesus pertaining to matters in heaven? Nicodemus' head must be swimming by now. He came to Jesus to find out a little more about Him and Jesus proceeds to make statements that thoroughly confuse Nicodemus. Jesus is exposing to Nicodemus, THE teacher of Israel, that he really doesn't know as much as He thinks he does. Yet, Jesus loves Nicodemus and He is challenging him to not be comfortable with what He thinks he knows but to pursue what he is finding out he doesn't really know at all.

Then, to top it all off, Jesus dropped one more statement on Nicodemus that must have completely confused him. Jesus said to Nicodemus, *"No one* ***has ascended into heaven,*** *but He* ***who descended from heaven: the Son of Man****"*.[166] Jesus is telling Nicodemus, and us, where He got His

---

[164] John 3:10-12 (emphasis mine)
[165] Jesus is The Prophet that Moses spoke of in Deuteronomy 18:15-18, Acts 3:19-23

information and spiritual training. Jesus tells us that since He descended from heaven, as a human, He has ascended to heaven to receive the information and training for what He knows, says and does, from the Father.

Jesus got His information and spiritual training, including His teaching about the new birth and everything else He talks about and reveals throughout His earthly ministry, from God the Father. Jesus went to the Father's throne to be taught, trained and mentored directly by the Father, face to face. Jesus took the Father's yoke upon Himself to learn from the Father and the Father taught Jesus face to face, in heaven. Is this so far-fetched, that Jesus would go to heaven from the time He was a young boy to be taught and discipled directly by God the Father? Well, let's look at a few facts that will make this easier to digest.

In the beginning, when God created Adam, He placed Adam in the garden to rule the earth as His regent. The scriptures tell us that Adam experienced an intimate, personal, face-to-face relationship and communication with God.[167] The earth was pure and righteous, just as God created it. Adam was holy, righteous and sin-free just as God created Him. There was nothing to keep God and Adam from enjoying their face-to-face relationship and the earth was in such a righteous state that God even came down here to enjoy fellowship with Adam.

Jesus enjoyed this same type of face-to-face relationship with the Father. Jesus was sinless and righteous, there was nothing to hinder him or restrict Him from having a face-to-face, intimate, personal relationship with the Father. Yet, since sin had such a profound effect on the earth by that time, instead of the Father coming down to the earth to fellowship with Jesus as God did with Adam, the Father brought Jesus to His throne in heaven in order to fellowship, communicate, teach, and disciple Him in what He was to know, say, and do.

In addition, we are told that the Apostle Paul was taken to the third heaven in order to receive teaching from God concerning the New Covenant truths that he taught and penned.[168] We also see that the Apostle John was caught up into heaven to see events and to be instructed concerning what would take place at the end of the age.[169] If Paul and John, as born again children of God, were taken to heaven to receive information and instruction from

---

[166] John 3:13
[167] Genesis 2:19, 22; 3:8-9
[168] 2Corinthians 12:2-4
[169] Revelation 4:1-4

God, why wouldn't God take His own Son, Jesus, into heaven in order to teach, train and mentor Him in the things he would need to know, do, and say on the earth? There was no one on earth capable of teaching and mentoring Jesus in what He was to know, do, and say.

Jesus took the yoke of the Father upon Himself to learn from Him. Once Jesus received His teaching, training and discipling from the Father, He was baptized by John, the Holy Spirit was sent upon Him by the Father, and Jesus went forth in His ministry as a human, discipled by the Father and empowered by the Holy Spirit. Jesus only did what He saw the Father doing and only said what He heard the Father saying. There was no human capable of training and preparing Jesus for what He was to do. Only the Father could disciple Him and only the Spirit could empower Him. Jesus took upon Himself the yoke of the Father to learn from Him, and it is this same yoke that Jesus wants us to take upon ourselves, to learn from Him.

We take the yoke of Jesus upon ourselves when we willingly submit ourselves to Him, to learn from Him. This yoke or discipleship is only revealed to us and forged within us through the Spirit of Christ, the Holy Spirit, in personal, intimate fellowship and relationship with Him. This is not an intellectual exercise nor is it a religious program with cookie-cutter methods, formulas and principles we simply memorize, recite, and implement. It is a relationship that costs both parties everything – where each party is made available to the other. The life of the disciple is placed completely in the hands of his teacher. Jesus tells us that the Holy Spirit, the Spirit of Christ, is our teacher and He will guide us into all truth. The Spirit will take what Jesus wants us to know, say, and do and will disclose it to us. The Spirit will conduct these direct discipleship activities with us as long as we are submitted to Jesus' yoke.

When we take on the yoke of the Father, through Jesus, we submit ourselves to the active discipleship of the Holy Spirit in our lives from that day forward. This is why we must grasp the importance of the Holy Spirit and yield to His sovereignty, authority, power, and influence in our lives. Otherwise, we short-circuit His discipling and transforming activities in our lives – relegating Him to a theological concept and ourselves to spiritually superficial and powerless lives. As followers of Jesus, the most important asset, the most critical influence, and the most intimate relationship in our lives should be the Holy Spirit.

In this life, we are disciples of the Spirit of Christ, first of all. Everything else is secondary and flows from this vital, practical, and prophetic discipleship relationship. With this in mind, here is something else to recognize. Jesus said, "Take ***MY*** yoke upon you and learn from ***ME***." If

Jesus wants us to take His yoke upon ourselves to learn from Him, then there must be other yokes, other masters and teachers available, that we can take upon ourselves and learn from.

The scriptures tell us that there are only two kingdoms (with authority and sovereignty) over the eternal lives of humans. These two kingdoms are the Kingdom of God and the domain of darkness, ruled by Satan. God possesses all sovereignty and authority and Satan only possesses the limited amount of authority and sovereignty that was given to him by Adam and Eve in the Garden. In fact, Jesus has already defeated Satan and his kingdom (authority and sovereignty) when He rose from the dead – defeating the power of sin and death over the hearts of people, once and for all.

The reason we still see the kingdom of darkness actively influencing the hearts of people is because once Jesus returns to establish His earthly rule, He must eradicate the domain of darkness and its disciples. Jesus is waiting until as many people as possible have an opportunity to submit to His Kingdom before He must return to earth in order to put an end to the effects of sin in the affairs of people, and to establish the Kingdom of God in its fullness on the earth.[170]

Nevertheless, the Kingdom of God and the kingdom of darkness are both present and working in the world and in the lives of humans, at the present time. There are only two kingdoms, masters, and yokes in this world, all other rulers and kingdoms are submitted to and living for one of these two kingdoms and yokes. Not only the earthly rulers and kingdoms but each individual in this world is either submitted to and living under God's yoke or Satan's yoke. We either spend our lives passionately pursuing God and His way of life or we spend our lives passionately pursuing Satan and his way of life.

Jesus confirmed this when He spoke to the religious leaders of His day concerning the motivation for their lives and activities. Jesus said to them, "***If God were your Father, you would love Me****, for I proceeded forth and have come from God, for I have not even come on My own initiative, but He sent Me. "Why do you not understand what I am saying? It is because you cannot hear My word.* ***"You are of your father the devil, and you want to do the desires of your father****. He was a murderer from the beginning, and does not stand in the truth because there is no truth in him. Whenever he speaks a lie, he speaks from his own nature, for he is a liar and the father of lies.*"[171] Either, God is our Father or Satan is our father. There are no other yokes that we can take upon our lives and hearts.

[170] 2Peter 3:8-10

Still, most people try to convince themselves that they serve a third kingdom and a third master, a third yoke that they can take upon themselves. This is their own personal kingdom, their own personal yoke where they are the master and do what's best for their own welfare, according to their own desires and lifestyles. Yet, we don't recognize that in serving ourselves we serve Satan because if we are not completely submitted to God and His Kingdom (authority and sovereignty) in our lives, we are submitted to and living for Satan.

Humanity was created for the Kingdom of God. We were created to thrive and prosper under the rule of God in our lives. We are absolutely lost if we try to live and function outside of the reign of God. We were created to possess the nature and character of God within our being and to display that godly nature and character to the rest of creation. As those created in God's image, we can only find our life's purpose and satisfaction in God and His righteous, holy rule. We have gone astray of that birthright and have settled for far less than God intended. Yet, He has given us a living example of who He is and what His Kingdom is like, in the person of Jesus.

Jesus knew that people were crying out for truth and reality in life. So He cried out to us, *"But seek first His kingdom and His righteousness, and all these things will be added to you."*[172] We are to submit ourselves to and passionately seek after His Kingdom and His righteousness, and all that God has created us for and has in store for us, from the beginning, will be given to us, once again. This is the yoke we are to take on ourselves. This is the yoke Jesus gives us, revealing it to us through His Spirit, who is present and working in our hearts and lives.

This truth is "good news" for all of us and restores in us a sense of eternal purpose and destiny; giving us confidence and hope as we seek to grasp a greater understanding of the Kingdom of God and how it impacts our lives and activities, as His Kingdom people on the earth. Jesus will make us into what He wants us to be – what God created us to be from the very beginning. We must remain under His yoke even when temptation and difficult, trying times come – when we feel like running from God's yoke in order to return to the yoke we grew up with and are very familiar with – Satan's yoke.

We think we will receive comfort and rest there but we forget that all Satan gives us is slavery, pain and death. If we stay with God's yoke, even when

---

[171] John 8:42-44
[172] Matthew 6:33

times get tough, the Spirit will reveal the nature and character of God to us, and will enable that same character and nature to be the foundation and motivation for our own lives.

Chapter Questions & Notes

Talk It Over....

1) Discuss within the group what the yoke of Jesus is, as mentioned in Matthew 11. What does this mean to us as followers of Jesus? What is Jesus' expectation for us as His disciples? How does this impact our lives and how do we respond to Jesus, based on this scripture? What is Jesus' responsibility to us and our responsibility to Him, based on this relationship? Write down your answers:

2) In this chapter, we see that Jesus lived His life on the earth as a human and as God. We see that Jesus, in His humanity, had to learn obedience through the things that He suffered. Like us, He needed to learn to respond to the will of God, even in the midst of temptation and difficulty. We are told, in Isaiah 53, that Jesus was a man of sorrow and acquainted with grief. Yet, we are also told that Jesus was tempted in all things as we are, yet He was without sin. Write down your thoughts and how this impacts you as a person and as a follower of Jesus:

(12)

Conducting Kingdom Activities Utilizing Representative Relationships

"Jesus said to them, "My food is ***to do the will of Him who sent Me and to accomplish His work.*** *""* John 4:34 (emphasis mine)

"Jesus said to him, "Have I been so long with you, and yet you have not come to know Me, Philip? ***He who has seen Me has seen the Father;*** *how can you say, 'Show us the Father'? Do you not believe that* ***I am in the Father and the Father is in Me****? The words that I say to you* ***I do not speak on My own initiative but the Father abiding in Me does His works****. Believe Me that* ***I am in the Father and the Father is in Me...*** *"* John 14:9-11a (emphasis mine)

"As You sent Me into the world, I also have sent them into the world…even as You, Father, are in Me and I in You, that they also may be in Us...I in them and You in Me, that they may be perfected in unity*, so that the world may know that You sent Me, and loved them, even as You have loved Me."* John 17:18, 21b, 23 (emphasis mine)

Understanding the relational dynamics of the Kingdom of God is one of the most important truths we can learn as believers in Christ, as it relates to our relationship to the Kingdom in this age and in the ages to come. Though very important, it is also one of the least understood truths today. When we grasp the truth of this relational dynamic and pursue it with all of our hearts, passion, and energy, we will see activities and manifestations of the Kingdom of God take place in and through our lives as never before, and we will see our intimacy and faith with God grow, in like manner.

Delegated Sovereignty & Authority

Humanity was created to be God's regents on the earth. We were to represent the nature and character of God as well as the sovereignty and authority of His Kingdom to all of creation. With this governmental calling, we were to represent the interests and purposes of the Kingdom of God on the earth. Therefore, as God's regents, we also function in an agent capacity for God, as it relates to His Kingdom purposes and interests on the earth. Humanity is established as regent, ambassador, and agent for the Kingdom of God on the earth.

How we grow in our personal relationship and intimacy with the Lord in the midst of laboring with Him in His current Kingdom activities, will determine our future rewards and level of rule and service in the ages to come.[173] This is not a trivial matter to be taken lightly. We have been called to a unique position and relationship within the Kingdom of God that will have astounding ramifications now, in this age, and in the ages to come. This is what God has ordained for us as His Kingdom people. We must seize it with faith and great passion if we are to see it come to pass in our lives.

Being brought into the council of God in order to hear, see, and execute strategic and tactical kingdom activities as they relate to the peoples and nations of the world – what an amazing blessing! What an amazing opportunity! What an amazing responsibility! God has determined this for us from the foundations of the world, according to His own sovereignty and authority. We must individually and corporately understand and passionately pursue God's purpose and plan for *conducting Kingdom activities utilizing representative relationships.*

I had a very strong prophetic experience in my last semester of college. I was about to graduate with a degree in Business Administration. I was taking one of my few remaining classes - Business Law. I am a "process" and "order" kind of person, so I found Business Law to be pretty interesting. During the semester we studied a number of relevant topics such as, contracts, torts, and business ethics. When we studied the subject of business ethics, we were introduced to an aspect of law known as Agency. Agency Law, as we know it in its formal sense, came to the US with the earliest English settlers. Agency Law has been practiced as an aspect of British common law for centuries.

Common Law is a body of laws and statutes that developed over a long period of time and came to set legal precedence for similar judicial decisions that would take place in the future. They were not established through

---

[173] Matthew 5:12; 1Corinthians 3:12-15; Ephesians 6:7-8; Colossians 3:23-24; Revelation 22:12

legislative action or executive order. Many of these laws have been established and recognized for centuries and have been found to be timeless in their application and relevance, with no need to be altered or repealed. Agency Law is one such body of law.

Over the next several class periods, as we studied Agency Law, the instructor described the scope of Agency law and explained the responsibilities those engaged in an agency relationship have toward one another. As he talked more about it and as I read more about it, I began to comprehend a relational dynamic I had never quite understood before. As my comprehension of this agency relationship dynamic grew and as the Holy Spirit brought specific scriptures to mind that paralleled what I was learning in class, I felt like my heart was going to beat out of my chest. Everything in me wanted to stand up in class and shout, "Do you have any idea what you're saying? Do you have any idea what this means?"

In this university Business Law class, God prophetically spoke to me about a foundational principle and relational dynamic of His own Kingdom. He wasn't speaking about Agency Law, specifically, but about something broader that was both critical and fundamental to His own Kingdom – the legal nature, functional aspects, and dynamic operation of the *representative relationship* within the context and activities of the Kingdom of God. What really got me excited about the relational dynamic between the principal and the agent was finding out that a strong synonym for *agent* is *intercessor* or *intermediary*.

As the King, President, CEO, and Supreme Court of the Kingdom of God, God has sovereignly established powerful *representative relationships* within His Kingdom that are supported by the legal authority and functional ability of God within their established spheres of influence and authorized scope. What we must recognize and embrace is this: these powerful representative relationships have been established by God to carry out His desired Kingdom activities and we (the Kingdom people of God) are the individuals charged with occupying these representative relationships and performing these necessary Kingdom activities. In His sovereignty, God has determined it to be this way. To not embrace this truth and walk in its reality is to walk in unbelief and resist the will and purposes of God for us.

When we look at the activities of God and His Kingdom in the scriptures, we see different types of representative relationships established to carry out His plans and purposes on His behalf. Yet, regardless of the particular representative relationship He utilizes, there are fundamental characteristics, responsibilities, and practices intrinsic and common to these relationships.

In the scriptures we see a number of representative relationships established which involve God and individuals or groups. Some of these relationships are: 1) *The relationship between God and angels;* 2) *the relationship between God and humanity*; 3) *The relationship between God and Abraham*; 4) *The relationship between God and the children of Israel*; 5) *The relationship between the Father and Jesus*; 6) *the relationship between the Holy Spirit and the New Covenant believers (the Church)*; and 7) *The relationship between Jesus and the New Covenant believers (the Church).* A few types of representative relationships established between God and these parties include: agency, regency, covenant partnership, adjudicatory representation, penal substitutionary atonement, intercession, and ambassadorial.

Again, regardless of the type of representative relationship, there are fundamental characteristics and responsibilities inherent within it. Let's take a look at what these characteristics and responsibilities are and how Kingdom authority and the force of law (the ultimate King and Judge) bolster these powerful relationships.

The Required Context For A Representative Relationship

There is one characteristic that must always be present if a representative relationship is to exist: *the presence of a third-party.* A representative relationship is only necessary and valid when there is a matter that involves a Principal and a Third Party. Therefore, a matter in which a representative relationship can legally and effectively operate can only have two parties involved, the principal and a third party. In such a matter, the principal's representative acts strictly as an intercessor or intermediary for the principal, acting on behalf of the principal in regards to his interests and activities with the third party.

In other words, there are only two parties with individual interests, activities, and desired outcomes involved in a representative relationship: the principal and the third party. The principal's representative to the third party is not considered a separate, individual party to the relationship but is considered an extension of or intercessor for the principal party, and is authorized by the principal to act and speak on his behalf as it relates to his activities and affairs with the third party. To say it plainly - as it relates to any matter involving the principal and a third party, ***the principal is IN his representative and the representative is IN his principal. They are one – they act as one, think as one, and speak as one...they are united...they act as a unit. The representative is the principal's intercessor in the matter involving the third-party.***

For instance, in a contract negotiation involving a professional sports team, there are only two parties to the negotiations: the sports team owner and the player. These are the only two parties whose individual interests, activities, and desired outcomes matter in the negotiations. Yet, there may be one or two agents involved in the negotiations: an agent for the player and an agent for the owner. The agent for the player, for all intents and purposes, is the player during the negotiations. When the owner is talking to the player's agent, he assumes that the agent is speaking and acting for the player in all respects, unless communicated otherwise.

Likewise, if the owner enlists an agent, such as a General Manager, to handle the negotiations with the player, the General Manager/agent speaks and acts for the owner in all respects toward the player regarding the negotiations. The player assumes that whatever the General Manager/agent says and does is completely authorized by the owner and is committing the owner to the results of the negotiations, whatever they may be.

In most cases, the principal's General Manager/agent will deal with the player's agent regarding the contract negotiations. This does not change the fact that the only two parties to the negotiations are the owner and the player. Their respective agents are extensions or intercessors of their principals and these agents conduct the negotiations on behalf of and for the benefit of their respective principals. The interests and desired results of the agents do not matter and do not enter into the equation.

This is the case in any representative relationship, whether it is regarding an ambassador representing his principal nation and its affairs with another host nation, or a regent representing and ruling in absentia for his principal sovereign who, for whatever reason, is not present to directly rule that particular geographic area or domain within his kingdom. The conditions, responsibilities, and results are always the same: 1) the principal and the third party are the only parties involved in the matter; 2) the agent involved is only an intercessor or extension of his principal, as it relates to the principal's interests, activities, and desired results; and 3) it is only the principal's interests, activities, and desired results that count when the matter with the third party is concluded. This is the essence of a representative relationship and the role of the representative as it relates to his principal and the third party.

With this in mind, let's take a look at some of the most important and significant attributes, characteristics, roles, and responsibilities involved in a representative relationship, regarding the principal and the representative. I will highlight the key principles and explain how these principles not only affect us as regents and citizens of the Kingdom of God but how they truly impact how we relate to the world around us, as His Kingdom ambassadors, regents, and agents.

Laboring Together With God – A Representative Relationship

Regarding a representative relationship, here are a few of the key principles *(all quotes regarding the representative relationship and the responsibilities of the principal and the agent throughout the remainder of this chapter, unless otherwise noted, will come from this single Business Law source material,*[174]*)*:

- *"Agency is the relation existing between two persons known as principal and agent by virtue of which the agent is the…representative of the principal."*
- *"An agent…is one who represents another, the principal, in…dealings with third persons. In his dealings with a third person, the agent acts for and in the name and place of the principal."*
- *"The parties to the transaction…are the principal and the third person. The agent is not a party but simply an intermediary. The result of the agent's functioning is exactly the same as if the principal had dealt directly with the third person and without the intervention of an agent."*
- *"When the agent is dealing with the third person, the principal, in legal effect, is present in the person of the agent."*
- *"Agency is a consensual relationship that may arise by contract or agreement between the principal and agent"*
- *"Whatever…activity a person may accomplish personally, he may do through an agent. Conversely, whatever he cannot legally do himself, he cannot authorize another to do for him. "Qui facet per alium, facet per se (Who acts through another, acts himself)"*[175]

When God said, *"Let us make Man in Our image, according to Our likeness, and let him rule…"*[176], and then elaborated on it by saying, *"Be fruitful and multiply, and fill the earth, and subdue it;"*[177], God, in His sovereignty and by His own free will, declared and established humanity as His ruling representatives of this planet. Humanity was to rule over the earth, subdue it, and keep it. Humanity's destiny was and still is to rule over and govern this planet as God's representative and intercessor. Our sin has not changed that. God has done or said nothing to change that. It will happen…we will once again

[174] *Business Law 6th Edition*, by: Smith & Robertson, 1985, West Publishing, pages 346-391
[175] Thesaurus.com – (http://thesaurus.com/browse/agency)
[176] Genesis 1:26
[177] Genesis 1:28

actively rule and govern planet earth as God's legal representative and intercessor.

In My Name

In John 10, Jesus has a confrontation with the Jews where they surround Him and demand that He tell them whether He is the Messiah or not. Jesus responds to them, saying, *""I told you, and you do not believe;* ***the works that I do in My Father's name,*** *these testify of Me...* ***I and the Father are one.*** *The Jews picked up stones again to stone Him. Jesus answered them,* ***"I showed you many good works from the Father;*** *for which of them are you stoning Me?" The Jews answered Him, "For a good work we do not stone You, but for blasphemy; and because You, being a man, make Yourself out to be God." Jesus answered them,* ***"Has it not been written in your Law, 'I SAID, YOU ARE GODS'? "If he called them gods,*** *to whom the word of God came (and the Scripture cannot be broken), do you say of Him, whom the Father sanctified and sent into the world, 'You are blaspheming,'* ***because I said, 'I am the Son of God'?*** *"If I do not do the works of My Father, do not believe Me; but* ***if I do them, though you do not believe Me, believe the works, so that you may know and understand that the Father is in Me, and I in the Father.""*** [178] (emphasis mine)

In this scripture, the Jews were ready to stone Jesus for blasphemy because they thought He, being a man, was making Himself out to be God. The reason they thought it was blasphemy was because Jesus said the works He did in His ministry were the works of the Father, and that He and the Father are One. Yet, Jesus responded to their accusation by saying that God called their forefathers gods and sons of God, quoting Psalm 82 which says, *"God takes His stand in His own congregation; He judges in the midst of the rulers... I said, "You are gods, and all of you are sons of the Most High."* [179] Jesus reasoned with them by saying, if God called your forefathers gods and sons of God, why do you want to stone Me because I said I'm the Son of God?

Jesus is not denying that He is God. Yet, what He is bringing up to them is that God established Israel as His chosen people, His representative people on the earth, through His blood covenant with Abraham, Isaac and Jacob. God even calls the children of Israel His first born son.[180] God established a representative relationship with Israel, where God (the principal) displayed

---

[178] John 10:25,30-38
[179] Psalm 82:1,6
[180] Exodus 4:21-23

His works through Israel (God's representative) to the nations around them (the 3rd party), at various times and in various ways. As God's representatives to the nations around them, Israel was in God and God was in Israel.

When Jesus said that He and the Father are one, he wasn't referring to He and the Father both being God; being in the trinity together. He was referring to the representative relationship He and the Father experienced together while Jesus was living according to His human attributes while on the earth; where the Father was the principal, humanity was the third party, and Jesus was the Father's representative to humanity. The Father was in Jesus and Jesus was in the Father, representing the Father's words and actions toward humanity as if the Father was here saying and demonstrating them to humanity, Himself. They acted as one toward humanity.

Jesus identifies with and communicates His representative relationship with the Father to the Jewish leaders by saying that the Father was in Him and He was in the Father. The Father was in Jesus displaying the activities of His Kingdom and reconciling the world to Himself,[181] while Jesus was in the Father listening to Him, relating to Him, and receiving the instructions the Father wanted Him to carry out, so Jesus could effectively represent the Father's desires, words and activities to humanity. Jesus and the Father were one, they functioned as a complete unit. Jesus told the Jews, even if they couldn't believe His words, look at the works He did; they were the same works the Father would do if He was here. He did what He saw the Father doing and said what He heard the Father saying.

Jesus confirms this is what He is doing and saying by His response to Thomas, when Thomas asked Jesus, in John 14, to show the Father to him and to the other disciples. Jesus responds by saying, *"Have I been so long with you, and yet you have not come to know Me, Philip?* ***He who has seen Me has seen the Father;*** *how can you say, 'Show us the Father'? Do you not believe that* ***I am in the Father, and the Father is in Me****? The* ***words that I say*** *to you* ***I do not speak on My own initiative, but the Father abiding in Me does His works****. Believe Me that* ***I am in the Father and the Father is in Me...*** *"* [182]

Jesus isn't saying He is God (even though He is God). Jesus is saying that He is here on earth to represent the nature, character, desires, intentions, words and actions of the Father to humanity as if the Father was here doing it, Himself. What the Father wants to say and do toward humanity, Jesus is here to do and say. As such, He perfectly represented the Father to

[181] 2Corinthians 5:18-20
[182] John 14:9-11a (emphasis mine)

humanity because He did so without failure (sin), unlike Israel, who continually rebelled against God (their principal) and didn't always represent Him effectively to the nations around them. Jesus confirms this by what he told the disciples, in John 4, where He says, *"My food is* ***to do the will of Him who sent Me and to accomplish His work."*** [183] As the Father's representative to humanity, Jesus accomplished the works the Father wanted and instructed Him to do on the Father's behalf toward humanity, as if the Father was here doing it Himself.

Jesus wasn't here to take the initiative to do what He thought was best, as God. Jesus was here as the Father's representative, to obey the Father, to represent the will of the Father to humanity, to reveal the Father's Kingdom, and to accomplish the Father's work toward humanity. There were only two parties involved with these activities, the Father and humanity. Jesus, the Father's representative, was in the Father and the Father was in Jesus (they were one in relationship, purpose, and were functioning as a complete unit), accomplishing the Father's work in the Father's way, toward humanity.[184]

We know this is what Jesus was doing and saying because when Jesus was preparing to go to the cross and then to return to heaven, He says the same exact thing to and about us, as His followers and representatives. Look at what Jesus prayed and asked the Father for, in John 17, before He went to the cross, in regard to all of us who would be His followers. You know what? The Father will answer Jesus' prayers because the Father always hears Jesus' prayers. [185]

- *"Holy Father,* ***keep them in Your name, the name which You have given Me,*** *that* ***they may be one even as We are."*** vs 11 (emphasis mine)
- ***"As You sent Me*** *into the world,* ***I also have sent them*** *into the world."* vs 18 (emphasis mine)
- *"I do not ask on behalf of these alone, but* ***for those also who believe in Me through their word;"*** vs 20 (emphasis mine)
- ***"that they may all be one; even as You, Father, are in Me and I in You, that they also may be in Us,*** *so that the world may believe that You sent Me."* vs 21 (emphasis mine)

---

[183] John 4:34 (emphasis mine)
[184] John 17:6-10
[185] John 11:41-42

- *"The glory which You have given Me I have given to them,* ***that they may be one, just as We are one."*** vs 22 (emphasis mine)
- ***"I in them and You in Me, that they may be perfected in unity,*** *so that the world may know that You sent Me,* ***and loved them, even as You have loved Me."*** vs 23 (emphasis mine)

In verse 18, Jesus says that in the same way the Father sent Jesus as His Kingdom representative into the world, Jesus is sending us as His Kingdom representatives into the world. The Father sent Jesus into the world to reconcile lost humanity back to Himself. In the same way, Jesus has sent us into the world to reconcile lost humanity back to God, through Jesus Christ.[186] What Jesus began as the Father's representative to humanity, we continue as the Father's and Jesus' agents to humanity. When Jesus said, in verses 11 and 22, *"that they may be one even as We are one"*, He wasn't saying, "that they may be God even as We are God". He was saying, "That they may be united and function as a complete unit, even as We are united and function as a complete unit." In the same way the Father (the principal) was in Jesus (the representative) and Jesus was in the Father, so the Father and Jesus (the principals) are in us (the representatives) and we are in them (vs 21).

Also, in verse 22, Jesus says, *"The glory which you have given Me I have given to them."* WHAT? "THE GLORY YOU HAVE GIVEN TO ME, I HAVE GIVEN TO THEM"? What Jesus is saying is, what Jesus had available to Him from the Father and utilized to demonstrate the reality and presence of the Kingdom of God and to accomplish all that the Father gave Him to do as the Father's representative to humanity; Jesus is giving to us, His followers and representatives, to demonstrate the reality and presence of the Kingdom of God and to accomplish what He has given us to do as His representatives to humanity. Are you kidding me? How awesome is that? The same Kingdom authority, empowerment, relationships, tools, capabilities and resources the Father gave Jesus, as the Father's Kingdom representative to humanity on the earth, Jesus is giving to us, His Kingdom people and representatives to humanity on the earth.

This is why we must understand and embrace the Kingdom of God and the fact that it exists and operates prophetically on the earth in this age. In the same way the Kingdom authority, empowerment, relationships, tools, capabilities and resources were available and active prophetically to and through Jesus when He was on the earth; so they are available and active prophetically to and through us, today. God in His sovereignty has chosen

---

[186] 2Corinthians 5:18-20

to establish it this way. It has nothing to do with us deserving or earning this. God wants us to be co-laborers with Him and He has sovereignly established and provided for it and us, for His own glory and good pleasure. All we have to do is accept it and walk in it, through faith.

As a result, as the Father's and Jesus' designated representatives and intercessors to planet earth and to a fallen humanity, we must understand our responsibilities toward God as the supreme ruler and our Principal, as well as God's responsibilities toward us as His representatives, ambassadors, and intercessors to humanity. Our governing responsibilities as His regents, our representation requirements as His ambassadors, and our intercessory activities as His agents are biblically substantiated for us through Jesus Christ's example and words to us, on the Father's behalf.

So, when Jesus says, *"If you ask anything in My name…"*, or *"In My name you will…"*, or *"If two or three are gathered together in My name…"*, or any such statement, Jesus is telling us that as His Kingdom representatives, we are authorized to act on His behalf and ask for what we need in order to act on His behalf toward the people around us and to accomplish what He wants us to do. The statement *"In My Name"* is Jesus authorizing us to act and speak on His behalf and engaging us in His Kingdom activities with those around us, as His Kingdom representatives, as if He was here doing the activities Himself. "*In My name*" isn't a term we ceremonially use at the end of a prayer. It is a statement of Kingdom reality; of who we are and what we are here to do as Jesus' representatives on the earth. It is as if He was here doing it and saying it Himself. What He would do or say, we are to do and say for Him, and if we lack the resources and ability to accomplish that activity for Him, we have been given the right, privilege, and authority to ask Him for it and He will *gladly* make the resources available to us.

Chapter Questions & Notes

Talk It Over….

1) As children of God and citizens of the Kingdom of God, we take the yoke of Jesus upon ourselves, to learn from Him. Likewise, we are representatives of the Kingdom of God to those around us, just as Jesus was when He was here. Jesus has much to say to us about how we live and act in this world, as Kingdom representatives and children of God. What are some of these responsibilities and expectations? What does Jesus say we are to do? How did He send us into the word just as the Father sent Him into the world? Write down your answers:

2) The Father gave Jesus everything He needed to adequately and effectively represent His nature, character, desires and activities to the human race, as if the Father was here doing it, Himself. As Jesus' representatives to the world around us and being sent out by Jesus in the same way the Father sent Jesus, what has Jesus provided to us in order for us to adequately and effectively represent His interests, desires and activities to the world, as if He was here doing it, Himself? As our Principal, He is legally bound to provide everything to be successful in what He has commissioned us to do. List His provisions for us:

3) Jesus gave us His name in order for us to go about His work and to accomplish His activities for Him, as if He was here doing it, Himself. When He gave us His name, what did He give us? When and how do we use His name, as His Kingdom representatives? How does using His name affect our prayers and what should we expect from our prayers, when we use His name in our prayers?

(13)

Serving From Love

"For even the Son of Man did not come to be served but to serve, and to give His life a ransom for many." Mark 10:45

In his New Testament writings, Paul often refers to himself as a bondservant or the bondservant of the Lord. The term "bondservant" is very unusual for us today but in the first century, it was understood what Paul meant when he said it.

The Lord gives us a wonderful word-picture and description of a bond-servant in Exodus and Deuteronomy. [187] In these two scriptures, God is speaking to the children of Israel through Moses. They are being led by God in the wilderness and God is instructing them so they may live a life that is pleasing to Him and that sets them apart from the other nations around them. God is leading and instructing them as a father would instruct and discipline his children – in how He and His Kingdom function, how they are to live as "a people for His own possession" compared to the other peoples around them[188], and how they are to live and act toward one another as His chosen people.

As God speaks to them, He instructs them, specifically, regarding the treatment of servants – especially those who are of the children of Israel and who owe a sizeable debt to one of their Hebrew brethren. When this situation occurred, the debtor was to serve the lender until he had labored enough to repay the entire debt. Yet, God put a provision in place which states that after a period of seven years, if the debtor was still serving the lender to repay his debt, the lender (or master) was to forgive the remainder of the debt owed by the debtor (servant) and set the servant free – regardless of how much he still owed. This instruction was given in order to build into the master, the God-like character qualities of mercy, grace and justice – reinforcing the truth that mercy triumphs over judgment.[189] God also put a provision into place intended to build into His people another

[187] Exodus 21:1-6; Deuteronomy 15:12-17
[188] Deuteronomy 14:2; 1Peter 2:9
[189] James 2:10-13

God-like character quality which provides for one to freely serve another, of his own accord – even if he is free and there is no debt of service to be repaid.

When the master sets his servant free after the seven years is completed, the servant may choose to continue serving his master because of his love for him and his house. Even though the servant is free to go, he freely chooses to remain with his master because of the heart-bond of love and gratitude he has developed toward his master. In his heart, he no longer considers it a burden to serve his master but considers it a joy and privilege to serve him. He is no longer simply a slave but is now a bond-servant to his master – having developed a heart-bond with his master; choosing to serve his master from a heart of love and gratitude rather than out of duty or fear.

When the servant declares this love and devotion for his master by choosing to serve his master for the rest of his life, the master takes his servant to the doorway of the house. The master then takes an awl and pierces the ear of his bond-servant – forever marking him as his bond-servant. From this time forward, when the bond-servant goes out in public, everyone who sees the mark in his ear knows that this servant loves his master and has chosen to freely serve his master and the master's family. He is no longer serving out of bondage - he is serving out of freedom with a heart of love, gratitude and devotion.

The servant's life and service is no longer focused on himself and his ability to get out of debt so he can pursue his own self-interests and plans. He has forever chosen to surrender his own self-interests and plans in order to dedicate himself to his master. He does not second-guess or regret his decision because he has come to know and love the nature and character of his master, and knows that he can place his trust and devotion in him. He knows that he will be loved, valued and cared for by his master. It is no longer about himself. It is all about his master. In all that the bond-servant does and says in serving and representing his master, his objective is to ensure that his activities enhance the credibility and reputation of His master's name.

This provision for serving from a heart-attitude of love and devotion is not new with the law given by God to the children of Israel. God is not going to require us to do something He Himself has not done or is not willing to do. God leads through example and, therefore, He leads through serving. Jesus instructs His disciples that, in the Kingdom of God, the greatest must be the servant of all. The greatest in the Kingdom of God is God, Himself. As a result, God is the servant of all and He leads us in being servants to those around us.

In order for God to lead through serving, He must possess a heart that serves out of love and devotion. We have no better evidence of this than in the covenants God established with humanity after Adam's rebellion in the Garden of Eden – especially His covenant to bruise the serpent's head (defeat the power or Satan, sin and death) and His covenant with Abraham (to bless all of humanity through Abraham's descendent – Jesus Christ).

After Adam's sin against God in the garden, humanity was totally incapable of acting on its own behalf to restore itself to a healthy relationship with God. Because our sin against God was a sin of rebellion conceived in the spirit of Adam, the sin that separated him and us from God was not the lone outward action of eating the fruit of the forbidden tree. The consideration and intent to rebel against God's lordship had already worked its way within Adam's heart before he ever ate of the tree. Since it was not, simply, the outward expression of his rebellion (the eating of the tree) that separated him from God but the formation of his rebellion in his heart; any outward expressions of remorse and sorrow (good works), alone, in an effort to atone for his sin, could not restore his relationship and fellowship with God. The human spirit which conceived the sin had to be dealt with, directly, if humanity was to truly fellowship with and live in God's presence again.

Two things had to happen regarding humanity and our sin before any intimate fellowship and relationship between us and God could be restored: 1) humanity must encounter the justice of God for our rebellion which is God's previously-established sentence for rebellion - death and eternal separation from God[190]; and 2) the human spirit had to be transformed and made alive toward God, again, since it had been polluted and hardened toward God because of sin.[191] God no longer ruled in our hearts – our own self-interests and self-gratification ruled our hearts. Satisfying these two criteria for restoration with God was completely outside of our ability to accomplish for ourselves.

If our relationship with God had any hope of being restored to its original standing, God was going to have to take the initiative and act on humanity's behalf. This is where we see the servant-heart of God take action. God had every right to completely destroy humanity and start all over again, if He wanted to. Instead, we see God come to our aid – to serve us when we were the most helpless and totally incapable of saving ourselves or repaying God for what He would do.[192]

---

[190] Genesis 2:16-17
[191] Isaiah 59:2; Ezekiel 36:25-27

The first instance of God serving humanity after our rebellion was His promise to defeat and destroy the power of Satan, sin and death, which ruled in our hearts and held humanity in its power.[193] Another significant instance of God's servanthood toward humanity appears in the life of Abraham. As God endeavors to reveal Himself (including His nature and character) to us, He establishes a covenant with a man named Abraham.[194] In this covenant God promises to bless all of humanity through a descendent of Abraham – namely, Jesus Christ.[195] This blessing involves God, Himself, providing a legal substitute for humanity's judgment; who would encounter and willingly accept the just judgment of God, on humanity's behalf. This legal substitute would and must be, Himself, completely sinless and willingly take upon Himself humanity's sin and the judgment and punishment of God intended for all of us.[196]

As a result of God's act of service to mankind, humanity had become a debtor to God. God paid a debt for us that we owed and we are totally incapable of ever repaying to Him. Yet, God is drawing each one of us to Himself, desiring to reveal Himself (His nature and character) to us so that we might come to know and experience Him as He really is. As we allow God to reveal Himself to us, we grow to love Him; choosing to serve Him – not out of duty or fear because of our debt but out of love, devotion and gratitude. When we choose to serve Him from the heart, we bond ourselves to Him from the heart – serving Him with love. He sets us free from the burden of debt that we owe Him and from our slavery to sin. Even though we are free from this slavery and debt, we choose to serve Him – becoming bond-servants of God, through Jesus Christ. As a result of this change of heart, God takes us and marks us (He transforms our inner-being and fills us with His Spirit) as His own. When we go outside the house, all who see us should see His mark upon us, recognizing that we now belong to Him.

As bond-servants of our Lord Jesus Christ, we have chosen to live for Him and not for our own self-interests and plans. We have forever chosen to surrender our will to pursue our own self-interests and plans in order to dedicate ourselves to Him, as our master, and his interests, plans and purposes. We do not second-guess or regret this decision because we have come to know and love the nature and character of God. We come to know that we can place our trust and devotion in Him. We know that we will be loved and valued by Jesus as our master. Our lives are no longer

---

[192] Romans 8:2-3
[193] Genesis 3:15
[194] Genesis 15:18; Genesis 17; Genesis 18:17-19
[195] Galatians 3:16
[196] 2Corinthians 5:21

about ourselves; it is all about Him. In all that we do and say in serving Him as His bond-servants, our objective is to ensure that our activities enhance the credibility and reputation of our Master's name – the name of Jesus. Whatever we do, we do it for the sake of His name.

When we make it all about Him and do all for the sake of His name, He, in turn, can freely make it all about us as His children. He can do this with confidence; knowing that we will not turn His Kingdom resources and blessings into tools we use to serve ourselves and to accomplish our own agendas. If we seek first the Kingdom of God and His righteousness, all these things He has designed for us to have and use will be given to us because we will not use them in a manner that will cause us to promote ourselves and to self-destruct. We will use them to serve Him and those around us. When we determine to make it all about Him, He will make it all about us.[197]

One thing we must remember. Since God is a servant because He has a servant's heart, we are also servants because we have been given His nature and character to dwell within our hearts. As we are bond-slaves to God because of our love and devotion to Him, so God will continue to serve us because of His love and devotion to us. This is the basis of His covenant with Abraham and all other covenants He has established with humanity. God loves us and is devoted to us and will be faithful to His covenants because it would be against His nature to do anything else. In all that God does, we see His nature and character shining through. Jesus told the disciples that He did not come to be served but to serve.[198] Jesus was the exact representation of the Father when He came to earth as a human.

He possessed the nature and character of God and demonstrated that nature and character perfectly to us.[199] Jesus came to serve humanity in His life, death and resurrection because that is the nature of God, Himself. If the nature and character of God dwells within us as His bond-servants, that same nature and character should drive and be demonstrated in all that we do toward Him and toward our neighbor.[200] When we are motivated by and demonstrate the nature and character of God within us, we will do all things for the sake of His name. As Paul said to the Corinthian church, *"Whether, then, you eat or drink or whatever you do, do all to the glory of God"*[201]

[197] Matthew 6:32-34; John 17:23; Luke 12:31-32
[198] Matthew 10:28
[199] Hebrews 1:3
[200] Mark 12:30-31
[201] 1Corinthians 10:31

Chapter Questions & Notes

Talk It Over….

1) Jesus tells us to love and serve one another, as His followers. Paul confirms and emphasizes this fact in his New Testament writings. The bond servant is to not only serve his master but he is to serve the master's family, just as he serves his master. As bond-servants of God and of Jesus, what does it mean that we are to serve our master's family as we serve our master? How does that affect our life as followers of Jesus? Do we see examples of Jesus serving people because He, also, served God the Father?

2) God chose to serve humanity because He is a servant. He does not ask or expect us to do something He, Himself, is not willing to do. How has God served humanity? How has this affected you and me as followers of Jesus? How does this instruct us and our behavior as those who have been forgiven and served by God?

Leaders: Since this is the last chapter in this book, discuss with the group what they have learned and how their knowledge and understanding of the Kingdom of God has increased? How has it effected their daily lives, their relationship with Jesus, and their relationships with those around them? What challenges have they encountered and how have they chosen to confront and overcome those challenges? How has this book affected their relationship with the Holy Spirit and how are they pursuing their relationship, moving forward? Have the members of the group write down their plans for moving forward with what they have learned, and for continuing their pursuit of the Kingdom of God in practical, effective ways.

VOLUME TWO

"Your Kingdom Come, Your Will Be Done"

The Presence & Activities of the Kingdom of God

(1)

Our Need For The Kingdom's Apostolic & Prophetic Foundation

"Therefore, holy brethren, partakers of a heavenly calling, consider Jesus, ***the Apostle*** *and High Priest of our confession."* Hebrews 3:1 (emphasis mine)

"So then you are no longer strangers and aliens, but you are fellow citizens with the saints, and are of God's household, ***having been built on the foundation of the apostles and prophets, Christ Jesus Himself being the corner stone,*** *in whom the whole building, being fitted together, is growing into a holy temple in the Lord, in whom you also are being built together into a dwelling of God in the Spirit."* Ephesians 2:19-22 (emphasis mine)

During the formative years of the Roman empire, as it was expanding into northern Europe and other more remote areas of the known world, Rome encountered a recurring problem within these regions where they had expanded. As Rome defeated the armies of these lands and endeavored to assimilate these indigenous peoples into the empire, they encountered frequent uprisings and rebellion. The manners and customs of these peoples were often very different from those of "civilized Rome". Rome was so far away, geographically and culturally, from these peoples and the manners and customs of these people were so engrained in them that they saw little reason and had no real incentive to become "Romanized".

In order to resolve this prevailing problem, Caesar established and commissioned "*apostolos*", or "*sent ones*", who would venture to these far off lands, in the name and authority of Caesar and Rome, in order to establish the Roman culture and lifestyle in the midst of these people, assisting them to more easily understand, identify with, and assimilate into the culture and lifestyle of the rest of the Roman empire. As these people gradually grew to understand and identify with Rome and the culture and lifestyle associated with it, Caesar discovered that he had instituted a very valuable and effective method for putting down revolts and uprisings, while bringing more established peace to all the peoples of the empire.

In His predetermined plan for humanity, which God established before the world began, including His provision for all that humanity would need even after sin entered the world; God established a very similar plan using the "*apostolos*". It was a plan for establishing and commissioning a "sent one" who would establish the culture and lifestyle of the Kingdom of God on the earth, and for effectively assimilating those who would choose to become citizens of His Kingdom. God commissioned His "*apostolos*", Jesus - the person He sent from heaven to bring the Kingdom of God to the earth and to establish a Kingdom culture and lifestyle for those who would become citizens of the Kingdom of God on the earth, throughout this present age.

Jesus, when He came to the earth, brought the Kingdom of God with Him. While He was here, He established the Kingdom culture as He taught, prepared and commissioned others who would further expand the Kingdom of God on the earth, once He returned to heaven. Shortly after Jesus began this apostolic activity, He was confronted by a large crowd of people who wanted to hear more from Him concerning the Kingdom of God. In response, Jesus took this opportunity to engage in what we have come to refer to as "The Sermon On the Mount." In reality, what Jesus did was to establish many of the foundational truths for what the culture and lifestyle of the Kingdom of God was to be like on the earth when He returned, at the end of the age. The culture and lifestyle that was already being experienced in heaven was to be planted, established and gradually expanded throughout the earth, by those who would follow Him – who He would train, commission, and send. Even though this Kingdom culture would exist alongside the culture of the domain of darkness throughout this present age, the culture of the Kingdom of God would be present and growing through the lives of God's Kingdom people, the Church.

What Jesus taught the people that day was much more than a sermon. It is the definitive prophetic revelation of the culture and lifestyle of the Kingdom of God in heaven, and that this culture and lifestyle is, likewise, to be established and experienced here on the earth by His Kingdom people. As the Father's "a*postolos*" (sent one) to mankind and the earth, Jesus began to establish this culture and lifestyle of the Kingdom of God on the earth. Later, in this "sermon", Jesus instructed and encouraged the people who were listening to Him to continue pursuing the Kingdom of God and to pray, asking the Father to establish this Kingdom culture and lifestyle on the earth. Jesus told them, *"Pray, then, in this way: 'Our Father who is in heaven, Hallowed be Your name.* ***Your kingdom come. Your will be done, on earth as it is in heaven.*** *Give us this day our daily bread. And forgive us our debts, as we*

also have forgiven our debtors. And do not lead us into temptation, but deliver us from evil. ***For Yours is the kingdom*** *and the power and the glory forever."* [202]
(emphasis mine)

The Kingdom of God is coming in its fullness to reside on the earth when Jesus returns. The will of God will be done on the earth, as it is being done in heaven, right now. The culture and lifestyle of the Kingdom of God in heaven will be the predominant culture and lifestyle on the earth when Jesus returns to establish His Kingdom rule, in its fullness. Yet, the Kingdom people of God are to begin experiencing this culture and lifestyle even now, while we are on the earth waiting for Jesus' return. This apostolic culture and lifestyle is to permeate the lives and activities of God's Kingdom people, now.

You could say that the followers of Christ are "counter-culture" in that we are to be pursuing the culture and lifestyle of the Kingdom of God, which is contrary to the prevailing culture of the world and its citizens who live and work all around us. We are the seeds of the Kingdom of God in this world. The culture and lifestyle of the Kingdom of God in the world is a seed within the prevailing culture and activities of the kingdoms of this world. We (these "seedlings") will continue to grow within our spheres of influence as we pursue the Kingdom and allow its influence and activities to touch our lives and the lives and culture around us.

The culture and lifestyle of the Kingdom of God will not overcome the world's system and culture in this age, before Jesus returns. Yet, it will have a tremendous effect upon our lives and upon those we come into contact with, as we live our Kingdom lives and demonstrate the reality and presence of the Kingdom of God to them. This is what Jesus taught those who followed Him and that is what the "Sermon on the Mount" is all about. The presence and activity of the Holy Spirit is impacting and changing the culture and lifestyles of God's Kingdom people, who, in turn, are to impact and demonstrate the presence and reality of the Kingdom of God to those who live throughout the earth, in this age.

If we are going to rule with Jesus here on the earth when He returns to establish His Kingdom in its fullness, it makes sense that we understand and experience what this Kingdom culture and lifestyle is to be like, before He returns. He has made a way and established the foundation for us to know and experience this Kingdom lifestyle, now. He has given us His word and His Spirit to teach us, train us, and empower us to be His Kingdom witnesses and "sent ones" in our generation.

---

[202] Matthew 6:9-13

Yes, when Jesus ascended into heaven after His resurrection, He gave gifts to His Kingdom people in order to equip His people for the work of Kingdom ministry. One of these gifts is the "*apostolos*", the apostle. This gift is not only the original twelve apostles of Jesus. It is not only the apostles written about and mentioned in the New Testament. Apostles are to be present and active among God's Kingdom people as long as we are on the earth, until Jesus returns. To deny or ignore this fact is to take on the "great commission" that Jesus gave us, with one arm tied behind our back and blind in one eye. It is a great hindrance to God's plan, for us to adopt and live according to this belief.

At the same time, being an apostle is more than a title. It's much more than going to a foreign country to tell people about Jesus, starting a church, or being the leader of a group of churches. The main purpose and focus of the Apostle, as well as for the other gifts that Jesus gave His people when He ascended into heaven (Prophet, Evangelist, Pastor, Teacher), is to equip His people for the work of Kingdom ministry and to build them into a spiritual force that will complete this great commission that Jesus gave us.

The purpose and focus of the Apostle is to establish the culture of the Kingdom of God as a foundation within and among God's Kingdom people, and to build upon this foundation in such a way that these people can take this Kingdom culture with them into the seven cultural kingdoms of this world. The apostle, as well as the other ascension gifts of Jesus, are not to do the ministry work while the rest of us stand by and cheer them on. These 5 ministry servants comprise less than 5% of the entire Body of Christ on the earth. Jesus never intended for this 5% to do all of the work of the ministry. They are to lead in the effort to train and equip the rest of the 95% of the Church who will do the work of the ministry.

Jesus (the model Apostle, Prophet, Evangelist, Pastor and Teacher) participated in these ministries and activities of the Holy Spirit as He taught, trained and equipped His followers to engage in these same activities once He was gone. Jesus didn't do all the work, nor did He expect His disciples to do all of the work. When the disciples came to Jesus and told Him to let the thousands of people go home to get something to eat, who had just spent all afternoon listening to Him teach on the Kingdom of God, Jesus said to them, "You feed them." Jesus knew that it was impossible for His disciples to feed all of these people through the natural means available to them.

When Jesus said to them, "You feed them," He was challenging them to assess and respond to the situation as He had been teaching them. He challenged them to respond with faith in the presence and power of the Kingdom of God. Miracles aren't miracles to God. They are His divine activities to meet the needs of people, at any given time and as they arise. Jesus didn't ask the disciples how much money they had. He asked them what food they had. The people needed food, not money, so God provided the food that the people needed, through the hands of His Kingdom representative, Jesus.

When the disciples reverted to their natural thinking and methods in a weak effort to meet the need, Jesus proceeded to engage them in another Kingdom training session. Jesus responded to the situation according to the will and desire of the Father, which was to exercise faith in the presence and power of the Holy Spirit, who was there to assist and empower Jesus. The Father wanted to engage and confront these thousands of people with the presence and power of His rule, so He instructed Jesus, by the Holy Spirit, to cooperate with Him so He could do what He wanted to do. Jesus cooperated with the Father by instructing His disciples to have the people sit down in small groups, and then He asked the Father to demonstrate His presence and power by feeding the people because they were hungry.

Yes, a miracle took place. Thousands of people were fed with a few fish and some loaves of bread. Again, a miracle isn't a miracle to God. Jesus had taught them to pray, *"…give us this day, our daily bread."* The Father wanted to do it. Jesus knew the Father wanted to do it because He knows the Father. Jesus cooperated with the Father by responding to the instructions the Holy Spirit gave Him. The Father, through the Holy Spirit, did the rest. That was the lesson for Jesus' disciples that day. It wasn't about how to feed thousands of people after preaching a long sermon to them.

It was Jesus instructing His disciples in the nature and character of the Father, and how to cooperate with the Father as He engages us and demonstrates through us, His presence and ability to meet the needs of the people around us. Jesus, living and ministering through the presence and power of the Holy Spirit, is our example for living a Kingdom life in this present age. When Jesus said, "You feed them", He was challenging His disciples to see and respond with Kingdom eyes and activities, allowing the Father to demonstrate His presence and power to those around them, as if He was here to do it, Himself.

Establishing and building upon this type of Kingdom culture is the purpose and ministry of the New Testament Apostle. The New Covenant ministries of the Apostle and Prophet are to, 1) build and establish the culture of the Kingdom of God in the midst of His people, and 2) to instruct and train

God's people in how to communicate with God and respond to the prophetic activities of the Kingdom of God in their lives. The Apostle and Prophet are the foundational ministries for the equipping and building up of God's Kingdom people, with Jesus being the chief cornerstone of this living building.[203] The Apostle instructs and trains God's people in the culture of the Kingdom of God, and the Prophet instructs and trains God's people in how to hear and respond to the prophetic activities of the Kingdom of God. Without these two ministries being present and active within the Church, especially the local church, God's people will not mature in the way Jesus desires and we will not accomplish all that Jesus wants us to accomplish.

What is most interesting is that, over the centuries, the two New Covenant ministries that the cultural, organized church has managed to remove from active ministry within the Church are the Apostle and the Prophet. The cultural, organized church developed erroneous doctrines that have taught us that the Apostle and Prophet are no longer necessary and relevant to the Body of Christ, the Church. We have been taught that since the death of the original Apostles, we don't need these two ministries. As a result of this "resistance" to the will and purpose of God, we find the Church, especially in the western hemisphere, spiritually weak and carnal. We have removed the two foundational ministries that Jesus gave us to establish us, equip us, and to build us up in our faith so we can engage in these prophetic activities of the Kingdom of God.

As we will see, we must once again recognize and welcome these two ascension gifts back into the Church, especially the local church, if we are to complete all that Jesus placed us here to accomplish for Him. We are only operating at 60% efficiency, at best, because we only have three of the five ascension gifts functioning effectively, among us. We need the Apostolic and Prophetic ministries of Jesus living and functioning among us. We must embrace them and what they bring to the Church. If we are to experience the culture of the Kingdom of God in our midst with any consistency and power, we must embrace these two ministries and allow them to engage in the ministry Jesus designated for them. We will only be "active" apostolic and prophetic people when these two ministries are present and active among us.

---

[203] Ephesians 2:19-22

Chapter Questions & Notes

Talk It Over….

1) Jesus is the original Apostle ("sent one") who came to instruct us and demonstrate to us what the culture of the Kingdom of God is really like. Jesus' words, lifestyle and activities effectively communicated to us what the "culture of the Kingdom" actually is and how we can effectively experience it ourselves, as well as communicate and demonstrate this culture to those around us, in our generation. In the Sermon on the Mount, Jesus continually used the phrases, "You have heard it said…but I tell you….", to communicate the differences between the "established, conventional culture" on the earth and the culture of the Kingdom of God.

   Review the Sermon on the Mount, identifying where Jesus draws these distinctions between the prevailing culture and the culture of the Kingdom, using these two phrases, and discuss these differences. Write down your observations:

2) The ministries of the Apostle and Prophet are to establish the cultural and prophetic foundation of the Kingdom of God within the communities of Jesus followers throughout the world. Jesus is to be the cornerstone of this foundation, as it is established by the Apostles and Prophets. Identify some of the apostolic and prophetic characteristics and building blocks the apostle and prophet should include and establish in this foundation, within the communities of believers in Jesus Christ.

Leader: Encourage the group to think about what the Apostle and Prophet do and how they can best build a foundation that encourages and provides for the instruction, training and equipping of believers to effectively experience, communicate and demonstrate the Kingdom of God within their individual spheres of influence. This may take some time, so encourage them not to be in a hurry. If this exercise requires time outside of the group meeting to effectively consider and identify these characteristics and building blocks, allow them to take this extra time, and to come back together to discuss.

(2)

The Holy Spirit – We Are To Know & Experience Him

"Now we have received…the Spirit who is from God, so that we may know the things freely given to us by God" 1Corinthians 2:12

For those of us who have assembled jigsaw puzzles, we know how challenging they can be. Sometimes we feel like tearing our hair out trying to put them together, especially the more difficult they are. The pieces seem so random and it is difficult to tell where the various pieces go and how they fit together, since many of them are the same color and have similar shapes. Seeing and comprehending the purpose, plans and activities of God is much like putting together a jigsaw puzzle. Everything seems to be so random and we have a difficult time putting together the pieces He has given us so we can clearly see the completed picture. Yet, He has given us some foundational keys to help us see the big picture of what He is doing and to reveal to us how the pieces of what He is doing fit together.

In the scriptures, God has given us the foundational keys for comprehending Him and His purposes for us in this age. He has given us the big picture of what He is doing, which is the expansion of the Kingdom of God on the earth. God has revealed to us what the finished picture will look like – the throne of God coming down to the earth where He will rule in the presence of His people forever.[204] He has also given us pieces of the puzzle that we need to frame that big picture, which are: 1) the initial establishment of His Kingdom on the earth through humanity; 2) the transfer of His Kingdom regents (humanity) to the domain of darkness, through sin; 3) the redemption of humanity and their transfer back into the Kingdom of God; and 4) the reestablishment of the Kingdom of God on the earth, through Jesus. The rest of the scriptures and what God has and is doing in human history reveal the remaining pieces of the puzzle so that all of creation and each individual person in this creation may comprehend His specific will, purposes and activities for them in this age. The key word is

---

[204] Rev. 21

"reveal" or "revelation" which implies that a personal relationship and communication is established between God and His people.

Embracing and experiencing the realities of the Kingdom of God is the glue that holds everything else together. Without embracing and experiencing the nature, character, purpose and operation of the Reign or God, the Scriptures will seem like disjointed pieces of a puzzle that never seem to fit together. We will see bits and pieces of truth from the Scriptures but we won't grasp the "big picture" reality and its relevance to our daily lives. Consequently, when difficult times come into our lives and these bits and pieces of Scripture are severely challenged, we will revert to what we *do* know – the pattern of behavior we have always followed and what our physical senses tell us is real.

In order to embrace and experience the Kingdom of God, we must first understand its nature and how it relates to us and to creation. The Kingdom of God is real and active, and it functions according to specific attributes and characteristics. Therefore, to discover the nature, character, attributes and abilities of the Kingdom of God, we must first discover the nature, character, attributes and abilities of God, Himself. God does not and will not change and, therefore, the defining attributes of the rule of His Kingdom will not change. The manner in which God rules his Kingdom will never conflict with his personal nature and character.

God values the free will He has sovereignly given to humanity and He desires each of us to willingly choose the rule of His presence in our lives. For those who willingly choose the rule of God, He provides all we need to be vital citizens of His Kingdom, to live lives in accordance with the nature and character of His Kingdom, to receive revelation from Him regarding Himself and His will for our lives, and to be engaged with Him in His Kingdom activities in this age and in the ages to come. This truth is exciting news for all of us and restores in us a sense of eternal purpose and destiny; giving us confidence and hope as we seek to grasp a greater understanding of the Kingdom of God and how it impacts our lives and activities, now.

The Holy Spirit – Our Most Important Possession As God's Kingdom People

In John 16, Jesus made an amazing statement to His followers just before He went to the cross to die for the sins of humanity. Jesus tells them, *"I tell you the truth, it is to your advantage that I go away…"* [205] What? How could it

EVER be to our advantage that Jesus would go away and leave us? While being here with His followers, speaking to them and doing powerful miracles among them, He completely changed their and our perception and understanding of God forever. People were flocking to Jesus by the thousands to hear Him talk about God and His Kingdom and to witness the miracles He was performing. How could it ever be a good thing for us that He would stop these activities and leave us? Did something happen to cause Jesus to say this to His loyal followers? As a matter of fact, something did happen to cause Jesus to not only say this but to consider this to be a good thing for us. Where can we find such an event? This event, too, is described in John's gospel, in chapter 12, not long before Jesus made that startling statement to His disciples.

"Now there were some Greeks among those who were going up to worship at the feast; these then came to Philip, who was from Bethsaida of Galilee, and began to ask him, saying, 'Sir, we wish to see Jesus.' Philip came and told Andrew; Andrew and Philip came and told Jesus. And Jesus answered them, saying, 'The hour has come for the Son of Man to be glorified. Truly, truly, I say to you, unless a grain of wheat falls into the earth and dies, it remains alone; but if it dies, it bears much fruit.'" [206] Up until this time, Jesus' ministry had been to the Jews, predominantly.[207] When a group of Greeks (Gentiles who were believers in the God of Israel and had come to Jerusalem in order to celebrate the Feast of Passover with the Jews) came to Jesus' disciples and requested an audience with Jesus, Jesus recognized that this request triggered a transition in His ministry, His life, and in the unfolding plan of God. His ministry as He knew it was completed. Now, what stood before Him was the cross and His sacrificial death for the sins of humanity. Yet, what was it about the request of the Greek followers that triggered this transition in Jesus' life, ministry, and the activities of God?

Jesus tells us, when He says, *"Truly, truly, I say to you, unless a grain of wheat falls into the earth and dies, it remains alone; but if it dies, it bears much fruit."* Jesus is telling us that the demands upon Him and the presence of the Kingdom of God through Him are too great for one person to satisfy. Jesus came to proclaim the presence and reality of the Kingdom of God to the Jews. Yet, when the Greeks (Gentiles) began placing demands upon Him, it was more than He, as one person, can satisfy – even as one who ministered in the presence and power of the Holy Spirit. As long as He was the lone representative of the reality and presence of Kingdom of God on the earth, the growth of the Kingdom would be limited to what He could do as that single representative. As one man, Jesus could only reach and minister to a

[205] John 16:7a
[206] John 12:20-24
[207] Matthew 15:21-24

finite number of people. He knew that humanity's demands on the Kingdom of God would only increase and the only way for Him to meet this demand was for Him to increase as well. As a result, He knew that the only way He could increase His Kingdom reach was to plant Himself as a seed so that His presence would grow and increase throughout the earth, to meet this demand.

This relates back to the parables Jesus taught the disciples about the nature and presence of the Kingdom of God on the earth, in Matthew 13.[208] *"The kingdom of heaven is like a mustard seed, which a man took and planted in his field. Though it is the smallest of all seeds, yet when it grows, it is the largest of garden plants and becomes a tree, so that the birds come and perch in its branches."* [209] The Kingdom of God, present on the earth in Jesus Christ, is the mustard seed. Jesus was one man who represented the presence and reality of the Kingdom of God to all humanity. Jesus was one man who the Father was able to work in and through in order to reconcile the world to Himself. Jesus was one man through whom the Father was able to communicate His words and display His works to a world who didn't know the Father. Jesus was one man who allowed the Holy Spirit to act through Him to demonstrate to the world that the Father is not a passive, disinterested being; who is uncaring and uninterested in the plight and peril this world is experiencing at the hands of the god of this world. As a result, the world was placing demands on the Kingdom of God, in Jesus, to communicate and act toward them as if the Father was here doing it Himself.

Jesus was all of these things to the world but He was only one man. Jesus knew the world and the demands the people placed upon the Kingdom of God through Him was too much for Him, as one man. He knew the world needed more who were just like Him, who would represent the presence and reality of the Kingdom of God to the people of this world. Jesus knew that the world needed more who were just like Him, who God could work in and through in order to reconcile the world to Himself.[210] Jesus knew that the world needed more who were just like Him, through whom God could communicate His words and display His works to a world who didn't know Him and who could communicate and act toward the world on His behalf.

Jesus knew that the world needed more who were just like Him, through whom the Holy Spirit could demonstrate to the world that God is not a passive, disinterested being; who is uncaring and uninterested in the plight

---

[208] Matthew 13:1-52
[209] Matthew 13:31-32
[210] 2Corinthian 5:16-19

and peril this world is experiencing at the hands of the god of this world. And, Jesus knew that the only way the world would experience more of these Kingdom representatives like Himself, was for Him to plant Himself as a seed in order to bring forth life and the growth of the Kingdom of God on the earth. In this way, He and the Father would have millions of Spirit-empowered Kingdom representatives who live and minister to the people of the earth as Jesus lived and ministered when He was here.

This is a tall order, to replicate Jesus' ministry and Kingdom representation many times over. These "little Jesuses" would need to represent the Kingdom of God to the people of this world in the same way Jesus did when He was here. Yet, God was up to the challenge. This is why Jesus tells His disciples, *"But I tell you the truth, it is to your advantage that I go away;"* [211] Even though the disciples were sorrowful that Jesus was going to die and go away, it was to their and our advantage that He do so. Not only because He was to die for the sins of all humanity. There was another reason, which Jesus goes on to tell His disciples in the rest of verse 7; *"...for if I do not go away, the Helper will not come to you; but if I go, I will send Him to you."* Who is this *Helper* that Jesus is going to send when He goes away? Who is this Helper who is such a benefit to us that it is worth Jesus going away from us so that this Helper might come to us? Jesus goes on to tell us who this Helper is; *"But when He, the Spirit of truth, comes, He will guide you into all truth; for He will not speak on His own initiative, but whatever He hears, He will speak; and He will disclose to you what is to come. "He will glorify Me, for He will take of Mine and will disclose it to you. "All things that the Father has are Mine; therefore I said that He takes of Mine and will disclose it to you."* [212]

This Helper that Jesus will send is the Holy Spirit. It is the same Holy Spirit the Father sent to Jesus and who helped and empowered Jesus to perform the works that He did on the Father's behalf.[213] Jesus told His disciples that the Helper, the Holy Spirit, was going to be sent so they would be able to carry on the work of ministry that He began; and they were to take this ministry to the entire world, not only to the Jews.[214] Just as Jesus was sent by the Father to be His witness and Kingdom representative to the Jews, Jesus is sending His disciples to be His witnesses and Kingdom representatives to the entire world and to each generation until the end of the age.[215] And, Jesus is giving them the same Helper, the Holy Spirit, to accomplish their work that the Father gave Him to accomplish His work.

---

[211] John 16:7a
[212] John 16:13-15
[213] Luke 3:21-22; Luke 4:1-2; Luke 4:14; Luke 5:17
[214] Acts 1:7-8
[215] Matthew 28:18-20

Remember, when a principal sends his representative to accomplish work for him with a third party, that principal is responsible to provide everything that representative will need to accomplish that work. Since Jesus came here to do the will of the Father and to accomplish His work, the Father was obligated to provide Jesus with everything He needed to do it. Since Jesus was living and functioning in ministry on the earth as a man, the Father was obligated to provide Jesus with whatever He needed to speak the words of the Father and to perform the works of the Father. This is why the Father sent the Holy Spirit to be with Jesus; that Jesus would be able to speak the words of the Father and do the prophetic activities of the Kingdom of God as if the Father was here saying it and doing it Himself.

Jesus (our principal) would not and does not expect His Kingdom representatives, the Church, to represent Him and His Kingdom to the people of this world without the same provisions the Father provided Him when He was here representing the Father. That is not just, righteous, or legal (the law of Agency). The throne of God is established on God's character, which is righteousness and justice, and God is the Supreme Court for the entire universe. Jesus must provide for us as His representatives. If He doesn't, then He is not our principal and/or we are not His representatives. Jesus has provided everything to us pertaining to life and godliness.[216] If we don't know what these provisions are or we aren't experiencing them as Jesus tells us we should, it is not Jesus' fault, it is ours.

There is a scripture in Luke 18, where Jesus is teaching His disciples on prayer. At the end of this teaching, Jesus tells them, "*"Hear what the unrighteous judge said; now,* ***will not God bring about justice for His elect*** *who cry to Him day and night, and will He delay long over them? "I tell you that* ***He will bring about justice for them quickly. However, when the Son of Man comes, will He find faith on the earth****?"*[217] The Father is just! Jesus is just! The Holy Spirit is just! If we do not know what the provision is that God has given us, or we are not experiencing that provision in our lives as their Kingdom representatives, then it is our fault. When God calls upon us to act for Him as if He was here doing it Himself, He must and will make sure we have whatever we need to accomplish it, even if it takes a "miracle" to do it. A miracle isn't a miracle to Jesus. It is simply Jesus providing what we need to accomplish what He wants us to do. It isn't us doing it. It is Jesus doing it through us. We are simply cooperating with Jesus in His works, as Jesus cooperated with the Father in the Father's works.

---

[216] 2Peter 1:3-4

[217] Luke 18:1-8 (emphasis mine)

At the end of this scripture teaching on prayer, Jesus says to His disciples, "***However, when the Son of Man comes, will He find faith on the earth?***" Jesus doesn't waste words and He doesn't say something rhetorically when He is teaching His disciples about something so important for them and their ministries as prayer and receiving the provision they need to accomplish their work, through prayer. What's interesting about this statement by Jesus is that He was speaking concerning the generation of Jesus-followers who would be living on the earth at the time of His return. He is asking the question, *"Will I find my Kingdom representatives living a life of faith when I return?"*

If you look at the context of that scripture teaching on prayer, and the question Jesus asks at the end of it; Jesus isn't asking about saving faith because He isn't talking about the born again experience. He is talking to His Kingdom representatives and preparing them for their ministry when He is gone. He is telling them that He will be righteous and just to provide everything they need to accomplish everything He as their principal requires, if they only ask in faith when they pray. Then He asks the question, "Will My Kingdom representatives who are on the earth at the time of My return have the faith to believe for and pray to receive my provision for them?" Jesus knew what the state of the world would be at the time of His return and how difficult it would be for His Kingdom representatives to possess and exercise the faith required to see His provision. At the end of the previous chapter, Jesus is telling His disciples what would be taking place on the earth at the time of His return.

In regard to Jesus being the Father's representative to humanity, we need to understand that Jesus was a perfect human living His life before the Father in perfect fellowship and relationship with Him. There was a perfect spiritual connection between Jesus and the Father from the time Jesus was a small child until just before He died on the cross. The nature of God was active and vibrant within Jesus all during this time, allowing Him to maintain this perfect relationship with the Father. In His ministry, Jesus was commissioned to go out as the Father's Kingdom representative to humanity, to speak the words of the Father and to do the works of the Father, as if the Father was here doing it Himself.

Placing this commission and requirement upon Jesus, the Father recognized that it was necessary for Jesus to possess an ability that was beyond His attributes as a human, even a perfect human, in order to demonstrate the Kingdom activities that the Father wanted to be performed toward humanity. The Father considered this to be necessary if Jesus was to successfully represent the Father and His Kingdom and to carry out His commission to humanity, as the Father desired. As a result, the Father sent the Holy Spirit upon Jesus and Jesus went forth from that day forward in the ability of the Holy Spirit to be the Father's representative to humanity, conducting the Father's business in the Father's provision, as the Father instructed Him. Jesus represented to humanity what the Father wanted to be said and done, and Jesus faithfully demonstrated and delivered the works and words of the Father, through the provision the Father gave Him – the Holy Spirit.

As our Principal, can Jesus justly and righteously do any less for us than what the Father did for Him, as His Principal? As Jesus' representatives, should we expect Jesus to provide any less for us than what the Father provided for Him, as the Father's representative? The Father's commission for Jesus required more ability than what Jesus' human attributes could deliver, and Jesus' commission for us requires more ability than what our own human attributes can deliver. Therefore, Jesus is obligated to provide what we need beyond our human attributes, if it is required to accomplish His commission for us, just as the Father was obligated to provide what Jesus needed beyond His human attributes, in order to accomplish the Father's commission for Him.

Now, we have to ask the questions; "Did Jesus give His first century Kingdom representatives the necessary provision to execute the same commission He has given us to execute? Do we see the first century Jesus-followers demonstrating abilities beyond their human attributes, being empowered by the Holy Spirit which Jesus gave to them, just as Jesus demonstrated abilities beyond His human attributes, being empowered by the Holy Spirit which the Father gave Him?" If so, then we have to ask ourselves the question, "Do we see the Jesus-followers of today demonstrating abilities beyond our human attributes, being empowered by the Holy Spirit which Jesus gave to us to execute our commission, just as Jesus and the first century Jesus-followers experienced?"

If we look at the Church in the western hemisphere, especially the Church in North America, we would have to answer "no". Did Jesus take away our provision, the Holy Spirit, sometime between the end of the first century and now? I believe the great majority of Jesus-followers today would say "no". Do the Jesus-followers of today have the same commission from Jesus that the first century Jesus-followers had? I believe the great majority of Jesus-followers today would say "yes". If we have the same commission from Jesus as the first century Jesus-followers had and they needed and demonstrated abilities beyond their human attributes, as empowered by the Holy Spirit to execute their commission; either we really don't have the same commission, or we really don't need the same provision beyond our human attributes to execute our commission, or we lack understanding of our commission and the faith to appropriate and experience the provision Jesus has given us to accomplish our commission. We really don't have any other options for why we aren't experiencing what Jesus and the first century Jesus-followers experienced in their ministries.

This brings us back to our scripture in Luke 18:8, where Jesus tells His disciples, "*However, when the Son of Man comes, will He find faith on the earth?*" If Jesus asked His disciples this question 2000 years ago, it must have been a legitimate question because Jesus doesn't waste words and He doesn't ask rhetorical questions about something as vitally important as this. There are many believers today who believe that Jesus doesn't do these kinds of miracles today; that we don't need them. Again, that means that we don't have the same commission and need the same provision that Jesus and the first century believers had and needed.

Again, if we ask believers today about our commission and Jesus' provision of the Holy Spirit, the great majority would say we have the same commission and we have the Holy Spirit today. That only leaves us with the third option, which is we lack understanding of our commission and the faith to appropriate and experience the provision Jesus has given us to accomplish our commission. Our commission includes being led by the Spirit of God and to appropriate His ability, where our human abilities and attributes fall short, in order to conduct the Kingdom activities Jesus wants us to demonstrate on His behalf to the people around us. This requires a relationship with the Holy Spirit and the ability to hear what He is saying and see what He is doing, just like Jesus did when He was here. This is part of the provision the Holy Spirit is here to supply to us.

We need to understand that God's provision is more than money, land and buildings. Not that He doesn't want us to have these things or anything we may need to accomplish what He wants us to accomplish for Him but are we praying and listening, consistently, so as to know what He wants us to do? Or, are we doing what everyone has been doing for years; assuming that it is what He wants us to be doing now? Do we question and wonder if what we are doing is really what Jesus wants us to be doing or are we caught up in the river of religious activity that isn't necessarily "tuned in" to Jesus' current will and Kingdom activities? In this scripture in Luke 18, Jesus is teaching His disciples how to ask and receive His provision for them. If we aren't actively and sincerely praying to hear what Jesus wants us to be doing on His behalf and, then, asking in faith to receive the provision to accomplish that activity; we may be caught in that cycle of religious activity and not Jesus' current Kingdom activities, where we can ask for and receive His promised provision. If we don't hear and see what He wants us to do, right now, we won't have the faith to ask and receive His provision. Faith comes by hearing the word of God…the living and active word of God as spoken to us by the Holy Spirit.

This is why Jesus needed the Holy Spirit upon His life if He was to be a successful witness and representative of His Father and the Kingdom of God. He couldn't speak the words of the Father and accomplish the works of the Father without the power of the Holy Spirit upon His life. Yes, the nature of God was working within Jesus in order to help Him maintain that spiritual relationship and fellowship with His Father. Yet, Jesus also needed the power of the Holy Spirit upon His life, working through Him to successfully accomplish all of the Father's activities toward humanity as if the Father were here doing it Himself.

This is why Jesus spent so much time teaching His disciples about the Holy Spirit, especially what the Spirit will do in and through their lives once He left the earth. It was very important to Jesus that His disciples understood what the Spirit was to do ***IN*** them but also what He was to do ***THROUGH*** them. They, and we, are to see the prophetic activities of the Kingdom of God operating in and through our lives. The nature of God *within* us, by the Holy Spirit, is to be witnessed by those around us. Yet, the prophetic activities of the Kingdom of God are to be witnessed and experienced by those around us, as they take place *through* us. We and the world need to see and experience the *inward* and the *outward* activities and manifestations of the Holy Spirit in our lives.

If anyone's internal spiritual life and the nature of God working within that person's life was enough to be a witness and persuade people to embrace the Kingdom of God, it was Jesus' spiritual life. His was a perfect life and people recognized the holiness and purity of His life as they witnessed it. Yet, the Father wanted to outwardly convey and demonstrate to the world the reality and presence of His Kingdom. The Father wanted the world to see and experience outward manifestations and activities of the reality and presence of His Kingdom. This is what the Father would do if He was here. Therefore, for Jesus to know what these activities and words were to be that He was to speak and demonstrate on behalf of the Father, the Father saw that it was necessary to send the Holy Spirit upon Jesus so the power and presence of the Spirit would empower Jesus, beyond the capabilities of His own human attributes, to conduct these outward prophetic activities and manifestations of the Kingdom of God, as if the Father was here doing them Himself.

The outward witness of the nature of God, residing on the inside of Jesus, did not satisfy the desires of the Father, who wanted to outwardly and prophetically demonstrate the reality and presence of His Kingdom to the world. The outward witness of the internal presence of the nature of God in the lives of Jesus' Kingdom representatives is not enough to satisfy the desires of Jesus, who wants to outwardly and prophetically demonstrate the reality and presence of His Kingdom to this world. There was an external, prophetic witness and demonstration of His Kingdom activities that the Father required from Jesus and the Father gave Jesus the Holy Spirit to empower Him, beyond His human abilities, to conduct and accomplish this outward, prophetic witness and demonstration.

Jesus requires an external witness and demonstration of His Kingdom activities, from us, and Jesus gave us the Holy Spirit to empower us, beyond our human abilities and attributes, to conduct and accomplish this external, prophetic witness and demonstration. Yes, Jesus wants the world to witness the internal work of the Holy Spirit in the lives of His representatives but He also wants the world to witness the external, prophetic witness and demonstration of His Kingdom's reality and presence through the lives of His people, empowered by the Holy Spirit whom He sent to us.

As The Father Sent Jesus, So Jesus Has Sent Us

In the Principal/Representative relationship, a strong, close relationship and communication must be in place between the Principal and his Representative. Without it, the current, revealed will of the Principal will not be effectively communicated to the Representative, and the provision required by the Representative to successfully accomplish the current, revealed will of the Principal will not be effectively requested and provided.

As a result, the relationship will collapse and the required activities will not be conducted and accomplished. The Representative may be involved with a lot of activities that he assumes the Principal wants him to conduct but they are fruitless because they are not confirmed, sanctioned and supported by the Principal. Likewise, the Principal may be trying to communicate the activities he wants his Representative to conduct for him but the Representative isn't listening or can't hear what the Principal is saying. As a result, the representative is not able to request and receive the provision he needs in order to successfully conduct the Principal's activities. Either way, the Principal/Representative relationship will not be successful in its purpose. The Principal will have to engage in the activities himself, or use another representative to accomplish what he wants.

Do we see this parallel Principal/Representative relationship and activity taking place and being spoken of by Jesus, concerning His Kingdom representatives? In the Gospels, we see the role that the Holy Spirit played in the life and ministry of Jesus, which the Father sent to Jesus as the Father's Kingdom representative to the earth. We see the power and enablement of the Holy Spirit in the prophetic activities that Jesus was engaged in. In John 9, Jesus said to His disciples, *"**We must work the works of Him who sent Me** as long as it is day; night is coming when no one can work. While I am in the world, **I am the Light of the world.**"*[218] Upon saying this to His disciples, Jesus healed a blind man by the power of the Holy Spirit. Notice, Jesus said that **WE** must work the works of the Father. Why would He say that unless He was planning to provide the same provision for His Kingdom representatives to conduct similar prophetic activities by the Power of the Spirit, as He experienced.

That is why Jesus says in another scripture, that, *"**You are the light of the world**. A city set on a hill cannot be hidden; nor does anyone light a lamp and put it under a basket, but on the lampstand, and it gives light to all who are in the house. "Let your light shine before men in such a way **that they may see your good works,** and glorify your Father who is in heaven."*[219] We tend to refer to this verse when we speak of our internal spiritual condition (the New Birth) being a light to those around us. Yet, it is clear from what Jesus said before healing the blind man that being a light in the world encompasses all aspects of life and ministry, as we are *transformed* and *empowered* by the Holy Spirit as Jesus' Kingdom representatives on this earth.

The Holy Spirit is here to take what Jesus wants to be said and done and disclose it to us as Jesus' Kingdom representatives. We are to speak and do what Jesus wants us to do, just as He did for the Father when He was here. Jesus sent the Holy Spirit to *help* us just as the Holy Spirit *helped* Jesus in His humanity. Jesus says that if we conduct and display the prophetic Kingdom activities of God, as He did when He was here, the Father will be glorified in them as if Jesus was here conducting them Himself. We are an extension of Jesus' representative relationship with the Father. What we do as Jesus' Kingdom representatives glorifies the Father, also. What Jesus did in His ministry to the Jews, we do to the entire world. The ministry we engage in and conduct is the same ministry Jesus was sent to engage in and conduct except we are to take the good news of the Kingdom of God and its prophetic activities and words to the entire world. Jesus and the Father will be glorified by what we accomplish on their behalf.

In John 14, Jesus says to His disciples, "*Truly, truly, I say to you, he who believes in Me, the works that I do, he will do also; and greater works than these he will do;*

---

[218] John 9:4-5 (emphasis mine)
[219] Matthew 5:14-16

because I go to the Father. "Whatever you ask in My name, that will I do, so that the Father may be glorified in the Son. "If you ask Me anything in My name, I will do it. If you love Me, you will keep My commandments."[220] In this scripture, Jesus tells His disciples that they are to do the very same prophetic Kingdom activities that He did, and even greater prophetic activities than He did, because He is going to the Father. This is why Jesus said that it is to our advantage that He goes away, so that the Holy Spirit can come. When the Holy Spirit comes, Jesus' Kingdom representatives will engage in the same type of prophetic Kingdom activities on Jesus' behalf, that Jesus engaged in on the Father's behalf; and even greater works.

The word "*greater*" (Greek: *Megas*), where we get our word "*mega*", means greater in number, demonstration, and impact. Jesus is telling His disciples that they will do "mega" works because He will go to the Father and send the Holy Spirit to empower them. We are to be Jesus' Kingdom witnesses in a more "mega" way than Jesus was the Father's Kingdom witness. We are continuing and extending Jesus' earthly Kingdom ministry for the Father, and He has given us the same provision the Father gave Him, the Holy Spirit, to carry out what He wants us to do and say, on His behalf.

Jesus goes on to say that if His Kingdom representatives will ask Him for whatever provision they need, to accomplish what He wants them to do, He will provide it. He is bound and obligated to do so as their Principal in the Principal/Representative relationship. It is a legally binding relationship because both Jesus and His representatives have chosen of their own free will to enter into this relationship and both parties have agreed to carry out their necessary functions as partners in this Principal/Representative agency relationship, just as Jesus and the Father had done while Jesus was on the earth.

Jesus goes on to say to His disciples, "*"If you love Me,* ***you will keep My commandments."*** This is not a suggestion from Jesus, it is a COMMAND! We are COMMANDED to do the works of Him who sent Jesus into the world as His Kingdom representative, just as Jesus did. Jesus told us that if there is anything we need from Him, to carry out these prophetic Kingdom activities on His behalf, we are to ask Him and He will GLADLY do it for us, that the Father may be glorified in Jesus' ongoing Kingdom representation of the Father, through us. We are not here to do our own thing. We are here to complete what Jesus started as the Father's Kingdom representative to the world. If the world is to believe that the Father sent Jesus as His Kingdom representative to the earth, we, as Jesus' Kingdom representatives, are to continue His representative ministry to the Father by

[220] John 14:12-15

taking the Kingdom of God message and the accompanying prophetic Kingdom activities, to the rest of the world, as if Jesus and the Father were here doing it themselves.

Do we believe that these same prophetic activities of the kingdom of God that Jesus carried out on the Father's behalf are valid for us today? Do we have the faith to pray for the provision we need to accomplish what Jesus and the Father have COMMANDED us to do, on their behalf? Do we recognize that we are not here to do our own thing, the way we want to do it and for our own benefit? Do we know that we are here to complete the ministry that the Father gave Jesus to accomplish as His Kingdom representative, as if the Father and Jesus were here to do it themselves? Do we think that Jesus, if He was here now, would believe that the miracles He performed 2000 years ago, being empowered by the Holy Spirit, are no longer for Him to conduct today and that He would still be able to complete the representative work the Father gave Him to complete, without them?

The Holy Spirit IN And THROUGH Us

There is a difference between the work of the Holy Spirit in the internal life of the follower of Jesus and the work of the Holy Spirit conducted outwardly through the follower of Jesus. One is a transforming work and the other is an empowering work. One is an internal work that is focused on the transformation of the individual follower of Jesus. The other is an outward work that is focused on the world and how the Father and Jesus want to engage and confront the people of the world with the reality and presence of the Kingdom of God. Jesus, Himself, taught on these two distinct functions and activities of the Holy Spirit in and through the life of the believer.

The first work of the Holy Spirit Jesus taught on is in John 4, where Jesus is talking with the Samaritan woman at the well. Jesus tells her, *"...whoever drinks of the water that I will give him shall never thirst; but the water that I will give him will become in him a well of water springing up to eternal life."* [221] Jesus describes the work of the Holy Spirit in the internal life of His disciples, by saying that the Holy Spirit will, *"...become in him a well of water springing up to eternal life."* This is the New Birth which Jesus spoke of to Nicodemus in John 3. This is the transforming work of the Holy Spirit in the internal life of the follower of Jesus Christ, recreating an individual's human spirit and bringing the

[221] John 4:14

individual back into a personal relationship with God, through the saving work of Jesus Christ.

We see this transforming activity of the Holy Spirit being initiated in the world, in the lives of Jesus' disciples, in John 20 where Jesus appeared to His disciples soon after He arose from the dead. *"He showed them both His hands and His side. The disciples then rejoiced when they saw the Lord. So Jesus said to them again, "Peace be with you; as the Father has sent Me, I also send you." And when He had said this, He breathed on them and said to them, "Receive the Holy Spirit.""*[222] Jesus had already died on the cross and had risen from the dead. Earlier, in John 20, Jesus appeared to Mary Magdalen near the tomb where He had been buried. As she went to touch Him, in her joy upon seeing Him, Jesus said to her, *"Stop clinging to Me, for I have not yet ascended to the Father; but go to My brethren and say to them, 'I ascend to My Father and your Father, and My God and your God.'"*

Jesus had risen from the dead but He had not yet ascended into heaven in order to present His blood in the heavenly Holy of Holies, as the atoning sacrifice for the sin and rebellion of humanity. He had not yet sprinkled His blood on the heavenly Mercy Seat once and for all, paying the price for humanity's sin and bringing humanity and God back into intimate relationship once again.[223] Jesus did not want Mary to touch Him, to cling to Him until He had ascended into heaven and had completed this High Priestly duty on behalf of humanity.

Once He ascended into heaven and presented His sacrificial blood to the Father, Jesus returned to the earth in order to appear to many people in order to show Himself alive, as proof that He is the risen savior of the world. Soon after returning from heaven, Jesus appeared to His disciples, as they were gathered together. Upon appearing to them, Jesus showed them His hands and His side where He had been pierced by the nails and the soldier's spear. Jesus allowed Thomas to place his hand into His side and into the wounds in His hands.[224] They were allowed to touch Him now.

Once the disciples saw and believed that it truly was Jesus, He said to them, *"Peace be with you; as the Father has sent Me, I also send you." And when He had said this, He breathed on them and said to them, "**Receive the Holy Spirit.**""* Jesus spent over three years training His disciples so they could go out and continue with the Kingdom representative ministry He had begun on behalf of the Father. He sent the twelve out with the authority the Father had

---

[222] John 20:21-22
[223] Hebrews 10:1-18
[224] John 20:26-29

given Him and with the empowerment of the Holy Spirit that the Father had given Him, so they could experience, first-hand, what they would do once He was gone.[225]

Later, Jesus sent seventy disciples out in order to do the same thing He sent the twelve to do. He was training all of His disciples to carry on the Kingdom representative ministry that He had begun on the Father's behalf, once He was gone. These seventy had the same authority of Jesus and His Holy Spirit empowerment that the twelve had, in order to conduct prophetic Kingdom activities on behalf of Jesus and the Father. Jesus was making no distinction between the twelve and the seventy when it came to carrying out the Kingdom ministry of Jesus, once He was gone.[226] Jesus sent all of them – the twelve and the seventy, in the same way the Father had sent Him and with the same authority and Holy Spirit empowerment that Jesus had received from the Father.

After Jesus told the disciples He was sending them in the same way the Father had sent Him, Jesus said to them, *"Receive the Holy Spirit."* Jesus had done everything necessary to deliver humanity from the domain of darkness into the Kingdom of God. Jesus had received from the Father the non-communicable attributes of God that he laid aside in order to become a human.[227] Jesus told His disciples, once again, that He was sending them in the same way the Father had set Him. Yet, the disciples had not been born again…they had not yet received the New Birth. Therefore, Jesus, breathed on them giving them the Holy Spirit, the Spirit of Christ, so they would be transformed by the work of the Holy Spirit in the inner man. His disciples were now born again and brought into intimate relationship with the Father. Now, they could truly be prophetic Kingdom representatives for Jesus and the Father, completing the work Jesus had begun on the Fathers behalf.

Yet, there is another work of the Holy Spirit that Jesus taught His disciples about. It was a different work from that which was to take place within the inner man of the follower of Jesus. This work of the Holy Spirit was to empower the followers of Jesus to be the Kingdom representatives that Jesus and the Father needed them to be. It is the same work of the Spirit the Father saw necessary that Jesus should experience and possess before He began His Kingdom representative ministry for the Father. We see Jesus proclaim this when He was in Jerusalem; *"Now on the last day, the great day of the feast, Jesus stood and cried out, saying, "If anyone is thirsty, let him come to Me and drink. "He who believes in Me, as the Scripture said, 'From his innermost being*

---

[225] Luke 9:1-6
[226] Luke 10:1-9
[227] John 17:5

will flow rivers of living water.'" But this He spoke of the Spirit, whom those who believed in Him were to receive; ***for the Spirit was not yet given, because Jesus was not yet glorified.*** *"* [228]

What Jesus says in this scripture is very different from what He said to the woman at the well in John 4. Here, Jesus is saying that the Holy Spirit will be like rivers of living water flowing from the disciple of Jesus. This is very different from a well of water springing up within them. This scripture is talking about rivers flowing out. Jesus is emphasizing the demonstration and power flowing out, when it comes to the work of the Holy Spirit in a believer's life. The scriptures say that Jesus was speaking of the Holy Spirit which Jesus' disciples were to receive at a later time. This manifesting and demonstrating work of the Holy Spirit in the believer's life had not begun because Jesus had not yet been glorified. When the disciples were sent out by Jesus to engage in these types of activities on His behalf as part of their training they went in the authority and the power of the Holy Spirit that had been given to Jesus by the Father.[229] Once Jesus left the earth to return to the Father, His disciples would need this same authority and power of the Holy Spirit given to them, as their own commissioning, if they were to continue to be Jesus' representatives on the earth doing the works of Jesus.

After His resurrection, Jesus ascended into heaven, briefly, to present His blood as an atonement for the sin of humanity. Then, He returned to the earth for a period of forty days in order to show Himself alive and to appear to His disciples in order to instruct them and to give them the Holy Spirit – the Spirit of Christ, so their inner man could be born again and transformed. Yet, Jesus had not yet been glorified. He had not yet ascended into heaven in order to remain and take His place at the right hand of the Father as the King of kings and the Lord of lords. He had not yet been given the name which is above every other name in heaven and on the earth. As long as Jesus was on the earth, after His resurrection, He was still the one man who had the authority of the Father and the enablement of the Holy Spirit to be the Father's Kingdom representative on the earth. The disciples had been born again but Jesus was still the one with the authority and power.

After being on the earth with His disciples for forty days after His resurrection, Jesus took them to the place where He was to leave them. When they arrived, Jesus said to them, *"These are My words which I spoke to you while I was still with you, that all things which are written about Me in the Law of Moses and the Prophets and the Psalms must be fulfilled." Then He opened their minds to understand the Scriptures, and He said to them, "Thus it is written, that the Christ*

---

[228] John 7:37-39
[229] Matthew 10:1-13; Luke 10:1-11

would suffer and rise again from the dead the third day, and that repentance for forgiveness of sins would be proclaimed in His name to all the nations, beginning from Jerusalem. "You are witnesses of these things. "And behold, ***I am sending forth the promise of My Father upon you;*** *but you are to* ***stay in the city until you are clothed with power from on high."*** *"He* ***commanded them not to leave Jerusalem,*** *but to* ***wait for what the Father had promised,*** *"Which," He said, "you heard of from Me; for John baptized with water, but you will be baptized with the Holy Spirit not many days from now." So when they had come together, they were asking Him, saying, "Lord, is it at this time You are restoring the kingdom to Israel?" He said to them, "It is not for you to know times or epochs which the Father has fixed by His own authority; but* ***you will receive power when the Holy Spirit has come upon you;*** *and* ***you shall be My witnesses*** *both in Jerusalem, and in all Judea and Samaria, and* ***even to the remotest part of the earth."*** [230]

Upon completing His words to them, Jesus ascended to the Father in heaven where He would remain until He comes again to fully establish the presence of the Kingdom of God on the earth at the end of the age. Again, what Jesus describes here is much different from what He describes when He talked to the Samaritan woman at the well; that the Holy Spirit would be within her a well of water springing up to eternal life. The focus of that work of the Spirit is upon the internal spiritual condition of the followers of Jesus. The Holy Spirit was to give them eternal life through the New Birth; transforming them and establishing a personal intimate relationship and fellowship between them and God.

The work of the Spirit described by Jesus when He met with His disciples prior to His ascension into heaven, was focused on the demonstration and manifestation of the power of the Holy Spirit that would enable Jesus' disciples to be His Kingdom witnesses beyond the borders of Israel; they were to go to the entire world. They were to continue to take the Kingdom representation of Jesus beyond the children of Israel as the Father sent Jesus to do. Jesus was sending His disciples to the entire world and to the succeeding generations of humanity until Jesus returns to establish the fullness of the Kingdom of God on the earth at the end of the age. Jesus' disciples were to go in the demonstration and power of the Holy Spirit on behalf of Jesus, just as Jesus went in the demonstration and power of the Holy Spirit on the Father's behalf. Just as Jesus was sent as a representative and witness of the Kingdom of God on the Father's behalf; we are sent as representatives and witnesses of the Kingdom of God on Jesus' and the Father's behalf.

[230] Acts 1:4-8; Luke 24:44-49

We are the continuation of the Kingdom ministry of Jesus. His earthly witness and ministry was limited to the children of Israel because He was only one man empowered by the Holy Spirit. Our witness and ministry as the Church and Kingdom representatives of Jesus is unlimited. We are to go to the world and to the succeeding generations of humanity being empowered by the Holy Spirit and with the same authority of the Father that Jesus possessed. Jesus planted Himself as a seed so the Kingdom and its witness could take root and expand on the earth through us, His disciples. Jesus needed the Power of the Holy Spirit on His life to accomplish the prophetic works of the Kingdom that the Father gave Him to do. We need the same power of the Holy Spirit to accomplish the prophetic works of the Kingdom that Jesus has given us to do.

This is how the Church will accomplish the mandate Jesus has given us. This is how the Church, the Kingdom representatives of Jesus on the earth, will take the good news of the Kingdom of God into the seven cultural kingdoms of this world as His witnesses. This is the ONLY way we can significantly impact these seven cultural kingdoms with the Kingdom of God. Satan has established significant strongholds over these kingdoms and it will take the power of the Holy Spirit working through the Kingdom representatives of Jesus Christ to make this desired impact. We cannot and will not successfully invade Babylon on behalf of Jesus as His Kingdom representatives apart from the powerful demonstration and witness of the Holy Spirit working through us. Persuasive words of wisdom alone will not be successful. We must have the demonstration of the Holy Spirit and power to accomplish this task.

Chapter Questions & Notes

Talk It Over....

1) The Holy Spirit is not an impersonal, non-living force or influence. He is a person; He is God, Himself. As God, He has a personality, is intelligent, has a sense of humor, is eternal, and possesses and displays the divine nature and characteristics of God. He speaks and listens. He has a will and exercises His will in conjunction and agreement with the Father and the Son. The Holy Spirit is the presence of God on the earth and He carries out the will of God as it relates to humanity and the activities of the Kingdom of God toward humanity. What is the nature, reality and purpose of the Holy Spirit and identify how He communicates and interacts with the earth and the people who inhabit it?

2) Jesus questioned when He returns at the end of the age, will He find faith on the earth? Why did Jesus ask that? If the Holy Spirit is the presence of God on the earth and empowers the people of God to experience and demonstrate the activities of the Kingdom of God, will the Spirit do these things apart from the active faith being exercised by the people of God? Will the Spirit carry out the activities Jesus wants His people to engage in apart from their active faith in and toward the Holy Spirit? If not, does that mean the Holy Spirit will not be working in and through the people of God when Jesus returns? Will Jesus find that His people are not engaging with and experiencing the activities of the Kingdom of God, through the ability of the Holy Spirit, when He returns to the earth? Is that a possibility? Write down your observations:

(3)

God Trains His Kingdom People To Obey & Cooperate With Him

"The LORD said to Gideon, "The people who are with you are too many for Me to give Midian into their hands, for Israel would become boastful, saying, 'My own power has delivered me.'"" Judges 7:2

When God told Joshua to lead the children of Israel into the Promised Land after the death of Moses, He encouraged Joshua not to rely on his own strength or to be timid and afraid of what was ahead of them. They knew there were giants in the land. They knew there were many enemies who had been entrenched there for a long time. He knew they weren't going to give up without a fight. He also knew God had promised this land to Abraham, Isaac, and Jacob, and to their descendants. God had led them through the wilderness for forty years and they were finally on the doorstep of receiving what God had promised them.

As Joshua was receiving the commission and authority from God to lead the people of God after Moses' death, God spoke to Joshua and said, ***"Only be strong and very courageous****; be careful to do according to all the law which Moses My servant commanded you;* ***do not turn from it to the right or to the left****, so that you may have success wherever you go. "This book of the law shall not depart from your mouth, but you shall meditate on it day and night,* ***so that you may be careful to do according to all that is written in it****; for then you will make your way prosperous, and then you will have success.* ***"Have I not commanded you? Be strong and courageous! Do not tremble or be dismayed, for the LORD your God is with you wherever you go."*** [231]

When Joshua and the children of Israel entered the Promised Land and began to capture the cities of those who inhabited the land, they came to one of the most fortified and protected cities in the land; Jericho. As Joshua was preparing to lead the people against Jericho, to take it, he had an encounter that would significantly impact his strategy and plans for taking the city. *"Now it came about when Joshua was by Jericho, that he lifted up his eyes and looked, and behold, a man was standing opposite him with his sword drawn in his hand,*

---

[231] Joshua 1:7-9 (emphasis mine)

and Joshua went to him and said to him, "Are you for us or for our adversaries?" He said, "No; rather I indeed come now as captain of the host of the LORD." And Joshua fell on his face to the earth, and bowed down, and said to him, "What has my lord to say to his servant?" The captain of the LORD'S host said to Joshua, "Remove your sandals from your feet, for the place where you are standing is holy." And Joshua did so." [232]

This person who stood before Joshua was the Lord, as He told Joshua to remove the sandals from his feet because the ground where he was standing is holy ground. Earlier, God told Joshua....no, God COMMANDED Joshua to be strong and courageous because the Lord was with him wherever he went. Now, the Lord stands before Joshua as the captain of the Lord's army. The Lord stood before Joshua in order to emphasize what He had told him earlier, not to fear or be dismayed but to be strong and courageous. The Lord was going to fight the battles for the Children of Israel against the peoples of the land that the Lord wanted removed. All God wanted His people to do was to be strong and courageous and to **cooperate** with Him in what He told them to do in the battles.

Later, as the children of Israel came to the city of Jericho to overthrow it, God told Joshua to have the people march around Jericho for seven days and on the seventh day they were to blow their trumpets as loudly as they could. Joshua also told the people, *"You shall not shout nor let your voice be heard nor let a word proceed out of your mouth, until the day I tell you, 'Shout!' Then you shall shout!" So he had the ark of the LORD taken around the city, circling it once; then they came into the camp and spent the night in the camp."* [233] *"Then on the seventh day they rose early at the dawning of the day and marched around the city in the same manner seven times; only on that day they marched around the city seven times. At the seventh time, when the priests blew the trumpets, Joshua said to the people, "Shout! For the LORD has given you the city." "So the people shouted, and priests blew the trumpets; and when the people heard the sound of the trumpet, the people shouted with a great shout and the wall fell down flat, so that the people went up into the city, every man straight ahead, and they took the city."*[234]

The children of Israel, God's Kingdom people, had to fight the battle. God didn't need them to win the battle but as God's Kingdom representatives on the earth at the time, God engaged them in the battle by having them conduct specific, tactical activities as their role in the battle. God wanted them to be **obedient** to what He commanded them to do and to **cooperate** with Him and His Kingdom activities because the battle was the Lord's, not theirs. Yet, they did not have to fight in their own strength and with natural

[232] Joshua 5:13-15
[233] Joshua 6:10-11
[234] Joshua 6:15,16,20

weapons. God was with them and demonstrated His power through the children of Israel as they were obedient to God's command, to do what He told them to do.

The children of Israel had to **cooperate** with God by being strong and courageous and by marching around the city as God commanded. They had to shout and blow trumpets as God commanded. They were **obedient** to do their part and God was faithful to do His part. The Bible tells us, "*By faith the walls of Jericho fell, after the people had marched around them for seven days.*" [235] God working, with the **obedience** and **cooperation** of His people, destroyed the wall and the city was taken. We cooperate with God through our obedience, faith, and any appropriate actions He instructs us to engage in. God fights the battle as we cooperate with Him through our faith and its corresponding actions.[236]

We are not smart enough, wise enough, or strong enough to do the works of God as we think they should be done and in our own ability. We don't have the eternal perspective or the eternal plan for the ages to come that the Father has. We don't see as He sees and we can't act as He acts in regard to His Kingdom plans and activities. He has given us some broad instructions for living a Kingdom life here on the earth. Yet, there is so much He has told us that He wants us to be engaged in on His behalf and for His Kingdom, strategically and tactically, that we are completely incapable of conducting unless He specifically communicates His present will, desires, and plans to us. This He does and will do prophetically since this is the nature of His activities and the activities of His Kingdom in this age.

The Father desired to do more to outwardly demonstrate the reality and presence of His Kingdom on the earth than what Jesus was able to conduct in His own human attributes and His perfect, internal spiritual condition. Jesus was God and He was human. Jesus laid aside His privileges as God in order to live His life in the capabilities of a human. Jesus was our example of how we are to live our lives before God, personally, as well as to live our lives as His Kingdom witnesses to the world. Jesus lived His inward life in perfect spiritual relationship and fellowship with the Father. Yet, Jesus had to rely on the outward demonstration and power of the Holy Spirit through His life if He was to be the effective witness to the reality and presence of the Kingdom of God to the world that the Father wanted Him to be.

---

[235] Hebrews 11:30
[236] James 2:14-26

God Has A Tailored Training Program For Each Of His Kingdom Representatives

In the Old Testament book of Judges there was a man named Gideon. He was a lowly, timid young man who at first glance would not be considered a leader by anyone. He looked down on himself, considering himself to be worthless and insignificant compared to everyone else. He was full of disappointment, disillusionment, doubt and questions – many, many questions; not unlike the people of God and our younger generation today. As soon as the angel of the Lord spoke to Gideon after appearing to him, Gideon immediately began asking questions and voicing his disappointment and disillusionment with God.

As far as Gideon was concerned, God was a million miles away and not remotely interested in what was happening to him and the rest of God's people. Sounds a lot like God's people today, especially the younger generation who are leaving our churches in droves because what they are being told about the God of the Bible and the Jesus of the New Testament seems irrelevant and God seems so distant and disinterested in them and what is going on in their world.

Let's take a look at the initial encounter between Gideon and the angel of the Lord as documented in scriptures; *"Then the angel of the LORD came and sat under the oak that was in Ophrah, which belonged to Joash the Abiezrite, as his son Gideon was beating out wheat in the wine press* ***in order to save it from the Midianites****. The angel of the LORD appeared to him and said to him,* ***"The LORD is with you, O valiant warrior."*** *Then Gideon said to him, "O my lord,* ***if the LORD is with us, why then has all this happened to us****? And* ***where are all His miracles which our fathers told us about****, saying, 'Did not the LORD bring us up from Egypt?' But now* ***the LORD has abandoned us*** *and given us into the hand of Midian."* ***The LORD*** *looked at him and said,* ***"Go in this your strength*** *and deliver Israel from the hand of Midian.* ***Have I not sent you****?" He said to Him, "O Lord,* ***how shall I deliver Israel? Behold, my family is the least in Manasseh, and I am the youngest in my father's house.*** *" But the LORD said to him,* ***"Surely I will be with you****, and you shall defeat Midian* ***as one man.*** *"* [237]

This is an amazing encounter between Gideon and the angel of the Lord. Many people believe that this "angel of the Lord" was actually the pre-incarnate Christ appearing to Gideon because of what He spoke and the

---

[237] Judges 6:11-16

authority with which he spoke. That is a discussion for another time, as that is not as important to us, now, as what was actually said to Gideon. Whether it was an angel or the pre-incarnate Christ, it is the words that were spoken to Gideon that we want to focus on. But, for the purposes of this scriptural example and what we want to glean from it, I will refer to the "angel" as "the Lord" because that is how the scripture itself refers to him when it says, "***The LORD** looked at him and said…*"

The thing that strikes me most about the initial interaction between the Lord and Gideon is what they were each focused on when they initially spoke to each other. The Lord's initial words to Gideon were, *"The LORD is with you, O valiant warrior."* This speaks **VOLUMES** about how the Lord saw Gideon and how He wanted to relate and interact with Gideon in their relationship. As far as the Lord was concerned, Gideon was a valiant warrior. Yet, when Gideon responded to the Lord and what He said, Gideon said, "*…if the LORD is with us, why then has all this happened to us? And where are all His miracles which our fathers told us about… the LORD has abandoned us…*"

Gideon was completely oblivious to what the Lord said to him except for the phrase, *"The Lord is with you…"* Gideon was so focused on his disappointment and disillusionment with God that he completely missed what the Lord said to him, how He saw Gideon, and how He wanted to relate to Gideon. When the Lord spoke, Gideon must have been thinking, *"Okay…good, this is the Lord; I can finally tell Him what I think of Him and how He has abandoned us to the enemy."*

Most of us, when we are honest with ourselves, think this way about God sometimes. When we look at the world around us and see how evil seems to advance unabated and the Church seems to be so powerless against it and irrelevant in the world; we want to confront God and ask Him these same types of questions. In prayer, when we are alone with Him and we know He is listening, we want to say, *"Okay…good, this is the Lord; I can finally tell Him what I think of Him and how He has abandoned us to the enemy."* Yet, just like Gideon, we don't hear what the Lord is saying to us; it doesn't resonate with us how God sees us and wants to speak and relate to us.

He sees us as and calls us *"O valiant warrior"*, and all we can think about and say is, *"Why, why, why…you have abandoned us."* Yet, just as the Lord didn't get offended by what Gideon said to Him, God doesn't get offended by what we say to Him. In fact, He keeps seeing us and talking with us as valiant warriors, not as we see ourselves; just as the Lord continued to speak with Gideon.

The scripture goes on to say, *"The LORD looked at him and said, "Go in this your strength and deliver Israel from the hand of Midian. Have I not sent you?"* Upon hearing the Lord say this to him, Gideon must have thought to himself, *"Go in* ***what*** *my strength? When did you send* ***me****? I must have missed something."* Gideon **DID** miss something. Gideon was so busy pondering the condition of everything around him and thinking about how he was going to give the Lord a piece of his mind, that he completely missed what the Lord said to him; that would be His strength. Gideon missed hearing how the Lord saw him and how He wanted to relate to Gideon.

He missed the words, "*The LORD is with you,* ***O valiant warrior****."* ***The Lord saw Gideon as a valiant warrior and He would be with Him****.* This is the strength Gideon was to go in! This is when the Lord sent Gideon, when He said, *"The Lord is with you…"* That's all the Lord had to say to Gideon, to send him to do what the Lord wanted him to do – to deliver Israel as a valiant warrior. If the Lord was with him, that's all he needed. That is Gideon's strength. That is our strength.

This is why the Father sent the Holy Spirit upon Jesus, when He was baptized by John. This is why Jesus sent the Holy Spirit upon His Kingdom representatives, the Church, on the day of Pentecost. This is why Jesus told them not to launch out into their ministry, yet, but to wait in Jerusalem until they received the power of the Holy Spirit upon them, once Jesus ascended and was glorified at the right hand of the Father in heaven. Then, the disciples could go as Jesus sent them. Jesus, the Spirit of Christ, was with them and He was their strength, just as the Lord sent Gideon and He was Gideon's strength.

Back in the scripture from Judges, Gideon responded to the Lord by saying, *"O Lord, how shall I deliver Israel? Behold, my family is the least in Manasseh, and I am the youngest in my father's house."* Gideon is still unable to see himself as the Lord sees him. He does not see himself as the valiant warrior the Lord sees. He does not feel *sent* because he sees himself as insignificant and powerless to do anything that could be useful to the Lord. Yet, the Lord responds to Gideon's objections and excuses by saying, *"****Surely*** *I will be with you, and* ***you shall*** *defeat Midian* ***as one man****."* **Surely**…**you shall**…**as one man**. These are the faith-building words that Gideon needed to hear! **Surely** (for certain, undoubtedly), the Lord will be with him. **You shall** (for certain, undoubtedly) defeat your enemy, **as one man** (united, as a complete unit). Hmmm…that sounds familiar, *"I and the Father are one."* [238] *"…that they may be one, even as we are one."*[239] *"We are one body but many members."* [240]

---

[238] John 10:30
[239] John 17:21

Gideon's strength was that he was not alone; the Lord was with him. Jesus' strength was that He was not alone; the Father was with Him through the Holy Spirit. Our strength is that we are not alone; Jesus is with us through the Holy Spirit, the Spirit of Christ. This is the strength of the Principal/Representative relationship as enacted, empowered, and supported by the reality and presence of the Kingdom of God. If God enacts such a representative relationship with anyone, for any reason, it is sure and will not fail in its purpose. That is why the Lord responded to Gideon with the words, "Surely, I will be with you."

This is why Jesus said of the Father, who sent Him, *"He who sent Me is with Me; He has not left Me alone, for I always do the things that are pleasing to Him."* [241] This why Jesus said, concerning His disciples who would follow after Him, *"Go therefore and make disciples of all the nations, baptizing them in the name of the Father and the Son and the Holy Spirit, teaching them to observe all that I commanded you; and lo,* ***I am with you always, even to the end of the age.*** *"* [242] In Principal/Representative relationships involving the Kingdom of God, God is the Principal and He is both *with* and *in* His representatives, whether it is Jesus (the Father's representative) or us (Jesus' representatives). God and His representatives are one and they operate as one…as a complete unit.

Jesus didn't say He would be with His disciples until the end of the first century, when the last original apostle died. Jesus isn't talking, only, about the work of the Holy Spirit that brings the New Birth to the human spirit. He said He will be with them always – to the end of the age, and He will provide them with everything they need to accomplish what He has sent them to do, which includes conducting the prophetic works of the Kingdom of God by the presence and power of the Holy Spirit. Jesus said He will be with us and providing for us until the end of the age when He returns to establish the fullness of the Kingdom of God on the earth.

This is what Gideon needed to hear and know, and this is what we need to hear and know. Gideon needed to hear and know the Lord was with him…this was his strength. Jesus knew the Father was with Him and He was trained by the Father to walk in this truth. We need to know this so Jesus can train us to walk in it.

Those who are progressively maturing in their faith are doing so as they practice their faith (they are doers of the word of God), training their

---

[240] 1Corinthians 12:12-27
[241] John 8:29
[242] Matthew 28:19-20

spiritual senses to discern good and evil (the nature and activities of the Kingdom of God and those of the domain of darkness). [243] We all grew up being trained by the domain of darkness, practicing its activities and living by its nature. When we experience the New Birth by the Spirit of God, we receive a new nature; the nature of God.

As a result, we need to be "reprogrammed" or trained to discern and act upon the influences of the Kingdom of God as opposed to the domain of darkness. We need to be able to discern the difference between the two when we encounter or are confronted by them. You think this would be easy but, often, our enemy and the ruler of the domain of darkness will come as an angel of light in order to deceive.[244] This is why we must be able to discern between the Kingdom of God and the domain of darkness. This is not a natural ability; it is a spiritual ability that must be developed. We must be trained to discern these opposing spiritual realities.

As we look at the encounter between the Lord and Gideon, we see the Lord *send* Gideon and we see the Lord begin to transform Gideon's understanding of himself; from worthless and insignificant in his own eyes to a valiant warrior in the Lord's eyes. The Lord is training Gideon so he can **cooperate** with God in what God wants to accomplish on the earth through him. Since God acts prophetically on the earth through His Kingdom representatives, He must train his representatives to **cooperate** with Him in His prophetic activities and how to discern His activities from those of the domain of darkness. One of the first activities God will engage in with His representatives is to train them to *trust* Him. He did this with Gideon. As time passed though, Gideon began to doubt what the Lord had said to him. As a result, Gideon asked the Lord to confirm what He said by performing a sign as a form of validation.

"Then Gideon said to God, "If You will deliver Israel through me, as You have spoken, behold, I will put a fleece of wool on the threshing floor. If there is dew on the fleece only, and it is dry on all the ground, then I will know that You will deliver Israel through me, as You have spoken." And it was so. When he arose early the next morning and squeezed the fleece, he drained the dew from the fleece, a bowl full of water. Then Gideon said to God, "Do not let Your anger burn against me that I may speak once more; please let me make a test once more with the fleece, let it now be dry only on the fleece, and let there be dew on all the ground." God did so that night; for it was dry only on the fleece, and dew was on all the ground." [245]

[243] Hebrews 5:14
[244] 2Corinthians 11:13-15
[245] Judges 6:36-40

The Lord was in the process now of training Gideon. In this scripture we see God training Gideon for what He would want Him to do on His behalf, at a later time. We have to be careful with expecting God to always confirm what He says and does by giving us a sign to validate it. Sometimes God may do this but it is usually based on a person's spiritual maturity. The less mature and trained an individual is the more likely God will give them a sign to confirm that a word or an action is from Him. Even then, God expects us to learn from our training so as we experience His activities in our lives, more and more, we will not need the sign for ourselves because we know it is from Him.

God wants us to be trained in such a way that over time we experience and interact with Him and the activities of His Kingdom through faith. He wants us to learn to be led by the Spirit of God and so prove to be sons of God.[246] As a result, the majority of signs that we will experience as we progress in our training and maturity in the Lord, will be for the immature and the unbelievers around us, not for us.

This is what Jesus said to those around Him when He was representing the Father to this world. When the audible voice of the Father was heard by those who were standing around Jesus, the scriptures tell us that Jesus said, *"Father, glorify Your name." Then a voice came out of heaven: "I have both glorified it, and will glorify it again." So the crowd of people who stood by and heard it were saying that it had thundered; others were saying, "An angel has spoken to Him." Jesus answered and said, "This voice has not come for My sake, but for your sakes."""*[247] Jesus had placed Himself under the Father's yoke as a young boy, in order to be taught and trained by the Father.

Jesus had His spiritual senses trained to discern the Kingdom of God and the domain of darkness. He had matured so as to be able to know the voice and activities of the Father without needing a sign from the Father to validate it for Him. Jesus had been trained to cooperate with the Holy Spirit and the prophetic activities of the Kingdom of God. He could hear what the Father was saying and could see what the Father was doing. He could discern what the Holy Spirit wanted to do in a given situation. He was a faithful and effective representative of the Father to this world.

God wants to do the same thing with us. We all start out completely immature in the spiritual realities and activities of the Kingdom of God. When God encounters us and influences us with His prophetic words and activities, how we respond and how we allow Him to train us through these

---

[246] Romans 8:14
[247] John 12:28-30

life-long "training sessions" will determine the spiritual growth and maturity we are able to achieve. The prophetic activity of the Kingdom of God taking place in our lives is not an indicator of the level of our spiritual maturity but we will not attain to the spiritual maturity we desire without this training and these prophetic activities taking place in our lives. We are here to do the works of Him who sent us. It is an important aspect of the spiritual maturing process because it requires an active faith to grow in these prophetic activities in our lives, as we believe and trust in Jesus' ability and willingness to provide what we need, when we need it, to conduct these activities on His behalf.

The more we practice what God is training us to do, the more we will grow and mature in the Kingdom of God and the more we will live by faith; not always needing His signs of validation for our own benefit. Not that we will see less and less of His prophetic activity in our lives, the more we experience and learn from His training. We will, actually, experience more and more of His prophetic activity in and through our lives because we will grow in our faith as we increasingly recognize His activity in our lives; being able to see and hear what He wants to do and say through us as His representatives. But, these prophetic activities and the signs that may accompany them will be for the benefit of those around us who need to see and experience the reality and presence of the Kingdom of God.

We will be His witnesses and will engage more and more in the prophetic activities of the Kingdom as Jesus engaged with the Father in the prophetic activities of His Kingdom, when He was here. This is what Jesus and the Father want from us and why they want to train us to walk in these prophetic activities. All we have to do is place ourselves under the yoke of Jesus to learn and be trained by Him, by the Holy Spirit. This is a lifetime endeavor but Jesus said that He will be with us to the end of the age.[248]

Another aspect of God's training of Gideon that we will look at is to observe and learn what type of people God is looking to engage with in order to take territory for the Kingdom of God and to move His Kingdom plans and purposes forward on the earth. To take territory for the Kingdom of God, such as the seven cultural kingdoms of this world, entails encountering and confronting God's enemy, the ruler of the domain of darkness - Satan and his followers. Satan is the god of this world's system and he has strategically placed his followers within the seven cultural kingdoms of this world.

[248] Matthew 28:20

To take territory for the Kingdom of God we must, of necessity, engage with the powers of darkness in order to displace them where they have been entrenched potentially for centuries. God will train us in this spiritual warfare but we must be willing to place ourselves under His yoke so He can direct us through this training. This training and this warfare will require us to be strong and very courageous, as we will encounter and potentially be confronted by the powers of darkness. Jesus was, and His Kingdom representatives should expect to be.

This training lesson is a tough lesson because it flies in the face of much of what we have been taught and want to believe about God. Yes, God is inclusive. Yes, God wants all of His Kingdom people to be involved in what He is doing on the earth. Yes, God doesn't play favorites; preferring one over another. Yet, there are times when God has to move forward with His Kingdom purposes and activities, leaving some of His Kingdom people behind. Why would God do this? What are these people like or what are they not doing that would cause God to have to move forward without them? Do they remain His Kingdom people? Will He ever use them again in what He wants to do on the earth? Let's see what God does with Gideon and how He trains Gideon in this scripture, to see if we can discover the answer to these important and troubling questions.

"Then Jerubbaal (that is, Gideon) and all the people who were with him, rose early and camped beside the spring of Harod; and the camp of Midian was on the north side of them by the hill of Moreh in the valley. The LORD said to Gideon, "The people who are with you are too many for Me to give Midian into their hands, for Israel would become boastful, saying, 'My own power has delivered me.' "Now therefore come, proclaim in the hearing of the people, saying, 'Whoever is afraid and trembling, let him return and depart from Mount Gilead.'" So 22,000 people returned, but 10,000 remained. Then the LORD said to Gideon, "The people are still too many; bring them down to the water and I will test them for you there. Therefore it shall be that he of whom I say to you, 'This one shall go with you,' he shall go with you; but everyone of whom I say to you, 'This one shall not go with you,' he shall not go." So he brought the people down to the water. And the LORD said to Gideon, "You shall separate everyone who laps the water with his tongue as a dog laps, as well as everyone who kneels to drink." Now the number of those who lapped, putting their hand to their mouth, was 300 men; but all the rest of the people kneeled to drink water. The LORD said to Gideon, "I will deliver you with the 300 men who lapped and will give the Midianites into your hands; so let all the other people go, each man to his home." [249]

The Lord is training Gideon in how to recognize those who are able be engaged in the activity required to take territory for the Kingdom of God,

[249] Judges 7:1-7

from those who are not prepared to be engaged in this activity. Something we need to understand about God, that is important to our over-all knowledge of the Kingdom of God and how it functions and operates, is that God really doesn't need anyone to fight His battles for Him. God is very capable of fighting His own battles and can remove Satan and his domain of darkness in a moment, at any time He desires. Satan is no match for God – he never has been and never will be.

The reason God wants to use His Kingdom people and representatives is because He placed humanity on the earth in the beginning to be His regents…His Kingdom representatives to this planet we call earth. This purpose and plan of God has not changed. Therefore, God chooses to conduct His Kingdom activities on the earth through the agency of people, and His plans and strategies to do so will always include people in some form or fashion. God doesn't need us but He wants to include us **if we are willing to obey and cooperate with Him and engage with Him on His terms, according to His plans and strategies, and for His glory and good pleasure**.

As a result, God can (and does) put conditions on the types of Kingdom representatives that He will use to accomplish His Kingdom activities and plans on the earth, in any given situation. God knows what He wants to accomplish and He is looking for Kingdom representatives who He can put through His "Kingdom Training Program" in order to prepare them to **engage with**, **obey**, and **cooperate with** Him in His prophetic purposes and activities on the earth.

The first thing the Lord tells Gideon in this scripture is, "*"The people who are with you are too many for Me to give Midian into their hands, for Israel would become boastful, saying, 'My own power has delivered me."* God knows humanity and the pride that is in our hearts. This pride is what motivated our rebellion against God in the first place. God is not opposed to using every single human being on this planet to accomplish His Kingdom purposes. God is inclusive and wants to engage all of us in what He is doing. Yet, He knows our tendency is to take credit for things we are engaged in even if we don't actually do the work to accomplish it.

God wants to include humanity in His activities on the earth including the activities that defeat and overthrow our enemy, the ruler of darkness. Yet, He doesn't want us to believe that we can actually defeat Satan on our own because we can't. As a result, God makes plans for working with us, His Kingdom representatives, to accomplish His Kingdom tasks without giving us the illusion that we can and are able to accomplish them on our own, without Him.

Therefore, God chooses to conduct His Kingdom activities on the earth, especially His activities involving the domain of darkness, using His prophetic Kingdom activities empowered by His Spirit. He chooses to accomplish this work Himself, with the **cooperation** of His human Kingdom representatives. So, we have this spiritual tension in which God plans and acts on the earth. He wants to engage all of His Kingdom representatives to accomplish His plans and purposes. Yet, He knows what He wants to accomplish is beyond the capabilities of His Kingdom representatives, on their own and in their own human attributes. He also doesn't want us to get the wrong idea when He accomplishes His activities through us; that we accomplished them according to our own means, strength and abilities. Plus, He doesn't want us to get prideful about what was accomplished because it hinders Him from being able to work through us in His future endeavors.

As a result, God incorporates His spiritual Kingdom realities, resources and weapons, prophetically, in order to accomplish His activities on the earth while engaging His Kingdom representatives. Yet, in order for His Kingdom representatives to **cooperate** with Him; to understand and recognize what He is saying to them and wants to do through them at any given time, God must train us in His prophetic Kingdom methods, character qualities, resources, and communications. This is what God is doing to train Gideon, and this is what we must understand and learn for ourselves as we watch what God does in Gideon's life.

God uses the lives of Moses, David, Abraham, Jesus, Paul, and all of His Kingdom representatives in the scriptures to teach and train us in His Kingdom methods and activities. As we read and learn from the scriptures, the Holy Spirit trains us in our individual lives to incorporate and experience these Kingdom methods and activities. God trains us so that we won't mistake His activities for our activities, thinking that we are accomplishing them according to our own means and strength. He trains us so we won't get puffed up with pride; hindering and limiting God from being able to engage us in His activities in the future.

We are told that God is not bound to save by many or by few. Jonathan, the son of King Saul, understood this truth when he spoke to his armor bearer as he was about to engage and attack the Philistine garrison, which greatly outnumbered his armor-bearer and himself. *"Then Jonathan said to the young man who was carrying his armor, "Come and let us cross over to the garrison of these uncircumcised; perhaps the LORD will work for us,* ***for the LORD is not restrained to save by many or by few."*** [250] Jonathan knew God didn't need him and his armor-bearer to defeat the Philistine garrison but chose to work through them to accomplish His purposes – to defeat the enemy of His people. This is the lesson God was about to teach Gideon as part of his Kingdom Training Program.

The next command the Lord gives to Gideon in this scripture is, *"Now therefore come, proclaim in the hearing of the people, saying, 'Whoever is afraid and trembling, let him return and depart from Mount Gilead.'" So 22,000 people returned, but 10,000 remained."* Fear is the enemy of faith. Joshua was gathering an army of people to confront the enemies of the children of Israel, as they were preparing to enter the land the Lord had promised them. For God to work through His people to accomplish His activities against His enemies, He needs people who are not afraid of the battles that will come; who are not afraid to confront and engage the enemy face to face. This takes faith. This takes the training of God in a believer's life because the enemy will do whatever he can to intimidate us.

Paul tells us, as God's Kingdom people and representatives, that our warfare is not natural; it I spiritual. *"...our struggle is not against flesh and blood, but against the rulers, against the powers, against the world forces of this darkness, against the spiritual forces of wickedness in the heavenly places."* [251] This warfare we are engaged in as God's Kingdom people is real and it is significant. Jesus engaged in this warfare when He was God's representative on the earth.[252] Jesus told us that we would be engaged in this spiritual warfare as His Kingdom representatives.[253] The early Church disciples of Jesus engaged in this warfare as Jesus' Kingdom representatives.[254] We saw earlier, in a previous chapter, that Patrick of Ireland encountered and engaged in this spiritual warfare with the evil kings and druids of Ireland, early in his ministry.

Believers today still engage in this spiritual warfare as Jesus' Kingdom representatives. I have encountered and have been openly confronted by demonic spirits over the years. Jesus told us we would be engaged in such warfare. It is in our job description as Kingdom representatives of Jesus, as He stated in Mark 16:14-20. Yet, Jesus will train His Kingdom people in these prophetic, spiritual activities if we recognize that this activity is real, relevant, necessary and important for Jesus to be engaged in through us, in the lives of people around us. People today have the same spiritual needs and strongholds in their lives as people in New Testament times. The

---

[250] 1Samuel 14:6
[251] Ephesians 6:12
[252] Mark 9:14-27; Matthew 17:14-21; Luke 8:26-39;
[253] Mark 16:14-20
[254] Acts 16:16-18; Acts 13:6-12

Kingdom of God and its ability to do warfare and overcome these evil spiritual forces is the only hope the people of this world have in order to escape the power and influence Satan has over them. We don't have to go looking for it. It is all around us, every day.

Yet, when the Lord was training Gideon, in preparation for leading the children of Israel against their evil enemy, the first thing the Lord told Gideon to do was identify those who are afraid and trembling at the thought of such warfare, to let them depart and go home. The Lord could not use them in the battle because their fear would keep them from successfully confronting and engaging in warfare with the enemy through faith. Jesus told His disciples the reason they were not able to cast the evil spirit out of the young boy was due to their lack of faith.[255] Faith cannot be effectively exercised when fear is present.

Jesus will train His people in such a way as to overcome the natural fear we have of such encounters, by placing us in situations where we must deal with our fear. We may not do it right. It may not be pretty. We will see how immature we are while we are in the situation but like any kind of training, we have to start where we are and God's Spirit and grace are enough to help us overcome our fears and to be successful in these activities, the more we encounter them and confront them.

If you notice, the people following Gideon didn't have to go home if they didn't want to. God left it up to the individual to decide if he/she was afraid enough to walk away from the upcoming battle. They could have remained and gone through the same training Gideon was about to go through. Gideon was afraid. We'll see in the next training session he has with the Lord that Gideon was still afraid, even after he completed this session where God removed those who, through fear, would hinder His Kingdom activities that would soon take place. God can't train us if we keep removing ourselves from the training sessions He has prepared for us. If we run from our tests, God will bring us back around to where we will face the test again until we pass it, or until we take ourselves out of His training program. In this test of courage, over 66% of the people decided that they were too afraid to engage in the upcoming battle. They took themselves out of the battle and out of God's training session because of fear.

God told Joshua, *"Only be strong and very courageous."* This is the first order of business when it comes to God's spiritual training sessions. Regardless of what it looks like and how fearful we may be, He will help us to trust Him

[255] Matthew 17:19-20

and who He is in and through us, as we set ourselves to be strong and courageous. This is how we proceed through His training; step by step, moving forward toward spiritual maturity. Our weapons are not natural weapons. They are spiritual weapons which God has given His Kingdom representatives. All we have to do is be strong and courageous and employ the weapons He trains us to use. *"For though we walk in the flesh, we do not war according to the flesh, for the weapons of our warfare are not of the flesh, but divinely powerful for the destruction of fortresses."*[256]

According to a Barna Research survey, the majority of American Christians do not believe Satan is a real being or that the Holy Spirit is a living entity. 59% of American Christians don't believe Satan is a real, living entity. Yet, 64% of American Christians believe that a person can be under the influence of evil spirits such as demons and evil spirits. Likewise, 58% of American Christians don't believe the Holy Spirit is a real, living entity. They believe He is "a symbol of God's power or presence but is not a living entity." 49% of those who agreed that the Holy Spirit is only a symbol but not a living entity agreed that the Bible is totally accurate in all of the principles it teaches.

The Bible states that the Holy Spirit is God's power and presence, not just symbolic. About these survey results, George Barna states, *"'Most Americans, even those who say they are Christian, have doubts about the intrusion of the supernatural into the natural world,' commented George Barna, founder of The Barna Group and author of books analyzing research concerning America's faith. 'Hollywood has made evil accessible and tame, making Satan and demons less worrisome than the Bible suggests they really are,' he said. 'It's hard for achievement-driven, self-reliant, independent people to believe that their lives can be impacted by unseen forces.'"* [257]

How do you instruct and train an army if they don't believe the enemy is real and that there is no real threat to their freedom and safety? Why would a people be concerned about combat training in order to encounter and confront an enemy that (in their minds) doesn't exist or doesn't pose a threat to them or their way of life? George Barna states, *"Most Americans, even those who say they are Christian, have doubts about the intrusion of the supernatural into the natural world."* If what Barna says is true, then the majority of American Christians don't believe in the prophetic activity of the Kingdom of God or the presence of the Holy Spirit in the world, whom Jesus said He sent to us after His resurrection. How can the Holy Spirit do or say anything, as Jesus claimed that He would, if He is not a real person with an

[256] 2Corinthians 10:3-4
[257] The Christian Post, April 13, 2009, by Jennifer Riley

intellect, a personality, and possesses the non-communicable attributes of God such as being all-knowing, all-powerful and ever-present?

If the Holy Spirit is just a force with no personality or attributes that distinguish Him as God, then Jesus is a liar and not who He says He is. If Satan isn't real and is not a tangible, serious threat to the world and to the people of God, then Jesus is a liar and not who He says He is. If the majority of American Christians don't believe the spiritual world is real, that the Holy Spirit is real, that Satan is real and that the activities of these beings intrude into this natural world in which we live and exist (their prophetic activity), then nothing that I have said, here, or that the Bible says has any relevance to our lives. Jesus is a liar and we, as Jesus followers, are of all people most to be pitied.[258]

Satan has done an effective job of making himself non-existent in the minds of a majority of Christians so he can continue wreaking havoc in our lives with little or no resistance from us. Satan has done an effective job of convincing Christians that the Holy Spirit is only a symbol or impersonal force that isn't relevant to us, so we won't recognize that the Holy Spirit is our liberator and emancipator from the mental, emotional and physical slavery we experience at the hands of Satan. Satan, through his cunning and deceptive tactics, has made, both, our slave master (himself) and our emancipator (the Holy Spirit) meaningless and irrelevant in our lives. Both deceptions have had a tremendous, negative effect on the Church and the lives of individual believers today. We can't afford to be deceived any longer. God is looking for Kingdom representatives to encounter and confront the enemy on His behalf. The question is, have we all decided to go home out of fear?

God told Gideon to let those of the children of Israel who were afraid and didn't want to fight in the upcoming battle, go home. They were looking at their ability to fight the upcoming battle in their own strength and were fearful because they didn't recognize the presence and ability of God, who was with them and who was going to fight the battle for them. They didn't have the faith to believe what He said and trust the provision He said He would give them. Their fear combined with their decision to go home, left no room for the faith they needed to hear from God and successfully carry out God's instructions for how to engage their enemy in the upcoming battle. There was not enough reality of the presence of God in their lives to counteract the fear they had. They thought they would have to fight the battle on their own, in their own strength.

---

[258] 1Corinthians 15:13-19

Is this why Jesus, after teaching His disciples on prayer and telling them not to lose heart, asked the question, *"When the Son of man comes, will He find faith on the earth?"*? [259] As I mentioned earlier, Jesus was teaching them about how to not lose heart in prayer, as we ask God for the provision we need to carry out His will and activities as His Kingdom representatives. The question is, "Why would Jesus ask a question about the faith of those living at the time of His return, after teaching His present disciples about prayer and not losing heart?" Well, if we look back at the end of the previous chapter, Luke 17, we get our answer. Here, Jesus is teaching His disciples about what was to take place in the last days, and the events and activities that would be experienced by the people on the earth at that time.

After telling them about the difficult activities taking place on the earth at His coming, as a result of Satan's rage against Jesus and His people, Jesus teaches them in Luke 18 how to pray for God's provision in difficult times and to not lose heart. Just as Gideon had to identify those who were fearful and wanted to go home instead of being trained to overcome their fear, Jesus instructed His disciples that fearful times would come at the end of the age. Yet, Jesus was training them, and us, in how to overcome the fear that can grip us by allowing Him to train us in how to have and exercise the faith necessary to believe and trust Him for the provision we will need to accomplish what He wants us to do, before He returns.

We can't wait until the last minute to submit to His training. It takes time and we must start now if we are to experience the benefits of His training when the onslaught of Satan comes, regardless of when it comes. This is why Jesus asked the question, as to whether He would find faith on the earth. Would His people place themselves under His yoke to learn from Him, or would they be afraid and go home, and not be prepared for what is coming. Again, these are decisions we as His Kingdom people must make – to place ourselves under His tutelage and training, to learn from Him, or be immature so as to listen to deceitful spirits and doctrines of demons; believing that the Holy Spirit is only a spiritual symbol and that Satan doesn't really exist.[260]

Now, moving on with God's training of Gideon, God says there are still some among the children of Israel who will not be able to cooperate with Him and what He wants to do in the upcoming battle. Therefore, He tells Gideon, "*"The people are still too many; bring them down to the water and I will test them for you there. Therefore it shall be that he of whom I say to you, 'This one shall go with you,' he shall go with you; but everyone of whom I say to you, 'This one shall not go*

---

[259] Luke 18:8

[260] 1Timothy 4:1-2

with you,' he shall not go." So he brought the people down to the water. And the LORD said to Gideon, "You shall separate everyone who laps the water with his tongue as a dog laps, as well as everyone who kneels to drink." Now the number of those who lapped, putting their hand to their mouth, was 300 men; but all the rest of the people kneeled to drink water. The LORD said to Gideon, "I will deliver you with the 300 men who lapped and will give the Midianites into your hands; so let all the other people go, each man to his home."

This remaining group of God's people consists of those who chose to stay when they could have gone home. Fear of the enemy and the upcoming battle was not enough to make them go home. Yet, when the Lord speaks to Gideon, He tells him, *"…bring them down to the water and I will test them for you there. Therefore it shall be that he of whom I say to you, 'This one shall go with you,' he shall go with you; but everyone of whom I say to you, 'This one shall not go with you,' he shall not go."* Here, we see more of what is involved in God's training program for His Kingdom representatives. First, the Lord says He will test the people for Gideon. He will place His people in a situation where their present spiritual condition and preparedness will be tested and exposed for what it is. Based upon this test, the Lord tells Gideon to keep those who pass the test but send home those who fail the test.

The people have no choice in the matter, after this test is completed. If they fail this test, it doesn't matter whether they are afraid or not, the Lord doesn't want them going into battle with Him against the enemy. As I mentioned earlier, God trains His Kingdom representatives so they will **obey** and **cooperate** with Him in His kingdom activities on the earth. If they do not enter into or complete the training and tests He has for them, individually, God may choose to keep them from engaging with Him in the upcoming Kingdom activities He conducts. They may be able to go only so far with Him in His activities, before He tells them to "go home".

In this test, God wanted to test each individual's preparedness for battle. He tells Gideon to, *"separate everyone who laps the water with his tongue as a dog laps, as well as everyone who kneels to drink."* One of the biggest risks to any military commander or leader is whether their troops are prepared adequately for the upcoming battles they will undoubtedly face. It was a major question and concern for military leaders in the American Revolutionary War, regarding the civilian militias which constituted much of the organized fighting force. It was a major concern and question for military leaders in the American Civil War because the men who comprised their ranks were fresh off the farm or were previously business and shop owners. Adequate preparedness is a major risk factor for any military leader, regarding those who would do the fighting in an upcoming battle or war. God is no different.

God and humanity have an enemy, Satan, who is out to do as much damage as possible to the Kingdom of God, God's Kingdom representatives, humanity as a whole, and to the earth before he is removed and cast into everlasting torment and punishment. Humanity is completely unable to engage and defeat Satan and the domain of darkness. Humanity is completely under the power of Satan so how can we defeat him? It is a spiritual war and humanity is under the spiritual authority of Satan and is unable to fight and win a spiritual war against him. The Father, through Jesus' death and resurrection, defeated Satan and his power so humanity can be free from his yoke.

Yet, even those who have been born again by the Holy Spirit, through faith in the death and resurrection of Jesus, are unable to defeat Satan in battle in their own strength, resources and human attributes. We still must rely on the ability, resources and power of the Kingdom of God through faith in the Holy Spirit working in and through us, if we are to realize and experience any spiritual victory and take any spiritual territory for God. We must **obey** and **cooperate** with the Holy Spirit and what He wants to do, to experience any sort of spiritual victory. This **obedience** and **cooperation** is learned and implemented through the training and instruction that comes only through the Holy Spirit. The Holy Spirit must prepare us…He must prepare each of us. Preparedness is the key.

Jesus prepared His disciples before He left them, to ascend to the Father. He trained them in the internal character qualities of the Kingdom that they were to demonstrate, and He trained them in how to **obey** and **cooperate** with the Holy Spirit so they could outwardly demonstrate the prophetic activities of the Kingdom of God, on His behalf.[261] They were to demonstrate **the internal character qualities** of the Kingdom of God as well as **the outward prophetic activities** of the Kingdom of God. Both were needed and expected in order to communicate the character of the King and the reality and presence of His Kingdom on the earth.

This is what the Lord was teaching Gideon on this day. God was instructing Gideon in how important it is for His people to be prepared and equipped to **obey** and **cooperate** with Him in the battles they would undoubtedly face as God's Kingdom representatives. God would fight these battles with the resources and ability of the Kingdom of God but He would work through His Kingdom representatives to fight the battle as if He were here to do it Himself. God needs a people who are instructed,

[261] Acts 4:18-20

trained and prepared to **obey** and **cooperate** with Him in how He wants to carry out these battles and to follow His instructions for doing so.

To expose the preparedness of each person continuing to follow Gideon that day, God tested each individual's ability to obey and cooperate, and He did so by testing their personal (spiritual) attentiveness and discipline. Each person had already chosen to stay by not allowing fear to disqualify them. Yet, there was another test they needed to pass – the test of preparedness. In order for each remaining person to demonstrate to Gideon their preparedness for battle, God had all of them go to the water to drink. Those who remained standing at the river and brought the water to their mouth with their hand to drink were separated from those who knelt down at the river to drink. Why was that a test of preparedness for battle?

Those who remained standing and brought the water to their mouths with their hand to drink, remained disciplined and attentive. Their weapons remained in their free hand and they could remain watchful as they drank the water. They were prepared to engage the enemy at any moment, even when they were getting a drink. If the enemy made a surprise attack while they were getting a drink of water, they were still prepared to fight, being watchful and having their weapons in their hand.

Those who knelt down to drink the water were not prepared; they were not disciplined and attentive. In order to kneel down to drink the water, they most likely put their weapons on the ground next to them and used both hands to get the water and bring it to their mouths. Or, even worse, they may have knelt down, put their hands on the ground, and put their faces into the water to get a drink. Either way, their weapons were on the ground, they were on their knees instead of on their feet, their hands were on the ground as they drank, they were facing the water and had their backs to the direction from where their enemy would have attacked them, and they were not attentive should a surprise attack occur while they were drinking. They were not prepared; they were not attentive and they lacked discipline. They let their guard down. They weren't watchful. They put down their weapons. They had their backs to the enemy.

This test exposed the lack of preparation in those who knelt down to drink. They wanted to fight. They did not let fear disqualify them. Yet, they weren't prepared for the fight in the way God needed them to be prepared. They lacked the preparation needed for the fight. They lacked the discipline and attentiveness to **obey** and **cooperate** with God and what He wanted them to do. God wanted to win the battle, yes, but He didn't want them to go to the battle if they weren't prepared. It would be dangerous for them and it would hinder God in what He wanted to do. They probably thought they were prepared and ready because they didn't let fear disqualify them.

Yet, God wasn't confident in their ability to **obey** and **cooperate** with Him in what He would ask of them, in the heat of the battle. In this case, God did not leave it up to the individuals who knelt to drink, to decide if they wanted to go home or not. After this test, God told Gideon to tell them to go home. There was no choice. They could not go to the battle. It was God's decision. They remained God's people but they were disqualified from this battle because they weren't prepared as God wanted them to be. Other opportunities would come their way if they would make the decision to enter God's training camp so He can prepare them for these spiritual battles against the enemy.

This is how important preparation is for God's Kingdom representatives on the earth. Jesus was a perfect man. He had no sin. He had no fear. He had an unbroken and vibrant relationship with the Father. He was the most qualified person to ever walk the earth, to engage with the Father in warfare with God's enemy Satan. Yet, God chose to train, instruct and prepare Jesus for thirty years before He released Him as His Kingdom representative to the people and to engage Satan in the spiritual battles to come.

In addition, the Father even saw fit to send the Holy Spirit upon Jesus in order to equip and empower Jesus with what He would need to be the Father's representative, as well as to cooperate with the Father in His battles with Satan and the domain of darkness. Being empowered by the Holy Spirit, Jesus needed to be instructed, trained and prepared to **obey** and **cooperate** with the Father and to allow the Holy Spirit to engage people and the domain of darkness, as if the Father was here doing it Himself. Jesus had to be prepared to **obey** and **cooperate** and the Father took the first thirty years of Jesus' life to prepare Him.

If the Father took thirty years to prepare Jesus for what He was to do, we must realize that there is training and preparation required for our lives. We never end our preparation. We are being prepared our entire lives to **obey** and **cooperate** with God because what God is preparing us for goes beyond this life, in this present age. God is preparing us for what is coming and what He wants us to do in the ages to come – in eternity. What we do in this life is just a moment, when we consider what we will be doing in eternity.

Yet, how we live our lives and how we let God instruct, train and prepare us in this life will determine what we do and the position we hold in the ages to come. We should not take this life and our preparation in this life lightly.

We may not be afraid of the enemy and the battle but are we allowing the Holy Spirit to instruct, train and prepare us to **obey** and **cooperate** with God in this life, and in the ages to come? What we do now has eternal ramifications.

Those who knelt down to drink, God considered unprepared to obey and cooperate with Him in the upcoming battle. So, He told Gideon to send them home. Of the 10,000 people who went down to the water to drink, only 300 were considered prepared and ready to cooperate with God in the upcoming battle. Yes, God said that 32,000 people were too many to fight the battle. God even said that 10,000 people were too many to fight the battle.

If all 32,000 people were tested and considered to be prepared to fight the battle, God would have fought the battle with all 32,000 because the people would have been trained and prepared in such a way that they would be able to **obey** and **cooperate** with God in the battle, and they would know that they didn't win the battle in their own strength. They would know that God won the battle in His ability and that they simply **obeyed** and **cooperated** with Him in what He wanted them to do. There were too many people to fight the upcoming battle because most of the people weren't prepared to recognize that it is God who fights and wins the battles.

As a result, God told Gideon to tell all but 300 people to go home. Out of 32,000 people, only 300 would go to the battle with God. That is less than 1% of all the people who started with Gideon. God would fight the upcoming battle with less than 1% of the people. We are told that God is not bound to deliver by many or by few.[262] He doesn't need us at all. God is not bound to engage in these activities with people who are not instructed, trained and prepared to **obey** and **cooperate with** Him. We choose whether we will be engaged with what God is doing by the decisions we make, including the decision to be instructed, trained and prepared by God. Military leaders train and prepare their troops to **obey** and **cooperate with** the plans, strategies and commands that they as leaders give them to carry out. The troops carry out the orders and fight the battles as if the military leaders were there to do it themselves.

This is why preparation is so important. It has nothing to do with God not loving His people. It has nothing to do with God not wanting His people to be engaged in the battles with Him. It has everything to do with the people being trained and prepared for the battle because they are representing God and they must **obey** and **cooperate with** Him in fighting the battles as if

[262] 1Samuel 14:6

God was here doing it Himself. God loves the people He sent home that day but they weren't ready to **obey**, **cooperate with** and **represent Him** in the upcoming fight. This is how important training and preparation is. This is how important OUR training and preparation is. This is one of the reasons why the Holy Spirit is here. This is one of the reasons why Jesus said, *"It is to your advantage that I go away."* If He doesn't ascend to the Father, the *Trainer* and *Preparer* doesn't come.

Now that this important test is completed, the scriptures tell us, "*The LORD said to Gideon, "I will deliver you with the 300 men who lapped and will give the Midianites into your hands; so let all the other people go, each man to his home."* The Lord said He WILL defeat the enemy with the 300 remaining people. It was a done deal. Now, all Gideon and his army had to do was go fight the enemy, right? Well, not quite. God wasn't finished with Gideon, yet. The Lord had something else He wanted to do in regard to Gideon's preparation, as the person who would lead this army. In His continued preparation of Gideon, God gives Gideon a greater experience of His prophetic Kingdom activities and the reality of these activities, within the plans and purposes of God for Gideon.

In this case God uses a prophetic event, a dream, in order to communicate with Gideon about the specifics of the upcoming battle but not a dream given to Gideon. God uses a dream given to an unbeliever, his enemy, in order to confirm what He had called Gideon to do and what He had told Gideon the eventual outcome of the battle would be. God uses His prophetic Kingdom activities to prepare us to fulfill our calling and to accomplish what He wants us to do. Let's see what this scripture says.

"Now the same night it came about that the LORD said to him, "Arise, go down against the camp, for I have given it into your hands. But if you are afraid to go down, go with Purah your servant down to the camp, and you will hear what they say; and afterward your hands will be strengthened that you may go down against the camp." So he went with Purah his servant down to the outposts of the army that was in the camp. Now the Midianites and the Amalekites and all the sons of the east were lying in the valley as numerous as locusts; and their camels were without number, as numerous as the sand on the seashore. When Gideon came, behold, a man was relating a dream to his friend. And he said, "Behold, I had a dream; a loaf of barley bread was tumbling into the camp of Midian, and it came to the tent and struck it so that it fell, and turned it upside down so that the tent lay flat." His friend replied, "This is nothing less than the sword of Gideon the son of Joash, a man of Israel; God has given Midian and all the camp into his hand." When Gideon heard the account of the dream and its interpretation, he bowed in worship. He returned to the camp of Israel and said, "Arise, for the LORD has given the camp of Midian into your hands." [263]

God is patient and loving in His training of us. He is waiting for us to recognize that we need His training, to engage with Him through the Holy Spirit, and submit ourselves to His yoke; His training and preparation. God moves us from one level of training to the next, as we respond to and obey what He tells us to do. He wants us to make progress. He wants us to cooperate with Him in His Kingdom activities. He wants us to be doers of His word. We will make mistakes. We may even take a step backwards at times but as long as we keep learning, doing, and seeking, God will continue to train and instruct us in His prophetic Kingdom activities.

In this scripture, God has placed Gideon near the camp of the enemy. God told Gideon earlier in the scriptures to tell the people to go home if they were fearful. Yet, we see here that Gideon, the leader of the people and the man God called to lead the battle against the enemy, was, himself, afraid. Gideon could have told God, earlier, that he was afraid and he could have gone home like the 20,000 others who went home. Instead, Gideon remained under God's training and preparation for him. Did God know Gideon was afraid? Yes.

In fact, in this scripture, God told Gideon that if he was afraid to go down to the camp, he was to take his servant with him. God knew Gideon was afraid but God honored Gideon's decision to stay in the training regardless of his fear. God's training and preparation of us will help us overcome our fear. In fact, God gave instructions to Gideon that would help Gideon overcome his fear. What was that instruction? God told Gideon to go down to the enemy camp! What? God told Gideon to take his servant, if he must, but go down to the enemy camp. This training exercise was God's way of dispelling Gideon's fear and sending him to the enemy camp was how God chose to do it.

God used a prophetic activity of His Kingdom to dispel the fear (the dream). God allowed Gideon to know that the enemy already considered himself defeated before the battle was ever fought. God used a dream, a prophetic activity of His Kingdom, to communicate to the enemy the eventual outcome of the upcoming battle. God told the enemy that they would be defeated by the hand of Gideon, before the battle ever got underway. In order to build Gideon's faith in God's ability to defeat the enemy, God allowed Gideon to hear this dream and its interpretation for himself.

---

[263] Judges 7:9-15

God used a prophetic event, a dream, to build faith in the heart of Gideon for what He was about to do, so Gideon, as the leader of the people, could **obey** and **cooperate with** God and what He wanted him and the people to do, on His behalf. Fear was keeping Gideon from being able to fully **obey** and **cooperate with** God, in faith. Yet, Gideon kept Himself in God's training program; he didn't run. Because of Gideon's growing and maturing faith in God and his faithfulness to God, God took Gideon to the next level in his training by taking the necessary steps to dispel Gideon's fear, using a prophetic Kingdom event and the testimony of the enemy, himself, to do it.

Experiencing the love and complete acceptance of God; experiencing the necessary training and preparation activities of God in our lives; allowing God to conduct and complete His training in our lives regardless of the situations we may find ourselves in during this training; trusting God in and during this training; allowing God to prepare us using His Kingdom resources, methods, and prophetic activities; and allowing God to train us in the best possible way, knowing that God knows the best way to train and prepare each one of us, is the only way we can and will be prepared to **obey** and **cooperate with** God in what He wants to do in and through us We can't train and prepare ourselves. We don't know ourselves well enough.

We can't be honest and objective enough with ourselves. We can't see the holes in our armor and the flaws in our character well enough to train and prepare ourselves. This is why Jesus sent the Holy Spirit; our instructor, trainer and preparer, to do this job in our lives and to instruct us in the prophetic activities of the Kingdom of God. This is why it is to our advantage that Jesus went way, so He could send the Holy Spirit to us. Gideon saw the outcome of God's training and preparation in his life…he was a new man. Gideon was faithfully leading the people through the faith God instilled within him through His training and preparation, and the people were faithful and prepared to **obey and cooperate with** God and Gideon during the battle.

The scripture goes on to tell us, *"So Gideon and the hundred men who were with him came to the outskirts of the camp at the beginning of the middle watch, when they had just posted the watch; and they blew the trumpets and smashed the pitchers that were in their hands. When the three companies blew the trumpets and broke the pitchers, they held the torches in their left hands and the trumpets in their right hands for blowing, and cried, "A sword for the LORD and for Gideon!" Each stood in his place around the camp; and all the army ran, crying out as they fled. When they blew 300 trumpets, the LORD set the sword of one against another even throughout the whole army; and the army fled as far as Beth-shittah toward Zererah, as far as the edge of Abel-meholah, by Tabbath. The men of Israel were summoned from Naphtali and Asher and all Manasseh, and they pursued Midian."* [264]

Three companies of 100 men each blew trumpets and smashed pitchers on the outskirts of the enemy camp. Again, God didn't need for them to do this in order to win the battle. He could have won the battle by Himself. Blowing trumpets and breaking pitchers isn't going to defeat any enemy unless God is fighting the battle with you. Marching around Jericho seven times and then shouting and blowing trumpets isn't going to defeat an enemy unless God is the one fighting the battle with you. God wanted the people involved but He wanted them involved ON HIS TERMS and IN COOPERATION WITH HIM! Remember, this is God's deal and He wants us **obeying** and **cooperating with** Him so He can conduct His Kingdom activities through us as if He was here doing it Himself.

He doesn't want His Kingdom representatives taking credit for something they can't and don't do. He doesn't want us to take credit (to think more highly of ourselves than we should) for activities and outcomes we can't conduct or control apart from Him. He wants us to be faithful to **obey** and **cooperate with** Him in what He does, so He receives the glory and we enjoy the opportunity of co-laboring with Him in His Kingdom activities on the earth. This is what it's all about. He doesn't expect us to do any of these activities ourselves because we can't do any these activities ourselves. We can't fight spiritual battles and take spiritual ground for God in our own human attributes and with our own human resources. God must do it with the resources and abilities of the Kingdom of God that He makes available to us.

We tend to look for ways to help God that we can do ourselves; that we are able to plan and accomplish with our own human attributes, resources, and ingenuity. God wants us to engage with Him where we can't accomplish what He wants us to do without Him and His provision. We don't see miracles and supernatural provision because we don't engage in the type of activities that require it. If we listen to and follow what God wants for us, we will experience these types of activities because these are the types of Kingdom activities He wants to conduct through us. God isn't looking for our human ingenuity and intellectual prowess. He's looking for our **faith**, **obedience** and **cooperation with** what He wants to do.

Jesus wants us to engage in humanitarian acts of kindness and brotherly love toward others **AND** allow Him to conduct His supernatural Kingdom activities through us, as if He was here doing it Himself. We can only do this by letting Him train and prepare us so we can **obey** and **cooperate**

---

[264] Judges 7:19-23

with Him when He wants to engage us in these prophetic Kingdom activities.

Again, all of us will not be doing all of the miracles, signs and wonders that Jesus did, all of the time. We will be individually and uniquely trained, equipped and prepared by the Holy Spirit to conduct the prophetic Kingdom activities that are aligned with the ministry and calling Jesus has designated for each of us, within His Body. Yet, as the Body of Christ as a whole, we will be engaged in and conduct even greater (mega) prophetic Kingdom activities than Jesus did, by the power and presence of the Holy Spirit who is with us. We will believe and act "as one man", just as the Lord told Gideon they would do; just as Jesus and the Father did, and just as Jesus told us we would do, with Him and the Father.

Yes, we should care for the poor and minister to one another, bearing one another's burdens by loving each other and showing the love of Christ toward each other. We do this through the transforming work of the Holy Spirit in our inner man. But, we are unable to engage in the spiritual battles and engage in the outward prophetic activities of the Kingdom of God without the instruction, training and preparation of the Holy Spirit, and apart from His ability working in and through us. He will train and prepare us and we must learn how to **obey** and **cooperate with** Him in these supernatural activities. Jesus learned to cooperate with the Father and the Holy Spirit in order to conduct His supernatural Kingdom activities.

The early Church believers learned to cooperate with the Spirit of Christ so they could engage in these supernatural activities with Him. It takes preparation to engage in these activities and only God can train and prepare us to cooperate with Him. God is not bound to deliver by many or by few. We each make the decision to engage in God's training and preparation activities for our lives. He won't do it apart from our willing participation. We may fail tests and have considerable fears to overcome but if we stay with Him and His training plan for our lives, He will prepare us to **obey** and **cooperate with** Him when the time comes.

From the very beginning, our enemy has been a spiritual enemy; our war has been a spiritual war; our battles have been spiritual battles, and they have always had to be fought with spiritual resources, spiritual weapons, and with spiritual strength and ability. Jesus won the war through the prophetic activities, resources and power supplied to Him by the Father. Jesus came to expose, overcome, and destroy the works of the devil.[265] As we see throughout the New Testament writings, Jesus exposed and overcame the

[265] 1John 3:8

works of the devil through spiritual means by the power of the Holy Spirit. Jesus defeated Satan and sin through spiritual means when He rose from the dead, defeating death itself. We cannot engage with God in His spiritual, supernatural battles and activities, today, using natural, intellectual and psychological resources and means, any more than Jesus could when He was here and the early Church believers could when they were here.

Our battles have always been the same, from the moment Adam and Eve sinned, to when Jesus was on the earth, and until now. They have been and always will be spiritual battles. Jesus trained and prepared His disciples to fight these spiritual battles as He did, with the same spiritual, prophetic resources and weapons He had, and being empowered by the same Holy Spirit that worked in and through His life. Jesus showed us how to do it. Jesus gave us the same prophetic resources and weapons that He had, to conduct the same prophetic activities that He conducted, in order to demonstrate the same reality and presence of the Kingdom of God to this world, as if the Father was here doing it Himself.

This is what Jesus has been doing since He ascended to the Father; equipping and training His Kingdom representatives to engage in the same prophetic, spiritual battles with the same prophetic, spiritual weapons, by the same prophetic, spiritual source of power as He used and experienced when He was here. He gave us the ascension ministry gifts (apostle, prophet, evangelist, pastor, teacher), in cooperation with the Holy Spirit, to conduct the necessary spiritual training and preparation that He provided to His disciples when He was here. This training and preparation is not relevant to this life, only. It is relevant for what God has in store for us, in the ages to come. We must not be short-sighted in our training, preparation and decision-making.

Jesus told us that the gates of hell will not prevail against His Kingdom representatives on the earth.[266] He said that the representatives of the Kingdom of God will confront the domain of darkness and that its gates will not prevail against them. We must take the Kingdom of God to the seven cultural kingdoms of this world, in the face of the domain of darkness that controls them.

The question is, are these ascension ministry gifts conducting this same spiritual training and preparation, today, using the same prophetic, spiritual resources and weapons that Jesus gave to His Church, in the beginning? If not; if we are trying to continue the same prophetic Kingdom training and equipping that Jesus engaged in, while employing only natural, physical,

---

[266] Matthew 16:18

intellectual, and psychological means to do so, then we will not be successful. As with Gideon's army in the Book of Judges, many followers of Jesus will not be engaged in the upcoming battles because they will realize, when confronted with the reality of these spiritual battles, that they are fearful of the enemy. Their fear will leave them intimidated and they will remove themselves from the battle.

Still others will not be effectively trained and prepared to cooperate with God in order to fight the kind of prophetic, spiritual battles they will encounter. They will be told by the Holy Spirit to "go home" because they lack the spiritual, prophetic training and preparation necessary to **obey** and **cooperate with** God in these battles. God is not bound to deliver by many or by few. He wants all of us to cooperate with Him in His prophetic Kingdom activities, using the weapons He has provided to us, in the manner in which He trains us to use them, to win the battles He will fight as we cooperate with Him. The decision is ours to submit to and engage in the necessary prophetic, spiritual training He has prepared for us. We must receive this training if we are to move forward with Him and cooperate with Him. He can't and won't make the decision for us. He has given that privilege to us.

Satan is not afraid nor affected by natural, physical, intellectual and psychological means and weapons. He is not intimidated by Kingdom representatives who use these natural means and resources to do battle. It is like using water to extinguish a grease fire. It will have little effect, or it can make the whole situation worse by allowing the fire to spread unabated by not attacking the source of the fire's life. Jesus attacked the source (Satan) through prophetic, spiritual weapons and the power of the Holy Spirit, as did the early Church believers. We must do the same and allow Jesus, through the Holy Spirit, to train and prepare us in these prophetic, spiritual resources, weapons and abilities. If we don't, will Jesus find faith on the earth when He returns?

Again, some say, we, the present-day Kingdom representatives of Jesus, are not to do the same prophetic Kingdom activities that Jesus and the early followers of Jesus did because God doesn't do those prophetic works anymore? Does that mean that Jesus, through the presence and ability of the Holy Spirit, isn't with us, as the Father was with Jesus and as Jesus was with the early Church believers? Does that mean that the Gospels and other New Testament writings were only for the early Church believers and not for us?

Either the New Birth is for all of Jesus' disciples until the end of the age or it is not for any of us. Either, the power of the Holy Spirit was sent by Jesus to be upon all of His Kingdom representatives, until the end of the age, or He was not sent to any of us. It's as plain as that. I do see the greater, "mega" works of Jesus taking place in the early Church, as documented in the New Testament, through the believers' lives. These "mega" works were in addition to the inward, transforming witness of the Spirit these believers displayed in their personal lives.

Jesus experienced and displayed, both, the inward and the outward witness of the Kingdom's reality to the people around Him. The early Church believers experienced and displayed both the inward and the outward witness of the Kingdom's reality to the people around them. Today, we must do the same or we run the risk of falling short in our individual calling and contribution in regard to "the great commission" Jesus gave us before He ascended to the right hand of the Father.

Jesus asked the question, *"When the Son of Man comes will He find faith on the earth?"* The early Church believers thought Jesus was returning in their generation. We are 2000 years removed from Jesus' question and much closer to the actual return of Christ. Many believe this is the generation in which Jesus will return. Faith must be active. Faith is exercised through decisions we make. God will not force these prophetic activities on us and He will not make the decisions for us that we need to make to exercise faith. God is sovereign and He has sovereignly chosen to give humanity a free will to choose and decide for themselves, and He will not violate that free will.

Will He find an active faith being exercised on His behalf, by His Kingdom representatives, when He returns? Will we be representing Him in the manner He describes and provides for in His words and actions, in the gospels and other New Testament writings? Or, will we have succumbed to the compromise and slow reprobating that leaves us unable to exercise an active and effective faith toward Jesus, or worse yet, susceptible to and believing in the seducing spirits and doctrines of demons of our day (such as believing that Satan and the Holy Spirit are not real), leaving us powerless and faithless representatives of Jesus?

I hope we can answer Jesus' question with an emphatic "yes" but we have a lot of work to do in order to be able to say that. The Lord is not bound to save by many or by few. He only needs a few and He will accomplish His will whether it is by many or by few. As individuals, we have to answer the question and decide if we are going to be of those who return to our homes because we are fearful and afraid of the battle ahead of us, or will we be sent home because we are untrained and unprepared to engage in the prophetic activities and spiritual battles that are ahead of us, or will we be of those who allow God to train and prepare us to **obey** and **cooperate with** Him when the battles come? Only we can answer that question. Only we can make the decision. *"For the eyes of the* LORD *move to and fro throughout the earth* ***that He may strongly support*** *those whose heart is completely His."* [267] (emphasis mine)

[267] 2Chronicles 16:9

Chapter Questions & Notes

Talk It Over....

1) Jesus has a unique plan and training program for each of His Kingdom followers. He orders our lives so we experience those things that best equip, train and prepare us to accomplish what He wants us to do. He establishes communication methods and a history with each of us, based on our calling, gifts, and place within the Body of Christ. He wants to prepare us for what He has for us to accomplish and he trains us to effectively cooperate with Him in what He is doing. Identify these unique methods and activities that God seems to be conducting in your life and experience with Him. Write down your answers:

2) God has a training plan and preparation activities designed to accomplish what He needs to, in each one of us, to bring us to the place where we can obey and cooperate with Him in His Kingdom activities and battles. He knows we are all fearful and unprepared when we begin this training course. He also knows that we each have to make the decision to let Him conduct and complete the unique training and preparation plan that He has for each of us. What does this mean to you, what do you think about this, how may it affect your life, and what kind of demands might this may place on your life, going forward? Write down your observations:

(4)

Pressing On To Spiritual Maturity

*"...**let us press on to maturity**..."* Hebrews 6:1 (emphasis mine)

*"Until we all attain to...**a mature man...**"* Ephesians 4:13 (emphasis mine)

*"Let us therefore, **as many as are mature**, have this attitude"* Philippians 3:15 (emphasis mine)

I've mentioned spiritual maturity several times, usually as it relates to experiencing the prophetic activities of the Kingdom of God. Specifically, that experiencing these prophetic activities isn't a sign of spiritual maturity. And, yet, we will not achieve spiritual maturity without experiencing these prophetic activities. We can't know Jesus experientially, apart from our prophetic encounters with the Holy Spirit. He reveals Jesus to us and makes it possible for us to connect with Him and experience Him. We can know about Jesus from the Bible but we can't know Jesus, experientially, apart from the prophetic activities of the Holy Spirit taking place in our lives.

What I want to address, here, is the subject of spiritual maturity. It is a very important subject and critical for us to know and understand as followers of Jesus. It is not to be taken lightly or approached in a flippant or haphazard manner, as if it is not important for us to embrace and pursue it in our lives. Jesus and the writers of the New Testament books spend a great deal of time on the subject of spiritual maturity and how to grow in it. It is imperative that we grow in spiritual maturity because our Christian experience in this life depends on it, as well as our place and function within the Kingdom of God in the ages to come.

What is spiritual maturity? How do we achieve it? If we were to ask several people, who identify themselves as followers of Jesus. these two questions, we will most likely get several different answers. We would get answers ranging from, "*an accurate systematic theology*", to *"loving everyone",* to "*being like Jesus*", to *"doing good things to help people"*, to "*being led by the Spirit".* Okay, assuming any or all of these answers are correct, they only address the first of the two questions, "What is spiritual maturity?" They don't answer the second question, "How do we achieve it?"

For instance, if we take the Systematic Theology text books taught in our seminaries and bible schools today, we will find many points of agreement between them but we will also find many points of disagreement. In other words, not everyone agrees on all areas of Christian theology. Is it possible, then, to attain to spiritual maturity if we can't even be sure that our systematic theology is correct? How do we love everyone? Does it mean that we are nice to everyone? Was Jesus nice to everyone? He called the Pharisees a bunch of snakes.[268] He took a whip to the money changers in the temple, driving them out of the temple and turning over their tables and throwing their money on the floor.[269] He told His disciples that if they didn't eat His flesh and drink His blood, they were wasting their time following Him.[270] What does it mean to love everyone and how do we do that?

Are we spiritually mature if we read the Bible and pray every day? Do we read our Bible for 10 minutes, or 30 minutes, or an hour? Do we say the same set of prayers every day or do we say different prayers every day? Do we pray for 10 minutes, or 30 minutes, or an hour, or two hours? What are the Bible reading and prayer requirements for achieving spiritual maturity? How is a person led by the Spirit? Do we sit in our room and wait for the Spirit to "move us" to do something? Is it based on how much and how often we are led by the Spirit, or is it based on the types of things He leads us to do and the quality of the results that come from those activities? What are the requirements for being led by the Spirit in order to achieve spiritual maturity?

Is spiritual maturity being like Jesus? Does it mean that we need to do miracles like Jesus? Does it mean that we learn to speak eloquently like Jesus so that we draw large crowds to our gatherings? He only had 120 people following Him when He ascended into heaven after His

---

[268] Matthew 23:33
[269] John 2:13-16
[270] John 6:52-58

resurrection. Do we consider that to be successful according to today's standards, and does it satisfy our "litmus test" for spiritual maturity? Does engaging in doing good things for people mean that we are spiritually mature? What is considered to be a "good work"? How many and how often should these good deeds be done to achieve spiritual maturity? Is it the level of impact or the scope of our good deeds that satisfies the criteria for achieving spiritual maturity? Is it the recognition of our deeds by others or the legacy of our good deeds that we leave behind after we're gone that determines spiritual maturity?

There are many opinions concerning spiritual maturity, what it is and how we achieve it. If we really want to know what spiritual maturity is, we need to go to the Person who has the answers, and to the place He has disclosed and documented His Kingdom communications to us; the Bible. Does the Bible tell us what it is? Does it tell us what it isn't? Does the Bible say what we are to do to achieve spiritual maturity? Does it say what we aren't supposed to do? Let's see what the Bible has to say about spiritual maturity.

Until We All Attain

Let's start with a scripture that we have already looked at, from the book of Ephesians. *"...until* ***we all attain*** *to the unity of the faith, and of the knowledge of the Son of God,* ***to a mature man****, to the measure of the stature which belongs to the fullness of Christ."* [271] In this scripture, Paul tells us that there is an activity that is to take place until, among other things, the entire Church, the Body of Christ, God's Kingdom people attains to spiritual maturity...spiritual adulthood...to a mature man. Paul is telling us that the entire Church is to achieve spiritual maturity or adulthood as a result of a specific activity taking place.

What does Paul tell us this activity is? In this scripture, there are two activities that Paul mentions; 1) "*the equipping of the saints for the work of service,* and 2) *the building up of the body of Christ*" [272] The individual members of the Body of Christ are to be engaged in activities designed to equip them for the work of Kingdom service, and to build them up in their Christian faith. What does this mean, to "*equip*"; to "*build up*"? To "*equip*", means to "*provide a complete furnishing, supplying or endowing*". To "*build up*", means "*to promote, stimulate and support another's growth*".

---

[271] Ephesians 4:13 (emphasis mine)
[272] Ephesians 4:12

So, the activities Paul talks about are to, 1) *"provide a complete furnishing, supplying and endowing to each member of the Body of Christ for the purpose of Kingdom service;* and, 2) *to promote, stimulate and support each member's faith and spiritual growth*".

As we saw earlier, these two activities are to take place until each member of the Body of Christ attains to, among other things, the spiritual stature of a mature man or spiritual maturity. If, according to Ephesians 4, spiritual maturity comes as a result of these two specific activities; 1) *"providing a complete furnishing, supplying and endowing to each member of the Body of Christ for the purpose of ministry;* and, 2) *promoting, stimulating and supporting each member's faith and spiritual growth*; where do these two activities come from or who is conducting these specific activities? Paul tells us that Jesus, after His resurrection, *"...ASCENDED ON HIGH, HE LED CAPTIVE A HOST OF CAPTIVES, AND HE GAVE GIFTS TO MEN. And He gave some as apostles, and some as prophets, and some as evangelists, and some as pastors and teachers,"* [273]

Jesus gave or "commissioned" these "ascension gifts" to the Body of Christ to focus on and engage in two specific activities; 1) *"providing a complete furnishing, supplying and endowing to each member of the Body of Christ for the purpose of Kingdom service;* and, 2) *promoting, stimulating and supporting each member's faith and spiritual growth.* These five commissioned gifts are to work hand in hand with the Holy Spirit to serve, support, and "come along side" of each follower of Jesus in order to supply what each member needs to engage in Kingdom service, and to promote and stimulate the faith and spiritual growth of each follower of Jesus.

Paul tells us, earlier, in his first letter to the Corinthians, that, "*...the body is not one member, but many...God has placed the members, each one of them, in the body, just as He desired...But now there are many members, but one body.*" [274] We are one Body but many members, and Jesus has placed each member in the Body as He desires. In other words, "one size fits all" training and equipping methods don't work in the Body of Christ because we aren't all a foot, or a hand, or an arm.

To put it another way, cookie-cutter programs and methods won't work when it comes to bringing the individual members of the Body of Christ to spiritual maturity because Jesus has placed each member into His Body with a unique function and purpose, based on His desire for

[273] Ephesians 4:8,11
[274] 1Corinthians 12:14,18,20

them and for His good pleasure. Remember, He is God, He is sovereign, and He can establish and provide for His Body any way He chooses. He has done that and we must come into agreement with what He has established.

He has commissioned these five ascension gifts to "come along side" of the members of the Body to supply and support them, in order to bring each individual member to spiritual maturity. Also, as I mentioned before, Jesus commissioned five gifts to the Body of Christ, not two or three. I don't see anywhere in the New Testament where He decided that the Church doesn't need two or three of these five gifts anymore, so He decommissioned them.

So, if each member of the Body is a unique member with a unique function, and Jesus commissioned five gifts to come along side of these individual members in order to engage in two specific activities designed to bring each member to spiritual maturity, we will not successfully bring the members of His Body to spiritual maturity with "one-size-fits-all", cookie-cutter programs and methods. Neither will we do it with only two or three of these five commissioned gifts functioning in the Body.

For instance, a baseball team has nine position players. All positions are not responsible for the same thing, all are not equipped with the same skills and resources, and all are not instructed and trained in the same way. An infielder is equipped with a short, small fielder's glove so he can easily remove the ball and throw quickly to get the runner out. The outfielder is equipped with a larger fielder's glove so he can reach more fly balls than if he had a shorter, smaller glove.

The catcher has completely different equipment than anyone else on the field because he must be able to block pitches thrown in the dirt, absorb foul balls without being hurt, and catch 100mph fastballs from the pitcher. Likewise, you teach, train and instruct each of the players differently, depending on their position. You don't want the hitting coach instructing the short-stop on how to turn a double-play; you don't want the pitching coach instructing the outfielders on how to play a fly ball off the wall; you don't want the outfield coach instructing the catcher on how to block a pitch in the dirt; and you don't want the team trainer instructing your clean-up hitter on how to adjust his stance so he can hit with more power.

The function and resources available to the Apostle are going to be different from that of the Prophet. The function and resources available to the Teacher are going to be different from that of the Evangelist or the Pastor. The training, instructing, coaching and supporting methods and results will be different for the Pastor than they are for the Prophet, and the methods and results of the Apostle will be different from the Teacher or the Evangelist. "One-size-fits-all" instructing, training, coaching and supporting methods and activities will only create frustrated and incompetent followers of Jesus, the five commissioned ministry gifts will not achieve the results they are expected to produce, and the individual members of the Body of Christ will remain spiritually and functionally immature.

Each player and each position requires specific equipping, training, coaching and support. "One-size-fits-all" methods, programs, training and coaching will do nothing but relegate a team to being a "cellar dweller" for years to come. Teams are always "re-deploying" resources and personnel, and evaluating their methods of operation in order to maintain their competitiveness and to utilize their personnel and resources in the most effective way.

The Church has tremendous personnel and resources at her disposal. Jesus has deployed His resources and personnel in a way that will achieve the results He desires. He has given the Church effective methods by which she can operate and be successful. We need to make sure we are implementing these resources and methods in the way Jesus intended. If not, we may find that He has brought in a new leadership team who will do what He wants, and we will find ourselves on the outside, looking in, like the Pharisees in Jesus' day.

We must all re-evaluate our approach; the individual followers of Jesus and the five commissioned gifts. We must take an honest look at, not only the programs, methods and organizational structures we have setup in our local churches, but we must passionately seek the wisdom and assistance of the Holy Spirit, the Spirit of Christ, in order to move forward in an effective way toward achieving spiritual maturity for the individual members of the Body of Christ. Again, this isn't about what we want to do and what is best for us. It is about Jesus, what He wants to accomplish, and how He wants to accomplish it. He will help us and provide what we need if we are serious about accomplishing what He placed us here to do. Let's take a look at another scripture that instructs us about spiritual maturity.

Leaving The Elementary Teaching About The Christ

The writer of the book of Hebrews tells us, in chapter 6, *"Therefore leaving the elementary teaching about the Christ, let us press on to maturity..."* [275] Immediately, we see two words that need our attention, "Therefore" and "leaving". Since "leaving" follows "therefore" in the statement, we will address "therefore" first, anticipating that we will receive insight from that exercise, concerning "leaving".

We have all heard it said, "When you see a "therefore", you need to find out what the "therefore" is there for." The word "therefore" is indicative of a follow-on action to be taken, based on the information previously stated or received. To find out what the information is that needs to be acted upon, we need to go back to the previous chapter, chapter 5. In the original manuscripts, there were no chapter and verse designations. These were added by scholars centuries later in order to better help us navigate the writings and to more easily find a specific place within the writings. As a result, there really is no Chapter 5 and Chapter 6. They all flow together in the original writings with no verse and chapter breaks.

What the writer of Hebrews begins with in Chapter 5, is a comparison of the New Covenant priesthood of Jesus and the Levitical priesthood in the Old Covenant. He compares the eternal priesthood of Jesus with the temporary priesthood of the Levites. Both priesthoods involve human beings but the eternal priesthood of Jesus is much better than the temporary priesthood of the Levites because Jesus will serve as a priest forever, without having to give up the priesthood because of death. The Levitical priests only served until their deaths. Then, others would take their place.

The priesthood of Jesus, in the New Covenant, is after the order of the priest Melchizedek, while the priesthood of the Old Covenant was after the order of Aaron, Moses' brother, and only included those from the tribe of Levi. The writer talks about how Jesus learned obedience through His suffering and, having been made complete, Jesus became a source of eternal salvation and a priest forever.

At this point in his teaching, the writer of Hebrews deviates from his subject matter in order to bring out an observation to his Hebrew

[275] Hebrews 6:1

Christian readers. He tells them that, even though he has much to say about this eternal priesthood of Jesus, it is difficult to explain it to them because his readers have become dull of hearing…they do not have an established foundation of the elementary principles of the Christ and the Kingdom of God, on which he can build. He goes on to say that, though they have been believers long enough to be teachers, themselves, they still need to be taught these elementary principles of Christ and the Kingdom. They still need the "milk" of the Kingdom of God.

The writer states that those believers who continually need to be fed on the elementary principles or "milk" of the word of God, are not growing in their ability to effectively exercise and experience these elementary truths on a consistent basis. The elementary foundation is never completely established in their lives. They keep going back to these same elementary principles without making the necessary progress to go on to the spiritual principles and activities that bring about their spiritual maturity. They cannot yet "stomach" the solid food of the Kingdom of God. It is this solid food of the Kingdom, received after the foundation of the elemental principles is established, that produces spiritual maturity. We need the strong foundation of the elementary principles of the Kingdom but once that foundation is built, we need to move on to the solid food of the Kingdom.

The writer then says that this solid food of the Kingdom is for those who are actively moving forward toward spiritual maturity, and then describes spiritual maturity being built into their lives by the training of their spiritual senses, through practice, to discern good and evil. So, again, we are told that there is a training and practice involved in the process of spiritual maturity. There is a training and practice that must take place in these elementary principles of the Kingdom in order for the firm foundation to be established.

Our spiritual senses must be trained through practice, to discern good and evil; to discern the Kingdom of God from the kingdom of darkness. It doesn't just happen. We can't get it through osmosis; by simply listening to the pastor's sermon on Sundays or by reading books, alone.

Jesus said that those who hear the word of God but don't act on it will have that seed of the word taken from them.[276] There must be a

---

[276] Mark 4:13-20

passionate pursuit, response and action on our part if that foundation of the elementary principles of the Kingdom is to be firmly established in our lives. The trainers, the equippers, the supporters…the five commissioned ministry gifts that Jesus gave the Church must come along side of the followers of Jesus to ensure the spiritual maturity of the Body of Christ and its individual members.

As I mentioned in Chapter 1 of the first book, we as followers of Jesus can engage in the process of reprobating by not responding to the influences of the Holy Spirit and the Kingdom of God in our lives. Even as we listen to the word of God being preached every Sunday and read books on these subjects, we can be slowly reprobating because we think that being at church and listening to the sermon, or reading a book on the subject is enough; that, somehow, it will automatically take root in our hearts and bring forth fruit without us doing anything to apply the word to our daily lives. What is actually happening is that our hearts are becoming more and more calloused to the influences of the Kingdom of God and the work of the Holy Spirit if we aren't regularly practicing what we hear and read.

We think that because we are listening and reading, God is able to do what He needs to do in our hearts. In reality, we are not practicing and training our spiritual senses in regard to what we are receiving, in order to build our faith in those areas. Hearing and reading aren't enough. Training in righteousness…training in the elementary principles of the Kingdom of God; practically applying and practicing the principles and truths we learn, and training our spiritual senses to respond as God desires are what brings spiritual maturity to our lives. James tells us that if all we do is hear the word of God and don't practice it or train ourselves in it, we are deceiving ourselves into thinking that we are making spiritual progress. In reality, we are actively reprobating. It may be slow but it is taking place.

The writer of Hebrews goes on to say that once the elementary foundation has been established in each believer, it's time to leave or move forward from the elementary teachings of Jesus and press on to spiritual maturity; to the solid food of the Kingdom. He goes on to list some of the topics and subjects included in the elementary teachings of Jesus and the Kingdom of God: repentance from dead works, faith toward God (including saving faith), instruction about baptisms, laying on of hands, the resurrection of the dead, and eternal judgment.

We must ask ourselves, "Are we instructing, receiving and acting on all of these subjects as elementary Kingdom principles and teachings?" If not, we are laying and establishing an inadequate Kingdom foundation. This exhortation in the book of Hebrews comes from a person who is most likely an Apostle (Paul, Apollos, etc.), so he or she knows how to build a firm, spiritual, Kingdom foundation.

There is a training and practicing that goes with teaching on these elementary principles of the Kingdom. And, there is training, practicing and supporting that goes with moving forward from these elementary principles to the solid food of the kingdom of God. Our spiritual senses must be exercised and trained to discern the Kingdom of God from the kingdom of darkness. It only happens through on-the-job instruction and training by the Holy Spirit.

How important is establishing a strong foundation of the elementary principles and teachings of the Kingdom of God in our lives, through their consistent and active practice? If we don't: 1) we can't move on toward spiritual maturity[277]; 2) we would continue to need teaching and instruction on these same elementary principles because we haven't become accustomed to or experienced with these principles…we are not doers or "practicers" of them but only hearers who have fooled ourselves[278]; 3) we are more susceptible to the worries, riches and pleasures of this life choking our spiritual life and making it very difficult to move forward toward spiritual maturity[279]; 4) we place ourselves in the precarious position of potentially falling away from the faith, to where we have little or nothing to show for our lives when we stand before Jesus at the end of the age[280], or worse, being accursed.[281]

If we look at these scriptures concerning the falling away of followers of Jesus, they all refer to those who do not have a firm foundation of the elementary principles of the Kingdom of God, and have not moved on toward maturity. They are susceptible to the lies and deceptions of this world's system and of our spiritual enemy. They have not been trained in the word of righteousness so as to recognize the truth and to stand for the truth in the day of evil.[282]

---

[277] Hebrews 5:11-14, 6:1
[278] James 1:22
[279] Luke 8:14
[280] 1Corinthians 3:12-15; Hebrews 6:8
[281] John 15:1-6; Hebrews 6:8; 2Thessalonians 2:1-3; 1Timothy 4:1-3
[282] Ephesians 4:10-17

Jesus warns us. Paul warns us. The writer of Hebrews warns us. We must establish a firm foundation of the elementary principles of the Kingdom of God in our lives, through the practice of them, and not simply listen to sermons and read books about them. We must move on toward spiritual maturity so we are equipped and experiencing the spiritual growth that leads to spiritual maturity and completion.

The Bible tells us that if we belong to Christ, no one or nothing can snatch us out of His hand.[283] But, remember, we are free will beings and we can make the decision to take ourselves out from under His care and protection…we can walk away if we so choose. As I said earlier in Chapter 1 of the first book, deception and ignorance are not acceptable excuses or reasons for reprobating. Regardless if we are deceived into believing a lie or are ignorant of what the scriptures say, we freely make our decisions to live and act the way we choose. We choose which yoke we are going to live under, the yoke of Jesus or the yoke of Satan.

God will influence us with His Spirit and the activities of His Kingdom as much as possible but we choose how we will respond and He will not violate that choice.[284] This is how important it is that all five commissioned ministries that Jesus gave as gifts to the Church function correctly and carry out their assigned duties, as Jesus established it. The spiritual maturity and strength of the Church, and each individual member, depends on it. Unlike baseball, this is not a game. We have an enemy who is roaming about seeking whom he may devour.[285] Now, let's take a look at one more scripture that talks about spiritual maturity.

That I May Know Him

In Philippians 3, Paul tells us, "*Let us therefore,* ***as many as are mature,*** *have this attitude.*"[286] Okay, here we have the word "therefore" again, so let's see what Paul says in the previous verses that, then, leads him to encourage those who are spiritually mature to have this same attitude. If we look back in chapter 3, beginning in verse 7, we see Paul write, "*…I count all things to be loss in view of the surpassing value of knowing Christ Jesus my Lord, for whom I have*

[283] John 10:27-30
[284] Hebrews 6:4-8
[285] 1Peter 5:8
[286] Philippians 3:15 (emphasis mine)

suffered the loss of all things, and count them but rubbish so that I may gain Christ, and may be found in Him, not having a righteousness of my own derived from the Law, but that which is through faith in Christ, the righteousness which comes from God on the basis of faith, that I may know Him and the power of His resurrection and the fellowship of His sufferings, being conformed to His death; in order that I may attain to the resurrection from the dead. Not that I have already obtained it or have already become perfect **(mature)**, *but I press on so that I may lay hold of that for which also I was laid hold of by Christ Jesus. Brethren, I do not regard myself as having laid hold of it yet; but one thing I do: forgetting what lies behind and reaching forward to what lies ahead, I press on toward the goal for the prize of the upward call of God in Christ Jesus. Let us therefore, as many as are perfect* **(mature)**, *have this attitude."* [287]

In a nutshell (and in one of the longest sentences I have ever seen) Paul tells us what spiritual maturity is. It is knowing Christ Jesus. It is not knowing about Him but knowing Him, experientially, in intimate fellowship and relationship. Paul doesn't stop there but goes on to list what is included in knowing and experiencing Jesus in intimate fellowship and relationship: 1) to know the power of His resurrection; and 2) to know the fellowship of His sufferings, being conformed to His death.

Spiritual maturity is the ongoing process of being spiritually strengthened, equipped and established in a life of enduring faith and Kingdom service, while choosing to engage in an ever-increasing intimate interaction and identification with Jesus, through the Holy Spirit; experiencing, both, the power of His resurrection and the fellowship of His sufferings, adapting to His example of Kingdom life and conforming to His example of obedience, even to the point of death.

This is why it is important for us, as followers of Christ, to accept and believe the fact that Jesus lived and functioned as a human being when He was on the earth. He experienced suffering throughout His life, not only when He went to the cross. He experienced the power of God working through Him, by the Holy Spirit, throughout His ministry; the same power of God that raised Him from the dead. If we are encouraged to accept and experience these same things, on our road to spiritual maturity, then we need to accept and believe that Jesus also experienced them. How can Paul encourage us to accept and experience what Jesus experienced, if Jesus didn't experience them?

This is why we must understand, embrace, and experience the prophetic activities of God and His Kingdom because we cannot know Jesus Christ in the manner Paul talks about apart from our revelatory experiences and

---

[287] Philippians 3:8-15 (emphasis mine)

encounters with the Holy Spirit. We can't know Jesus in this way by reading and knowing what the Bible says, alone. We can't know Jesus in this way by listening to sermons and reading books, alone. This must be more than intellectual exercises and humanitarian pursuits. There must be spiritual practice and training in what we learn and in what He reveals to us.

I can't read the Baseball rule book, alone, and expect to go out and play baseball at a high level. I can't read a biography about Babe Ruth or Stan Musial and expect to go out and play baseball at the high level at which they played. Now, if they were alive and were to come along side of me and teach, instruct, and train me in how to play; and I practiced and practiced and practiced; I would have hope that I could attain to their level of play at some point in my life. It doesn't happen by osmosis; it happens with teaching, instruction, training, a passionate pursuit[288], and practice, practice and more practice.

Now, the question comes up, "How am I supposed to practice knowing the power of His resurrection, and practice knowing the fellowship of His sufferings? That's not like playing baseball." Oh, yes it is! When you play baseball, you have a coach who comes along side of you and teaches and explains the game and rules of baseball to you. You spend time with that coach to where you trust him and that what he is telling you is the truth. You trust that the way he is teaching you the game is, in fact, the correct way to play.

Then, you begin to practice what you have been taught and the coach continues to instruct you and train you in the game, as you practice. You can read the instruction manual and listen to what the coach tells you all day long but until you put into practice what the manual says and what the coach tells you and instructs you to do, you will not mature in the game. As you learn more, the coach puts you in "live game situations" where you test your knowledge and what you have been practicing to see if it really works that way in a real game. You have to make decisions based on what you encounter and what confronts you in the game, and you learn more from these encounters and confrontations than you would by just reading, listening, and practicing because you have an actual opponent, an adversary, who will test you because he doesn't want you to win.

You find that you make mistakes, so the coach is right there to help you make the necessary adjustments. You don't stop playing the game when you make a mistake or fail. You make the necessary adjustments as you keep going…on-the-job training. You keep at it; building up your strength,

[288] Philippians 3:12

coordination, speed, and knowledge of the game, even as your coach teaches you more advanced aspects and nuances of the game. You have come to trust the coach, more and more, because what he has taught you and trained you to do, so far, has been successful. As you embrace, incorporate and practice these advanced aspects and nuances of the game, you move out of the "amateur" status as a player and advance into the "professional" status. You are no longer immature but have become a mature player, playing the game, interacting with your teammates, and confronting your adversaries in a mature manner.

When we are engaged in the process of growing and maturing in baseball (or any sport), we will find ourselves laboring, tripping over our own feet, getting a sore arm from throwing so much, and getting thrown out stealing second base because we were getting a late jump from first base. Then, suddenly, everything seems to "click" into place. Our bodies get used to the physical demands placed upon it, and our mind and emotions come into agreement with what we discover was necessary to grow and mature as a player. The game seems to "slow down" for us so that we are able to do what is expected of us as a professional, and we continue to grow in our skills and abilities.

The game becomes "second nature" to us because we learn, train and practice until it does. We achieve maturity and we realize and know there is no other way to achieve it. There are no shortcuts to athletic maturity. Likewise, there are no shortcuts to spiritual maturity, and we have a Coach who will never leave us or forsake us. He knows how to get us from the sandlots to the major leagues if we will pursue a relationship with Him and let Him teach, instruct and train us in what it will take for us to achieve that spiritual maturity.

Again, as those who are moving toward spiritual maturity in Christ, we will make mistakes; we will experience failures. We will experience what appear to be setbacks along the way. Yet, we need to have the same attitude that Paul had, and that he encourages us to have, in Philippians 3, "*Brethren, I do not regard myself as having laid hold of it yet; but one thing I do:* ***forgetting what lies behind and reaching forward to what lies ahead, I press on toward the goal for the prize*** *of the upward call of God in Christ Jesus.*"[289] If we sin, we must turn our backs on that sin and keep moving forward, toward maturity. If we make a mistake, fail, or don't do as well as we think we should be doing, we go to THE Coach and see what He wants us to do to enhance our training so we can be more successful.

[289] Philippians 3:13-14

Then, we turn our back on the failures and mistakes and keep moving forward to maturity. No committed athlete is going to let a few mistakes and failures keep him or her from moving forward as far as their talent and preparation will take them. Jesus wants us to succeed in our Christian life and He will be there for us and will do everything He can to help us succeed. Yet, He can't make the decisions for us and He won't force us to do something or go somewhere we don't want to do or go.

A number of years ago, as I was praying at an all-church prayer meeting, the Lord gave me an experience that helped me understand the importance of being connected to Him and the need to live my life based on this spiritual connection. This all-church prayer meeting was scheduled for an hour. About twenty minutes into the meeting, as I was praying to myself with my eyes closed, I saw what looked like a black and white movie begin to play in my mind's eye.

I have had this type of experience happen to me a number of times over the years and, through the communication history I have developed with the Lord over the years, I have come to understand what these experiences are and why He gives them to me. God will develop a communication history with all of us, throughout our lives, as we seek Him and respond to the subtle and not-so-subtle influences He engages us in, in our personal time of fellowship and prayer with Him.

So much of this communication history is based on who we are as a person - the personality, gifts, temperament and calling that He has placed on and within each of us. The more we get to know ourselves and Him, based on our experiences with Him as we allow Him to be actively engaged in our lives, the more we will recognize these communications and influences and are better able to respond to Him, participating in the Kingdom activities that He has in store for each of us. It is all based on developing our faith through our spiritual interaction and fellowship with Him within our daily lives.

As I watched this black and white movie playing within my mind's eye, I saw a vine with ripe grapes, ready to eat. I could see the internal workings of the vine and the branches, as if I was looking at an x-ray. I watched the nutrients flow from the vine, through the branches and into the fruit. As I watched, the flow of nutrients slowly changed direction. I watched the nutrients flowing into the fruit, from the branch, change direction and flow out of the fruit, back into the branch. As this reverse process continued, I watched the fruit slowly shrivel and dry up until it was completely dead and, then, fall off the branch. Then the vision ended.

As I stood there (I often like to stand as I pray), I wondered what the Lord was trying to tell me. Suddenly, a scripture from Revelation chapter 3 popped into my mind…and as I thought about it, I received a very strong impression that this is the process that often takes place when a follower of Jesus starts down the road of "leaving their first love." This vision communicated to me what often takes place during the spiritual process of reprobating in a believer's life. Just like grapes are the visual expression of the relationship between the grape vine and its branches, the spiritual fruit in our lives is the tangible expression of the spiritual and practical relationship and interaction we experience with God. Our spiritual life and health comes from that relationship and consistent interaction with God.

In the vision, where the "normal" process flow of life within the grape vine changed, I saw a reprobate process take its place. The branch tried to draw life from the fruit it was producing instead of from the vine. The branch "sucked" the life out of the fruit, causing it to wither and die. The Kingdom activities we engage in and the fruit we produce for the Kingdom of God are to be an outward expression of the active, vital relationship we experience with God. The Kingdom activities we engage in and the fruit we produce cannot give us life and sustain us, spiritually.

That is not God's process of life; it is the process of reprobating. This "reprobating" may take a while. We may not initially recognize what is happening because we still seem, to ourselves, to be spiritually vital and active. Yet, the true source of our spiritual vitality is no longer producing real fruit. The reprobate process has taken over and it only leads to an individual slowly withering, drying up, and becoming fruitless, or even worse, dying.

Experiencing the power of Jesus' resurrection only comes from the branch being actively, vitally and experientially connected to the Vine, continually. The fruit we bear for God and His Kingdom are simply the visual expression of this active and vital spiritual relationship and connection we experience with Him. We can't do anything for God. The best we can do is willingly and actively cooperate with Him in what He is already doing. As Jesus, Himself, said, "The Father is working until now, and I am working."

Jesus knew that the activities He was involved in and the results He was experiencing were a result of His relationship with the Father and His cooperation with what the Holy Spirit wanted to do through Him. That is why Jesus accomplished what He did and experienced the power of the Holy Spirit working through His life, as He did. Jesus and the Father were one…they operated as a complete unit. Jesus was in the Father and the Father was in Jesus.

We can practice the power of His resurrection when we encounter and engage with the opportunities He gives us to obey and cooperate with Him, that call for us to trust in and exercise His power that He has made available to us. God's prophetic Kingdom activities working in and through our lives will often call for us to engage with and trust in His presence and power to see the results He desires, come to pass. He will be there to support us and work with us, if we let Him.

We can practice the fellowship of His sufferings, being conformed to His death, when we encounter or confront the opportunities that call for us to die to our own wants and desires in order to allow Jesus to have His way and do what He wants in and through our lives – often, prophetically. Jesus' body was repulsed by the thought of hanging on a cross for crimes He didn't commit. Yet, He despised the shame of the cross by embracing it and resolutely marching up the hill to die a death that none of us could die for ourselves. He had a hope of what the Father had in store for Him, if He was successful.

As a result of His successful mission to die for mankind's sin, the Father, *"...highly exalted Him, and bestowed on Him the name which is above every name, so that at the name of Jesus* EVERY KNEE WILL BOW, *of those who are in heaven and on earth and under the earth, and that every tongue will confess that Jesus Christ is Lord, to the glory of God the Father.*[290] God has the same type of reward for us, if we press on to spiritual maturity by experientially knowing Jesus, the power of His resurrection, and the fellowship of His suffering, being conformed to His death. It is a wonderful reward.[291]

[290] Philippians 2:9-11
[291] Revelation 3:21

Chapter Questions & Notes

Talk It Over….

1) Discuss this dynamic: engaging in an outward activity and experience, alone, compared to engaging in the spiritual maturing process which may or may not produce that same outward activity or experience – personal desire vs. spiritual obedience. Write down your observations:

2) Jesus has a unique personal training and equipping program for each of us as His follower and Kingdom representative. Discuss how these unique training and equipping activities are defined and impacted by the spiritual maturation process. How does this affect our approach to ministry? Does this change how we perceive our place and ministry within the Body of Christ and how we pursue it? In what way? Write down your answers:

(5)

Kingdom Leadership: Whose Church Is It?

"and ***in the middle of the lampstands*** *one like a son of man…"*
Revelation 1:13 (emphasis mine)

*"****the one who walks among*** *the seven golden lampstands says this."*
Revelation 2:1 (emphasis mine)

"He who has an ear, let him hear what the Spirit says to the churches."
Revelation 1:7a

Before we begin the subject of Kingdom Leadership, there are a few general things that I need to say about the Church in the western hemisphere, especially at the local church level. I have been an active member, participant, and leader in the local church for over forty years and I am not unaware or unconcerned regarding the spiritual condition that much of the Church finds herself in today. I have a sincere concern in regard to this condition because, as one who has contributed to the proliferation of this unfavorable condition, I want to see the Church turn things around and operate in all that Jesus has ordained for her.

I believe that if a person experiences or observes a problem situation or condition and is willing to be part of the solution, whatever that solution may be, then they should have the opportunity to voice their perspective of that situation or condition as well as their thoughts on possible solutions. I want to be part of the solution to this particular condition in the Church. I believe that the general disregard for the prophetic activity of the Kingdom of God and for the complete ministry of the Holy Spirit in the lives of believers today, within the local church, is a contributing factor to the larger condition in which the Church finds herself.

We in the Church can point to many symptoms and ailments regarding our spiritual condition. We are very aware that things are not as they should be. Yet, in most of the areas where we sorely come up short of the revealed will and purposes of God, we can trace part of the cause back to a lack of effective leadership in these areas. Again, as a leader in the local church for many years, I acknowledge that some of my own actions and attitudes, especially in my early years, contributed to this condition. There are specific capabilities and characteristics that Jesus built into the fabric of His Body, the Church, when He established her on the earth 2000 years ago of which we are ignorant, dismissing them outright as irrelevant, or simply putting them aside because they are inconvenient.

These particular attitudes and actions exist for many reasons, some of which are understandable but none of them are legitimate. How can we have a legitimate excuse for putting something aside that Jesus purposely built into the fabric of the Church? Is it legitimate to plead ignorance in regard to something that God has stated plainly in the scriptures? Can we consider something irrelevant that Jesus says is important enough to lust for? None of us are perfect and I don't believe God expects us to be. I do believe He wants and expects moral courage, spiritual integrity, and intellectual honesty from us, especially from His leaders in the Church.

One of my seminary professors said something one time that has stayed with me and I believe may apply to this current condition in which we find ourselves. He said that the orientation of the Hebrew/Middle-Eastern mind is much different than that of the Greek/Western mind. We in the West live in a cultural orientation based on the ancient Greek way of thinking.

When a person says the phrase "lack of knowledge" to someone with a Western orientation, the result will most likely be expressed in the word "ignorance". On the other hand, when a person says the phrase "lack of knowledge" to someone with a strong Hebrew/Middle-Eastern orientation, the result will most likely be expressed in the word "rebellion". You see, we in the West are much more passive in our response to not having the required knowledge to make a necessary decision or to take a necessary action. We say, "What we don't know won't hurt us." The Hebrew/Middle-Eastern mind is much more active and aggressive in their response to not having the required knowledge. They say, "What we don't know will destroy us! "

God, through the prophet Hosea, speaks to His people through the Hebrew/Middle-East orientation when He says to them, in Hosea 4:6, *"My people are destroyed for lack of knowledge. Because you have rejected knowledge, I also will reject you from being My priest. Since you have forgotten the law of your God, I also will forget your children."* What God accused the nation of Israel of doing, and threatening to forget their heritage as a result, forgetting His Law, we have also done by ignoring, dismissing, and putting aside so much of what Jesus purposely designed into the fabric of His Body. The children of Israel put aside His Law because they didn't feel that it was relevant for them anymore.

As a result, God destroyed them (He let them be taken into captivity so that they were no longer a nation). We have ignored, dismissed, and put aside His functional tools and resources designed to bring us success as His Body. As a result, God has allowed us to become virtually impotent to the world around us, teetering on the very brink of irrelevance, with little true success and very little respect from the people we have been sent to minister to on behalf of the Kingdom of God.

We cannot continue down our present path and expect to complete what Jesus commissioned us to do, as His Kingdom representatives. We pray for God to move and work among us but we aren't willing to accept and implement all that He has given to us to accomplish the work. We embrace those things that aren't too difficult or too inconvenient to implement but the things that are more difficult to comprehend and are more difficult and inconvenient to implement, we dismiss, push aside, and claim ignorance, saying; "What we don't know won't hurt us". But in reality, what we are ignoring, dismissing, and putting aside is destroying us (making us irrelevant and inconsequential to the world around us).

I believe that what I am discussing in this book, in regard to the prophetic activity of the Kingdom of God, is both scriptural and necessary for the Church to be a vital, active, and successful force on the earth. If you believe that only a portion of what I am saying is valid, there is still enough here to make considerable headway in bringing the Body of Christ to maturity and to making us relevant again to the world around us. There is more that needs to be addressed and fixed than just this subject of embracing and conducting the prophetic activity of the Kingdom, but I am willing to start with this and go on from here. I am willing to commit myself to seeing this take root again in the local church, and I will do what I can to see it happen.

There is a foundational truth of the Kingdom of God at risk in the Body of Christ today. This risk can best be stated in the question, "Who is the head of the Church, including the local church? Is it Jesus or is it the local church leadership?" Even though Jesus commanded church leaders to watch over and feed the flock of God (I Peter 5:1-4), church leaders don't own the flock of God. The flock of God, including the local church, is owned by Jesus Christ the Chief Shepherd and Head of the Church.[292]

The decisions that we make on a daily basis as church leaders and leaders of other Christian ministries, organizations and institutions, regarding the direction and activities of our ministries, must be made with the keen understanding that Jesus is the functional head of the entire Church and we

[292] Ephesians 5:23-24

are but the under-shepherds and leaders who are responsible to Him for the health and welfare of those we lead. This is His deal, not ours. He is the owner and we are His representative leaders.

I want to take some space here to reinforce the fact that Jesus is scripturally, theologically and functionally the Head of the Church on the earth, which includes the local church and other Christian ministries, organizations and institutions. These scriptures will establish the fact of: 1) the truth concerning Jesus' ownership of all aspects of the Church, and 2) His intimate knowledge of and concern for the people, condition, and ministry of each local church, ministry, organization and institution.

In The Middle of the Lampstands

In this first chapter of Revelation, John saw a vision (a prophetic manifestation of the Kingdom of God, by the way) of seven golden lampstands which represent seven local churches in Asia Minor, at that time. We tend to look at these seven churches in a prophetic sense, meaning these seven churches may represent seven spiritual "dispensations" or universal conditions in which the Church has found herself throughout her history up to the present day, or they may represent seven distinct spiritual conditions or environments in which individual churches may find themselves at any given time, since the day of Pentecost. Yet, there is far more that Jesus wants us to see and understand from this part of John's prophetic experience. It should be significant to us that John refers to and speaks of Jesus' relationship to and interaction with these seven lampstands several times within these first few chapters.

He also comments that Jesus is always together with these lampstands, placing Himself clearly in the center of them. Jesus, in His letter to one of the churches, also identifies Himself as the one who walks about in the midst of the lampstands. These local churches, represented by the lampstands, were of great value and of considerable interest to Jesus, represented by the fact that they were golden lampstands. He identified them by name, knew what was going on within them, naturally and spiritually, and He made specific, unique remarks to each of them. They were very important to Jesus and they had His undivided attention, as only God can give.

In Revelation 1:13, Jesus is said to be standing in the middle of these lampstands. When we read that Jesus is standing in the middle of this group of lampstands, it speaks of Jesus' ownership authority in relationship to these churches. Jesus, as the Head of the Universal Church, is the head of each local church, ministry, organization and institution that recognizes and submits to Jesus as Savior, Lord, God and King. He is not some distant CEO or Owner who is so busy with other things that He can't be involved in the day-to-day activities of each of His churches around the world. Jesus is the functional head of every local church and ministry and He signifies that fact by standing in the midst of them.

After John describes Jesus standing in the midst of the lampstands, Jesus tells John to write a letter to each one of these churches, telling them specifically what He wants them to know and what it is they must do, if they want to continue experiencing His presence and activities (or He will remove their lampstand from His presence). This is the kind of statement you would expect to hear from one who has the privilege and authority of ownership. He is giving them instructions on what He wants them to do in order to keep their local church vital, active and in right relationship with Him, who is the owner. These were not suggestions. These were commands.

The One Who Walks Among The Seven Golden Lampstands

In the first part of Revelation, in the letters that are written to these seven churches, John is writing the letters while the content he is to include in them is being dictated to him by Jesus. Not only is Jesus described as the One who stands in the midst of His local churches (the lampstands), Jesus is identified as the One who walks among His churches; He watches and knows their activities and their spiritual condition. The fact that Jesus walks about in the midst of His churches tells us that He is intimately acquainted and familiar with everyone and everything having to do with His churches. That is why He told the church at Ephesus that He knows their members, their activities, their attitudes, and their spiritual condition. These seven letters were dictated by Jesus and sent directly to the leaders of these seven churches.

Jesus is vitally active in the day-to-day activities of all of His churches and ministries. He not only wants to be involved in the decision-making process, He requires it. That is why He is requiring every one of these churches to make specific decisions that will impact their relationship to Him and their relationship to the world around them. If they do not make the required decisions and take the required actions, Jesus spells out to them the potential repercussions they will experience as a result (their lampstand will be removed from its place in His presence).

This is why I want to emphasize the point, again, that we as leaders cannot keep Jesus out of our decision-making process by purposely ignoring, dismissing, and setting aside direct commands and requirements that He has placed upon us. If we do, we can expect there to be repercussions. Jesus tells us if we do not heed His word and His will, He will remove our lampstand from its place in His presence. No CEO or Owner would ever consider letting his/her direct orders and requirements be summarily dismissed or ignored within the company he/she runs. Therefore, do we honestly think Jesus will sit idly by and do nothing while we ignore Him, implementing our own decisions and plans with little regard for what He may want us to do, or setting aside what He has plainly established within His Body, the Church, from the very beginning of her existence?

He has so much in store for us but we are the ones who are hindering His blessing. We are the roadblock to our own success. We must recognize and accept the fact that true success, in the eyes of God, comes through obedience to Jesus and what He has and continues to tell us He wants us to do on His behalf. This includes our faithfully appropriating the gifts, resources and abilities He has provided for us since the day of Pentecost, and continues to provide for us so we can accomplish what He has placed us here to do.

Needless to say, this obedience isn't always easy and often comes with a price, which includes difficulty, inconvenience, and trouble. Yet, the result of our success is the completion of Ephesians 4:11-16. What God is asking us to do as leaders in the local church and other ministries is no different than what an owner expects from those he places in charge of his business assets and resources while he is away.

As Jesus' delegated and representative leaders in the Church, we are to watch over the flock of God, the Body of Christ, on the earth. There will be difficulty, inconvenience, and trouble when we endeavor to raise immature children in such a way as to bring them to spiritual maturity and adulthood. Yet, once they are mature adults and able to care and provide for themselves and their own families, those difficulties, inconveniences, and troubles don't seem as inconvenient and overwhelming anymore. As Jesus' representative leaders, the level of success and accomplishment we will enjoy as a result of pursuing, introducing, and integrating the prophetic activity of the Kingdom of God into our churches and ministries will far surpass the difficulties and inconveniences we will experience along the way.

He Who Has An Ear, Let Him Hear

This scripture in Revelation 2:29, by its very message, declares that the Church of Jesus Christ, God's Kingdom people, is a prophetic people. *"He who has an ear, let him hear what the Spirit says to the churches."* We must hear what His Spirit is saying. It is His prophetic people, the Church, who are instructed to exercise their prophetic capabilities, to hear what the Spirit of Jesus is saying to them. He expects us to hear with our prophetic ears and see with our prophetic eyes. Otherwise, why would He have given us this command? God is continually speaking to His people concerning the activities of His Kingdom. We just need to exercise our spiritual "senses" in order to "tune in" to what He's saying and doing. Let me illustrate what I mean.

In the world around us, communication is taking place all of the time. Communication waves are transmitted continuously in order to carry the content of the communication to its desired destination. This communication can contain audio, visual, data or all three types of content, simultaneously. Yet, in order to receive this communication and to enjoy the benefit of the content, we must have the necessary type of communication receiver. Without having the proper receiver in our possession, having it powered on, and understanding how to operate the receiver effectively, this communication continues to take place all around us but we are oblivious to it and cannot enjoy the benefits of the communication's content.

We are all prophetic people. The spiritual, prophetic activity of the Kingdom of God is taking place all around us. God is zealously acting and passionately speaking all of the time. Angelic activity is taking place all around us as God works to move His Kingdom forward on the earth through His prophetic people. If we are believers and followers of Jesus and have been born again by His Spirit, we each have the Holy Spirit living inside of us in order to help us get "tuned in" to and receive from God and His Kingdom's activities. God has spiritual communication and activity that He sends specifically to us and for us, and we need to be able to receive and act on that activity. But, we must have our spiritual receivers turned on and tuned in to God's frequency, if we are going to know what He's doing and hear what He's saying.

The writer of Hebrews tells us about Jesus, *"In the days of His flesh, He offered up both prayers and supplications with loud crying and tears to the One able to save Him from death, and He was heard because of His piety. Although He was a Son,* ***He***

learned obedience *from the things which He suffered. And* ***having been made complete,*** *He became to all those who obey Him the source of eternal salvation."* [293] Even for Jesus, it was **a process** to learn obedience. It was **a process** to grow in wisdom and favor with God and people. It was **a process** to be made complete (mature), as He learned obedience through the things which He suffered. Living prophetically as a child of God takes time. It is counter-culture. It is **a process**. *"For the gate is small and the way is narrow that leads to life, and there are few who find it."* [294]

We all have the Kingdom of God "Receiver" living on the inside of us – the Holy Spirit. He was given to each of us as a free gift. He will guide us into all truth; He will show us things to come. [295] We have to realize that we already have Him residing inside of us, learn how to hear what He is saying and see what He is doing, and learn to cooperate with Him so we can respond when the Kingdom of God places its demands upon us. God wants to use each of us to engage with and impact those around us. Let those of us with spiritual ears hear what the Spirit is saying to us.

[293] Heb. 5:7-9 (emphasis mine)
[294] Matt. 7:14
[295] John 16:13

Chapter Questions & Notes

Talk It Over....

1) In 1Corinthians 6:20, Paul tells us that, as faithful followers of Jesus, we are no longer our own; we have been bought with a price. This is true individually and corporately. Even though God has given us, each, a free will and the capacity for self-determination, we were originally created to reflect His glory and find our complete fulfillment and satisfaction in Him. When God redeemed us from sin and death, we became His prized possession once again. Reflecting God's glory and finding our complete fulfillment and satisfaction in Him became the willing desire and purpose for our lives, once again. Whether it is as a representative leader placed within His Church to shepherd His flock, or as an individual child of God and representative of His Kingdom here on the earth, we belong to God and He has ownership rights and privileges over our lives.

   Discuss what this means and how it applies to how we conduct our lives as individuals and our ministries as leaders (or potential leaders) within His Church. After reflecting on this, do you see a need for change? What are these changes?

2) Being prophetic Kingdom people, as a result of the Holy Spirit living within us and being actively involved in our lives, it is our responsibility to embrace and engage in the prophetic preparation and training activities that the Holy Spirit desires to conduct in our lives. Yet, as free will beings, we choose whether we are going to embrace and participate in these prophetic training activities, or not. What are the ramifications of these decisions? What are our prospects, should we choose to participate in these spiritual

activities? What are our prospects, should we choose not to participate?

Leaders: Facilitate the group conversation in order to encourage all group members to actively participate in and contribute to the discussion. This is a very important topic that requires periodic personal assessment throughout our lives so we can consistently place ourselves in a position to spiritually grow, mature and increase our capacity and ability to engage with the Holy Spirit in the prophetic activities of the Kingdom of God. Facilitate the discussion and encourage each member to engage in this assessment process so they can keep moving forward in their prophetic relationship and activities with the Holy Spirit.

(6)

Kingdom Leadership Is Shared Leadership

"Therefore it says, "When He ascended on high, He led captive a host of captives, And He gave gifts to men…And He gave some as apostles, and some as prophets, and some as evangelists, and some as pastors and teachers, for the equipping of the saints for the work of service, to the building up of the body of Christ; until we all attain to the unity of the faith, and of the knowledge of the Son of God, to a mature man, to the measure of the stature which belongs to the fullness of Christ." Ephesians 4:8-13

From the beginning of creation, we see that God's Kingdom leadership is a shared or plurality of leadership. When God created humanity and placed them in the garden, the scriptures tell us, "*Then God said, "Let* ***Us*** *make man in* ***Our*** *image, according to* ***Our*** *likeness."* [296] God is one God in three persons. He is not three gods working together. God is one God and He does all things after the counsel of His will. [297] He lives in unity, harmony, and humility together - preferring one another. [298] When He acts, He acts as one and when He speaks, He speaks as one. [299]

God has one agenda - to expand, enjoy and share His Kingdom with those He has created. As a result, the Father does not have a different agenda from the Son, nor does the Son have a different agenda from the Spirit. The Son is not selfish so as to demand His way above the Father, nor is the Spirit selfish so as to demand His way above the Son. God's vision and purpose is shared and established, having determined the necessary plans and tactics after the council of His will. God lives, works and makes decisions in unity or as a complete unit.[300] God is not fractured, divided or in disarray. His DNA, His nature, character and attributes permeate His Kingdom, and His creation was made to function at peak performance only as it allows Him to transform and rule within it. Paul spoke the truth when he said to the Greek philosophers in Athens, "*…for it is in Him that we live and move and exist."* [301]

---

[296] Genesis 1:26a (emphasis mine)
[297] Ephesians 1:11
[298] Hebrew 1:8-9; Luke 12:10; John 16:13-14; John 6:38
[299] Genesis 1:26a
[300] John 17:21-22

God's leadership is based upon His nature, character and attributes. Therefore, He is the leadership model for all of us who are His bond-servants and whose hearts are being transformed by His Spirit. We are to display the same godly nature and character qualities in our lives as we co-labor with Him in His Kingdom activities here on the earth.

Those who do not know Christ and have not received His Kingdom into their hearts are unable to effectively comprehend or sincerely demonstrate the leadership qualities of God and His Kingdom. They cannot truly comprehend Kingdom leadership since it must be spiritually evaluated,[302] and they cannot practice Kingdom leadership, from the heart, because their lives are not ruled by the character of the King. [303] They may try to practice Kingdom leadership principles but they will ultimately fail because the character of Christ does not rule them and their hearts are not being transformed by the Spirit of God. Their efforts to practice Kingdom leadership will be mechanical and "unnatural" since their hearts do not possess the Kingdom, which gives life and sincerity to their leadership.

Kingdom leadership, to be effective toward others, must first begin in our own hearts. Just as God rules Himself and His own activities through the nature and character qualities that reside within Him, we as individuals must allow the nature and character of God within us, through the Holy Spirit, to rule our hearts, thoughts and activities. This doesn't happen immediately when we are born again. The Holy Spirit removes the "DNA" or nature of sin and darkness from our spirit and infuses us with the "DNA" or nature of God. This "DNA" of God, empowered by the Holy Spirit, begins to re-orient our spirit, mind, emotions, affections, will, and body to that of the Kingdom of God. This process of conversion transforms our very thoughts, words and motivations. The nature of God is imparted to us – giving Kingdom life to our whole being. [304]

As a result of this transforming work of the Spirit, the Kingdom of God steadily increases its rule and leadership in our lives. This Kingdom activity begins to work itself out in our daily lives in very practical ways. The sinful and evil addictions and habits we are enslaved to begin to grow weaker and weaker in our lives. These addictions and habits are replaced by the addictions and habits of the Kingdom – as we talk to and share our lives with God, finding out more about Him through His word, spending time

---

[301] Acts 17:27-29
[302] 1Corinthians 2:13-15
[303] John 8:43-45; Romans 8:5-9
[304] Hebrews 4:12

talking about God with other believers, and telling others the Good News that the Kingdom of God is here to change their lives and bring them into a relationship with God that will last forever.

Yet, this transforming work doesn't stop with us as individuals. It spills out of us and into other areas of our lives, including our families, neighborhoods, communities, and culture. The Kingdom of God within each of us actually begins to engage the people and environment around us, impacting and transforming them through the Kingdom leadership working in us and being displayed through us. [305] This is how Kingdom leadership works. As the Kingdom leads each of us and we respond to its leading, this transforming activity flows from us and begins to engage, transform and lead those around us. It is a natural outflow of the life and Kingdom of God within each of us. It is not a program, method, or formula. It is organic…it is life.

God's Kingdom Leadership Serves

As we saw, previously; God is the supreme-being in the universe and, yet, He is a servant. He is a servant because He possesses a servant's heart. The motivation of His heart is to serve. He does not serve as a form of manipulation in order to get what He wants. He serves as an extension of His character, and all of His plans and purposes are established with this godly characteristic of service as a foundation. Even in His leadership, He leads through serving. Because God is also just and righteous, He does not command us to do something He Himself does not do. Paul tells us to be perfect (complete, mature) even as our heavenly Father is perfect (complete, mature).[306] If an aspect of God's completeness (maturity) is that He is a servant, then we must also be a servant if we are to truly be complete (mature). We have no choice.

Jesus came to reveal and demonstrate to us the nature and character of God.[307] He was the exact representation of God's nature and character.[308] When Jesus came to earth as a man, He laid aside His divine attributes and became a bond-servant – to serve His Father and humanity.[309] He told us that He did not come to be served but to serve.[310] As He instructed, trained and

[305] 2Corinthians 2:14-16
[306] Matthew 5:48
[307] John 14:9
[308] Hebrews 1:3a
[309] Philippians 2:7
[310] Matthew 20:27-28

mentored the disciples, Jesus commanded them to be servants as He was a servant.[311]

As the Holy Spirit lives within our hearts to deposit within us the Kingdom or active rule of God, He also empowers or enables the nature and character of God within us. One of these godly characteristics He empowers or energizes within us is the characteristic of a servant. Yet, the Holy Spirit doesn't simply enable this characteristic of a servant within us and then expect us to go out there and do it all ourselves. He actually leads us in the practical application of this and the other characteristics of God in our daily lives. He leads us, not by standing at a distance in order to dictate to us and watch to see how well we do. He leads us by coming along side of us, as a servant, to help us. In fact, when Jesus told us that the Holy Spirit would come after He left earth to return to heaven, He told us that the Holy Spirit, *The Helper* would come.[312] The Greek word translated *Helper* in these verses is *Parakletos*, which means; *"…summoned, called to one's side, called to one's aid; in the widest sense, a helper, succorer, aider, assistant."*[313]

The Holy Spirit, God Himself, the presence and power of the Kingdom of God in this age, operates in the ministry of a servant. The amazing thing is that He is here to serve you and me – to help us as we endeavor to become conformed to the image of Christ and to demonstrate the nature and character of God and His Kingdom to this world. He doesn't stand far away to see how we do. He comes alongside of us (dwells within us) to help us and to accomplish God's eternal purpose within us. This is the servant-heart of God. This is the leadership style of God on display for the whole world and all of creation to see and witness.

God leads us by "coming alongside" of us to serve and help us. He helps us in many ways. He guides us.[314] He instructs us.[315] He communicates with us.[316] He counsels us.[317] He reveals Himself to us.[318] He imparts His Kingdom resources to us.[319] He watches over us to protect us.[320] He does none of these things from a distance – disengaged from us and our lives. He does them while completely engaged with us; right next to us; within us. All we have to do is realize the reality of it, believe it, seek Him and submit

---

[311] Matthew 20:25-27; Galatians 5:13-14; John 20:21
[312] John 14:26; John 15:26; John 16:7
[313] The NAS New Testament Greek Lexicon – Crosswalk.com
[314] Isaiah 30:21
[315] John 14:26
[316] John 16:13
[317] Psalm 32:8
[318] John 16:14-15
[319] 1Corinthians 12:4-7
[320] Isaiah 49:15-17

our lives to His will and purposes, and make the necessary decisions each day that allow Him to transform our lives and accomplish His purposes in and through us. Without faith it is impossible to please Him because those who come to God must believe that He is and that He is a rewarder of those who diligently seek Him.[321] Now that we have seen that God's leadership style is one of coming alongside of and serving those He leads, let's take a look at several instances where God came alongside of others to lead, serve and help them.

In Genesis, God created humanity and placed them in the Garden to rule over it and keep it. God created humanity with a tremendous intellect, as well as a spirit completely alive to God and the Kingdom of God. Humanity was capable of experiencing and enjoying the manifest presence of God, completely. Yet, even though God created humanity with these innate spiritual and natural abilities, He still considered it necessary to come alongside of humanity in the Garden in order to instruct and mentor them in the application of Kingdom leadership and rule, and to support humanity as they applied what they were learning.

In Genesis 2, God created the animals and birds and brought them to Adam to see what he would name them. [322] This is a unique action by God because it shows that He was serious about Adam exercising Kingdom rule in the Garden – to the extent that God, Himself, submitted the naming of His own creations to the authority He had delegated to Adam. Instead of God naming each one and then telling Adam their names, God came alongside of Adam, allowing His Kingdom regent and co-laborer to exercise his delegated authority to name each one of them. God is so secure in Himself that He not only delegated Kingdom authority to Adam over the Garden, but He also submitted His own naming rights and privileges, as Creator and King, to Adam's authority.

Adam was learning how to rule effectively through the exercise of God's servant leadership. God came alongside of Adam to mentor him in Kingdom rule and authority. After God placed Adam in the Garden, anything that took place in the Garden He submitted it to Adam so he could exercise his delegated Kingdom rule and authority. God did not usurp Adam and his responsibility; He supported and empowered him.

When God saw that His friend, co-laborer and Kingdom regent did not have a suitable companion, He served the needs of Adam by creating Eve. Again, instead of creating and naming her before He brought her to Adam,

---

[321] Hebrews 11:6
[322] Genesis 2:19-20

He brought her to Adam and submitted the naming rights to him - to see what he would name her. God displayed His servant leadership style to Adam so Adam could learn, experience, and instruct others in this servant leadership. Let's take a look at another example of God's servant leadership; this time involving Adam's son, Cain.

In Genesis 4, Cain and his brother Abel each made a sacrifice to the Lord – Cain made a sacrifice of what he had grown from the ground and Abel brought a sacrifice of one of the firstlings from his flock. [323] The Lord accepted Abel's sacrifice but He rejected Cain's sacrifice. The scripture account does not specifically tell us why God accepted one sacrifice and not the other but we know enough about God that it most likely had to do with the type of sacrifice God expected from Adam and his seed (an animal sacrifice as a sin offering), or the attitude of Cain's heart was not acceptable to God when he offered his sacrifice. Regardless of the reason, we know God's judgment is righteous and that there was ample reason why God rejected Cain's sacrifice.

The scripture goes on to tell us that Cain became angry because God rejected his sacrifice. We then see that God came alongside of Cain in order to help Him by instructing him in the dynamics of sin and its results. God asked Cain why he was angry. Cain must have understood why his sacrifice was rejected and that he had no one to blame for it but himself. Yet, God encouraged Cain by telling him that if he repents and changes the attitude of his heart, he will escape from the temptation to sin.[324] If Cain does not change his heart-attitude, then "sin is crouching at the door" and the temptation will lead to the development of evil intentions – giving birth to the sinful act.[325]

God displayed His Kingdom leadership and love for Cain by taking the initiative to come alongside of Cain; to serve him and instruct him in how to overcome the temptation that he was confronted with. God, both, exposed the attitude of his heart and encouraged Cain to make the right decision, by submitting to God, so he could overcome the temptation. Even though God showed servant leadership toward Cain, God could not make the necessary decisions to deliver Cain from his temptations. Cain, only, could make those critical decisions, yet God had given him the way of escape.

This example instructs us about the nature and character of God, and His respect for man's free will that He has given each of us. God will come

---

[323] Genesis 4:1-8
[324] 1Corinthians 10:13
[325] James 1:14-16

alongside of us in order to instruct us, encourage us, and provide us with the way of escape from sin and temptation.[326] But He will not make the decision for us or force us to make the correct decision against our wills. Kingdom leadership will take the initiative to come alongside to help and serve but it will not and cannot do the other person's job for them.

We must each exercise our own wills to submit to God, His Lordship and His reign in our lives – He will not force it on anyone. When we submit to Him and allow His servant leadership to guide and mentor us, we will see His nature and character being developed in our lives. We will become more like Him and we can, then, exercise the same servant leadership toward others, as God brings them into our sphere of influence. True servant leadership is secure and at peace with itself, and is able to freely focus on the growth and success of those they lead. Let's look at one more example of God's servant leadership; this time in the life of Jesus.

Jesus was the exact representation of the Father's nature and character when He was on earth.[327] When we see Him, we see the Father.[328] In the Old Testament we see prophecies that tell us much about the activities, character, and life of the coming Messiah. One of these prophecies predicts that the coming Messiah would be betrayed by one of His close friends.[329] As we read through the gospels, we see references made of the disciple of Jesus named Judas. Judas is one of the twelve who Jesus called to be his closest followers and friends. And just as we see with all of the twelve Jesus had chosen, Judas has his own character flaws. In his case, it was in the area of greed. Yet, when Jesus gave the twelve their various ministry responsibilities within the group, Jesus gave Judas the responsibility of managing the ministry purse. In other words, Judas was put in charge of the ministry bank account.[330]

If we look at the other disciples who made up the twelve, there were several others who were probably more qualified to manage the ministry funds. Matthew was a tax collector who knew how to squeeze the most out of every cent. Peter, James and John were fishermen and knew how to manage a business and its finances. Yet, Jesus chose a religious zealot who had a problem with greed to manage the ministry finances. Most of us would consider this to be a serious lapse in judgment and contrary to sound Biblical financial principles. Regardless of these seemingly glaring

---

[326] 1Corinthians 10:13
[327] Hebrews 1:3
[328] John 14:9
[329] Psalm 41:9; John 13:18; Mark 14:18-20
[330] John 12:4-6

inconsistencies, we know that Jesus is the exact representation of God's nature and character and that when we see Jesus, we see the Father.

We also know that Jesus only did what He saw the Father doing and only said what He heard the Father saying.[331] Did Jesus miss or ignore the will of God and, therefore, sin by putting Judas in charge of the ministry purse? Was Jesus totally oblivious to the fact that Judas was pilfering from the ministry? Was Judas predestined by God to betray Jesus and, therefore, Jesus totally wasted His time, effort and the ministry funds that were pilfered – making Jesus a fool for putting Judas in charge? The answer to these questions is an emphatic "NO". Therefore, the Father had a purpose for having Jesus put Judas in charge of the ministry funds, even though it SEEMS to fly in the face of all scriptural wisdom and prudence.

There are two more scriptures that I believe are also relevant to this example of servant leadership, in the case of Judas. The first scripture says, *"First of all, then, I urge that entreaties and prayers, petitions and thanksgivings, be made on behalf of all men…This is good and acceptable in the sight of God our Savior, who desires all men to be saved and to come to the knowledge of the truth."*[332] The second verse says, *"For all who are being led by the Spirit of God, these are sons of God."*[333] Even though God, in His foreknowledge, knew that Judas would be the one to betray Jesus, He still loved him and wanted to give Judas every opportunity to overcome his greed. As an example of God's nature and character toward all humanity, Jesus came alongside of Judas during their 3 ½ years together in order to: 1) serve him, in an effort to instruct Judas in the truth; 2) model the correct way to overcome temptation and to live a life before God; and 3) encourage Judas to repent of His greedy heart-attitude, submit to God's truth regarding personal needs and finances, and resist the temptation that would give rise to sin and the intent to make unwise decisions to satisfy his greed.

Just as God did in the case of Cain, Jesus came alongside of Judas to serve him and lead him into what God had for him. Yet, Judas was responsible for dealing with the temptations that confronted him. Regardless of what some say, that Jesus put Judas in charge of the ministry purse in order to "give him enough rope to hang himself", that is not the case because that is not the nature and character of God. When temptation comes (and it will come because we have an enemy who hates us), God will always give us the way of escape if we submit to Him and look for the escape.

---

[331] John 5:19; John 12:49-50
[332] 1Timothy 2:1-4
[333] Romans 8:14

As a religious zealot that Jesus had called to follow Him, Judas most likely hardened his heart toward Jesus when he realized that Jesus was not going to be the one to physically establish the Kingdom of God in Jerusalem and deliver Israel from the power of Rome. As a result, he allowed his disappointment in Jesus to lead him down the path to get back into his former lifestyle and the greed that controlled him. Judas knew the Jewish leaders didn't like Jesus and were looking for a way to discredit and silence Him, so he may have seen this as an opportunity to make some money at Jesus' expense.

Regardless of what the exact motives were, Judas allowed greed to take hold of him in such a way that he was willing to betray one of his best friends in order to acquire some money. As a result, he willingly betrayed Jesus, as God had foreseen, and fulfilled the prophecy God had spoken as a proof-point that Jesus was truly the Messiah who was to come. Sometimes, being a servant leader means being taken advantage of and hurt. But as Jesus did, we must love those who hurt and betray us because God loves us, who hurt and betray Him.

As children of God, we have the nature and character of God dwelling within us. This includes the character quality of a servant. We are to lead through service to others as God leads through service to others. We are to come alongside of others and lead them into a relationship with God and into the activities of God, by serving and encouraging them and being a model of the nature and character of God. We cannot make their decisions for them but we can encourage them to make the right decisions for God, if they are willing to submit to God and resist those things that desire to hinder and hurt them. We are bond-servants of God and as such, we are free to serve others in order to bring them into a greater experience with God and His Kingdom.

As sons of God, we are to be led by the Spirit of God because God desires all people to be saved and to come to the knowledge of the truth. God is concerned about the hearts of all people and will go to great lengths to reach them with the truth of His word. Since God knows every heart and what needs to be done in order to draw each person to Himself, we must find out what God wants us to do with each person we lead so we are effective in allowing the Spirit of God to minister to their hearts and bring them to the saving knowledge of Jesus Christ. That is God's style of leadership. That is Kingdom leadership.

Chapter Questions & Notes

Talk It Over….

1) The Holy Spirit is called "the Comforter", "the One who comes alongside to help" those who are followers of Jesus. This implies that *relationship* and *community* are involved in His training, instructing and mentoring activities. The Holy Spirit is directly engaged in these activities in each of our lives and He works through those around us to conduct these same activities, through relationships within the context of community. What affect can these activities have upon us, our community relationships, and the Kingdom activities we engage in throughout our lives?

2) We see that God gives each of us a free will. God desires that we all mature in our faith and in our relationship with Him so He can instruct, guide, train and mentor us effectively, and so we can enjoy a vital, active and growing interaction with Him. We must freely choose to engage with Him and to respond to Him when He comes alongside of us, directly, or through others He places in our lives. What kind of response does this require of us? What character qualities does this require of us? What results should we expect to see as a result of these activities in our lives?

Leader: Share with the group, examples from your own life where God came alongside of you, personally or through others He sent into your life, in order to engage you in a particular Kingdom activity or to work a particular character quality into your life. Describe what was involved with this "engagement", the nature of the engagement, what you were asked to do, what your attitude was when you were confronted with this request, how you responded to the request, and what the result was. What did you learn, about God and about yourself? What would you have done differently? How did it change your relationship with the Lord and with the community of believers you were engaged with, at the time? Has it affected how you live your life now?

(7)

Preparing The People Of God For Kingdom Living

"And He gave some as apostles, and some as prophets, and some as evangelists, and some as pastors and teachers, for the equipping of the saints for the work of service, to the building up of the body of Christ" Ephesians 4:7-13

The ministry of Jesus on the earth was a course in Kingdom discipleship, leadership, and service. His ministry is the example for all followers of Jesus, especially for the Ascension gifts of Jesus listed by Paul in Ephesians 4. Jesus was focused on training and preparing people to live Kingdom lives and to carry out the Kingdom activities that God desires and intends for each of us. This was the main focus of Jesus, outside of His death, burial, and resurrection.

He spent His time preparing His followers to carry out the activities of the Kingdom, once His time on earth was completed. This is the main focus of the Ascension gifts of Christ – to prepare individuals and families of believers, as Jesus did, to carry out the activities of the Kingdom on the earth, from generation to generation, until Jesus returns to establish the fullness of His Kingdom on the earth.

Jesus was THE apostle, prophet, evangelist, pastor, and teacher. He was the fullness and embodiment of all of these ministries in one package. He is our example to follow. As the Father sent Jesus, Jesus has sent us. His focus was on instructing, discipling, mentoring, and preparing individuals and families to carry out the Kingdom work. This is what we are to do, as His Kingdom representatives. It's not about us as leaders, it's about the individuals and families we are to serve and prepare.

This is why we must understand our place as Kingdom representatives who are here strictly to represent the desires and intentions of Another, and not as individuals who are out to fulfill our personal dreams, pursue our desired lifestyle, and to carve out our ministry "niche". The true mission and purpose of the ascension gifts of Christ is to serve and prepare the Body of

Christ for Kingdom service and representation. These gifts encompass more than the ministries of the Pastor, Teacher and Evangelist.

There are more than three ministry gifts that were given by Jesus, that are necessary and relevant to the Church today, especially the local church. Jesus gave us all five ministries and we need all five ministries active and functioning effectively if the Church is to be successful and accomplish all that Jesus wants us to do. The Apostle and Prophet must be embraced, active and functioning in the local church, as well, if we are to fulfill all that Jesus wants and expects from us.

To understand the purpose and place of the Prophet in the New Testament and in the local church, we must go to the place in Scripture where his/her role and function is identified and explained. This is done for us by the Apostle Paul in Ephesians 4:7-13. In this scripture, Paul tells us that after Jesus had put the New Covenant into effect, He ascended into heaven to be seated at the right hand of the Father. It was after His ascension that Jesus gave specific servant leadership gifts to the Body of Christ.[334] These ascension gifts are the Apostle, Prophet, Evangelist, Pastor, and Teacher. All five of these gifts were given: 1) for the equipping of the saints for the work of service, 2) to the building up of the body of Christ, 3) until we all attain to the unity of the faith, and of the knowledge of the Son of God, to a mature man, to the measure of the stature which belongs to the fullness of Christ.

We could say it another way. If the saints are not fully equipped for the work of service, and the Body of Christ has not attained to the unity of the faith and the knowledge of the Son of God, if it has not grown up into a mature man, to the measure of the spiritual stature that belongs to the fullness of Christ, then all five of these leadership ministries should still be present, relevant, vital, and active within the Body of Christ, and specifically the local church.

The question is, then, "If the Church has not attained to the measure of the stature that belongs to the fullness of Christ, then where is the Prophet? Where is the Apostle?" If we go to any local church, we will most likely find at least one Pastor and probably a Teacher. We have Evangelists in the field (even though you won't find many located and functioning within the local church). Many believers identify the missionary as the modern form of the Apostle but is it the Apostle Christ gave as a gift to the Church? Is the culture of the Kingdom of God effectively being planted and established within the local church as Jesus desires and instructed?

[334] Ephesians 4:7-8

There are few of us who can honestly say we have met or heard a New Testament Prophet, much less have one located and functioning on a regular basis within our local church. Paul tells us that all five of these leadership gifts are to be located, functioning, and equipping the saints within the local church, if the Body of Christ is to attain to its mature spiritual stature and fulfill the mission for which Christ has placed her here.

Another question that now arises is, "If the NT Prophet is to be present and active in the Church today, should we expect the NT Prophet to function in the same way as the Prophet in the OT? Do the same rules apply and are the OT and NT Prophets responsible in the same way before God for their ministries?" If we look closely at Ephesians 4, we will see something very important.

The servant leadership gifts Christ gave to the Church in the NT, after His ascension, were new gifts in their purpose, scope and function. They had not existed before, as Christ was now giving them to the Church, as a gift. They were commissioned to function within a new paradigm called the New Covenant Kingdom of God and within a new environment known as the redeemed community of Jesus Christ, the Church. Therefore, we cannot and should not assume that the NT Prophet will necessarily have the same function, responsibility, and operate by the same guidelines as the OT Prophet.

With this in mind, we must ask ourselves, "Do we see an example of the ascension leadership gift of the Prophet in the NT? The answer is "yes", and his name is Agabus. In the book of Acts, we are told some prophets, including Agabus, came from Jerusalem to Antioch where Paul and Barnabas were ministering in the church. Once there, Agabus stood up and prophesied that there would be a great famine all over the world. This prophecy was fulfilled years later during the reign of Claudius.[335]

As a result of reading this scripture, we see that one aspect of the NT Prophet's ministry is the aspect of foretelling the future, as enabled by the Holy Spirit, in regard to God's plans and purposes. It is not the only aspect nor the most important aspect of the Prophet's ministry but it is one aspect of this ministry. As I mentioned earlier, the Prophet's most important aspect of ministry is to instruct, equip and train the followers of Jesus in the prophetic nature and activities of the Kingdom of God so believers can successfully accomplish the work of ministry, and to be built up and encouraged as vital members of the Body of Christ. The servant leadership

[335] Acts 11:27-28

and ministry of the Prophet is just one aspect of the prophetic activity of God's Kingdom on the earth today.

There is another scripture relating to the Prophet Agabus, in the book of Acts.[336] Here, Paul is in Caesarea, in the house of Philip the Evangelist. Agabus came down from Judea and seeing Paul, he took Paul's belt and bound his own feet and hands, and said, "This is what the Holy Spirit says: 'In this way the Jews at Jerusalem will bind the man who owns this belt and deliver him into the hands of the Gentiles.'" [337] In this instance Agabus is, again, foretelling by the Holy Spirit, what will take place in the future but this time it is in reference to Paul's ministry activities.

What is unique about this prophecy from Agabus compared to the first prophecy mentioned earlier is that this second prophecy did not take place exactly as Agabus had prophesied it. Here Agabus says the Jews in Jerusalem will bind Paul and deliver him into the hands of the Gentiles. If we look at Acts 21:27-36 we will see the incident about which Agabus prophesied, play itself out. In this scripture we don't see the Jews at Jerusalem bind Paul and deliver him into the hands of the Romans. Instead we see the Romans bind Paul with two chains and carry him away in order to deliver him from the hands of the Jews, who were intending to kill him.

In essence what we have here is Agabus, a recognized and respected NT Prophet from the church in Jerusalem, who had established a credible prophetic ministry and reputation throughout the churches in that area, delivering a prophecy to Paul at Caesarea that was not completely accurate. As a result of this partially inaccurate prophecy, was Agabus to be declared a false prophet and stoned to death by the leaders of the Jerusalem church, according to Deut. 18:20? Was he prophesying presumptuously in the Lord's name, which was the reason why false prophets under the Old Covenant were to be stoned? Agabus' prophecy was not completely false, yet it was not entirely correct.

I do not believe Agabus was stoned or removed from the Church as a false prophet as a result of this inaccurate prophecy. The reason for this is given to us by Paul in 1Cor. 14:29 which says, "And let two or three prophets speak, and let the others pass judgment." Here we see a major difference between the OT prophet and the NT prophet. In the OT, if a prophet was found to be wrong, by speaking presumptuously in the Lord's name, he was to be immediately stoned.

---

[336] Acts 21:8-12
[337] Acts 21:11

But, here in the NT, not only is it possible for the prophet to be partially or completely wrong but the other prophets in the local church are to evaluate the prophecy so the church can benefit from it if it is correct, or they can dismiss it if it is incorrect. In 1Thessalonians 5:19-21, Paul again exhorts us regarding the exercise of the prophetic gifts within the local church, "Do not quench the Spirit; do not despise prophetic utterances but examine everything carefully; hold fast to that which is good."

The reason the NT Prophet functions differently and is not held responsible before God in the same way as the OT Prophet is because God has placed the NT Prophet within a different spiritual and ministry paradigm in the NT. The NT Prophet is called, first, as an equipping leadership ministry within the local church and is to function within a team ministry structure with, and held accountable by, the Apostle, Evangelist, Pastor and Teacher. The NT Prophet is not a "lone ranger" as the OT Prophet was. Foretelling future events is only a small part of the ministry of the NT Prophet.

The Prophet is also to: 1) forth-tell the mind and heart of God in such a way as to call God's people to a course of action, based on what God has revealed regarding the current purpose and plans of His Kingdom, and 2) to assist in the spiritual instruction, training and mentoring of believers, specifically in the area of the prophetic nature and activities of the Kingdom of God, both, with individuals and the local church, corporately. Yet, all prophecy is to be evaluated and judged within the environment of team ministry.

Each individual believer in the NT possesses the Spirit of God within him or her, unlike the children of Israel in the OT, and is therefore to be led by the Spirit of God as sons of God.[338] They do not need to go to the NT Prophet to "inquire of the Lord" regarding God's direction for their life, as people did with the prophets in the OT. The NT Prophet is to assist in the equipping and training of believers in such a way that the individual believer is able to know and understand the scriptural ways in which God speaks to His people, and how to hear the voice of God and to follow Him in His plan for their lives.

The NT Prophet operates, grows, and matures within his or her ministry in the same way the other ascension leadership gifts and all NT believers do; by grace through faith.[339] Just as the NT Pastor, Teacher, Apostle and Evangelist grow and mature in their ministries, by grace through faith, so the NT Prophet grows and matures in his or her ministry, in the same way.

---

[338] Romans 8:14
[339] Romans 4:16

The main purpose of the NT Prophet, just as it is for the Apostle, Evangelist, Pastor and Teacher, is to equip, train, and build-up the Body of Christ, and they are to do so within the context of the local church. If the NT Prophet is not recognized, embraced, and allowed to function within the local church as Christ has ordained, the individual believers within the local church will not receive the necessary prophetic instruction, training and equipping Jesus intends. The ministry of the NT Prophet is just as important within the local church as that of the Pastor and Teacher. In fact, the Pastor and Teacher will not receive the necessary prophetic instruction and training in their own lives and ministries because, as individual members of the Body of Christ, first, and Ascension gifts, second, they are personally missing out on the equipping ministry of the Prophet.

Now, regarding the gifts (manifestations) of the Holy Spirit, including prophecy; it is necessary to understand their place in the life of the local church as well as the individual believer, today. Paul tells us in 1Cor. 13:9-12, that now, *"…we know in part, and we prophesy in part; but when the perfect comes, the partial will be done away."* The spiritual gift or manifestation of prophecy, just like all of the spiritual gifts given to the Church by the Holy Spirit, is incomplete and temporary. These gifts are not intended to provide us with everything there is to know about God and all that He is doing now or is going to do in the future.

These gifts are intended to provide us with the necessary "glimpses" of God, His plans and purposes, that we need in order to have hope, to walk by faith, and to possess the necessary "abilities" to accomplish His plans and purposes in this age. Therefore, these spiritual manifestations are only given, and only needed, until "the perfect (complete) comes"[340]. It is all or nothing. The Scriptures do not tell us that the Holy Spirit will take some gifts away and leave the rest, or that we can keep some of the manifestations and put the others aside or ignore them. Either the Spirit removes all of them or He leaves all of them. That is why Paul tells us they are all present with us until the complete comes. Therefore, it is important for us to know what this "perfect" or "complete" is that is to come because it impacts the duration of time the Church can expect to partake of these spiritual manifestations and ministry gifts, including the ministry of the Prophet.

It is not obvious from this scripture in 1Cor. 13:9-12 what the "perfect" is. The Greek word translated "perfect" can also be translated "complete". Therefore, we should first look elsewhere within the letter of 1Corinthians and within the context of Paul's reference to the Corinthian church's

[340] I Corinthians 13:10

exercise of these spiritual gifts, to see if we are able to ascertain what the "perfect" or "complete" is, to which Paul is referring. In 1Corinthians 1, Paul is greeting the Corinthian church and is encouraging them in their walk with the Lord and in their exercise of the spiritual gifts within their church.

One of the exhortations he gives them says, *"...in everything you were enriched in Him, in all speech and all knowledge...so that you are not lacking in any gift,* ***awaiting eagerly the revelation of our Lord Jesus Christ."***[341] Here, Paul encourages them by telling them that they, as a church, do not lack in any spiritual gift or manifestation. He goes on to exhort them to continue in these gifts as they *"wait eagerly for the revelation of our Lord Jesus Christ."* When Paul is speaking of the revelation of our Lord Jesus Christ, he is speaking of the Second Coming of Jesus Christ to the earth at the end of the age.

To gain more insight, let's look further within the context of Paul's teaching on spiritual gifts. In 1Cor. 13:12, Paul goes on to elaborate on the "perfect" or "complete" that is to come, by saying, *"For now we see in a mirror dimly, but then face to face; now I know in part, but then I shall know fully just as I also have been fully known."* We see from this scripture, in regard to the exercise of the spiritual gifts, that Paul and the Corinthians are only able to "see dimly" and "know in part" but then (when the complete manifestation of the Kingdom of God comes) they will see and know fully or completely (the spiritual gifts will no longer be needed) because they will see Him "face to face".

We are part of the same Body of Christ, now, as Paul was in the year 65 A.D., and it is evident that the Body of Christ today is still only able to "see dimly" and "know in part" regarding the current and future plans and purposes of God. Therefore, it is obvious that the "perfect" or "complete" has not yet come.

We also see that the Ascension leadership gifts of the Apostle and Prophet are still present, vital, and foundational elements of the Body of Christ and the local church, in particular. Without these critical ministries functioning properly, the individual believer, the other Ascension leadership gifts, and the Body of Christ as a whole will not fulfill her designed purpose on the earth. We also see that all of the spiritual manifestations of the Holy Spirit, as mentioned in 1Corinthians 12-14, including prophecy, are still present, vital, and critical to the success of the individual believer and the entire Body of Christ, today.

The Prophet must take his/her place as a vital ministry within the local church environment because, as God's prophetic people, the Prophet is our

[341] 1Corinthians 1:5,7 (emphasis mine)

leader when it comes to the prophetic activities of the Kingdom of God. The Prophet is the one who is responsible before God for making sure this spiritual aspect of the church is developed and maintained. Without the Prophet, we will continue to settle into an immature, short-sighted, and intellectual existence, devoid of the Spirit and oblivious to the presence and activities of the Kingdom of God going on around us. Remember, God is not bound to save and deliver, by many or by few. This prophetic training is important and necessary in the overall training Jesus desires for each of us.

The scriptures teach us that God first created Adam, as an individual, and then He put Adam and Eve together as a family. That is the original order of creation and that is the chemistry of the local church, as well. The local church is made up of individuals and families. Jesus knew this when He sent the Ascension leadership gifts to the Church. Therefore, success in ministry for these leadership gifts means individuals and families within the local church are being adequately trained and equipped to live and minister effectively within their individual spheres of influence. It doesn't mean these ministry leadership gifts are to personally train each individual in the church. It does mean that the specific spiritual resources given to these Ascension gifts by God, for their unique equipping responsibility within the Body of Christ, must find their way to each and every believer and family in the local church.

What does this mean, practically? Apostles are to ensure that the proper foundation and culture of the Kingdom of God is established in the life of the local church and each of its members and families. This means parents and individuals are taught and trained in how to establish a proper Kingdom foundation and culture for spiritual growth and maturity, in their own personal lives and within the life of their families. In the same way, Prophets are to ensure that parents and individuals are taught and trained in the prophetic nature of the Kingdom of God, how to live prophetic lives, and how to establish families that are Kingdom focused and prophetic in nature.

The same is expected of Evangelists, who are to ensure that parents and individuals are taught and trained in how to evangelize within their own spheres of influence, and how to establish a family environment that evangelizes those around them. Pastors are to ensure that parents and individuals are taught and trained in how to address their own spiritual nurture and care, and how to effectively nurture and care for their families. Teachers are to ensure that parents and individuals are taught and trained in the word of God and in how to instruct, mentor and train their families in the word of God.

Moses couldn't effectively minister to the spiritual needs of a million people, who were of the children of Israel, until his father-in-law taught him to train, mentor, and delegate these responsibilities to other leaders and elders among the people.[342] There are ways in which the Body can minister to itself, in regard to these Ascension ministry resources, so everyone is receiving the instruction and resources they need to grow and mature. That is the only way Ephesians 4:11-13 will come to pass. The ministry resources of all of these Ascension ministry gifts, including the Prophet and Apostle, must find their necessary place and function within the local church.

Individuals and families are paramount in the mind of God. If they are not successful, the Ascension ministry gifts are not successful. If the individual believers and families in our churches are not living and ministering effectively within their personal spheres of influence, it doesn't matter how big of a ministry or church we have, or how many books we write, or how many conferences we speak at, as Ascension gifts. Jesus Christ wants spiritual maturity in His Body, and He wants it one believer, one family, and one local church at a time. The five Ascension gifts must come together and work together for this to occur and the local church is the place where Christ established this to take place.

[342] Exodus 18

Chapter Questions & Notes

Talk It Over….

1) In Exodus 18, Moses' father-in-law, Jethro, visited Moses and after seeing the daily activities that Moses was engaged in, as the leader of Israel, he suggested to Moses a more effective approach to leading God's people. He suggested to Moses that he share the leadership and oversight duties, over the children of Israel, by assigning other leaders to give oversight to varying groups of people. Some of these leaders gave oversight to larger groups, while other leaders gave oversight to smaller groups, while Moses continued to give general oversight over all of the people.

   With this leadership model in mind, discuss within your group how this model could assist with the instructing, training and mentoring of the followers of Jesus within the local church environment. How do you see this functioning? What would be the benefits of this model? What would be the challenges of this model? How would this model function over the long term and what would be its benefit? Would this assist in the equipping and training of believers in the word of God, in the raising up of future leaders, in the training and mentoring of emerging Ascension gifts within the local church, and in equipping and training believers in the prophetic activities of the Kingdom of God? If so, how?

2) The spiritual gifts or manifestations of the Spirit mentioned by Paul in 1Corinthians 12-14 are supernatural manifestations – they function outside of normal human attributes and capabilities. They require the participation and empowerment of the Holy Spirit to be active and effective in and through a believer's life. Believers must learn to cooperate with the Holy Spirit as He participates with and enables these manifestations in and through the believer's life. How does this activity effectively function within the

leadership and oversight model established by Moses, within the local church environment?

Leader: Read Exodus 18 and 1Corinthians 12-14 before they discuss these two questions, so they understand the context of both scriptures and are able to effectively discuss the questions, applying what they learn from these scriptures. Encourage full participation so the group appreciates a wide perspective and are able to effectively discuss the pros and cons of what the scriptures communicate.

(8)

Taking The Kingdom Of God To Earth's 7 Cultural Kingdoms

"Why are the nations in an uproar and the peoples devising a vain thing? ***The kings of the earth take their stand and the rulers take counsel together*** *against the Lord and against His Anointed, saying, "Let us tear their fetters apart and cast away their cords from us!""* Psalm 2:1-3 (emphasis mine)

*"Then the seventh angel sounded and there were loud voices in heaven, saying, '****The kingdoms of this world*** *have become the kingdom of our Lord and of His Christ; and He will reign forever and ever.'"* Revelation 11:15 (emphasis mine)

In 1975, Bill Bright, founder of *Campus Crusade for Christ*, and Loren Cunningham, founder of *Youth With A Mission* each had an encounter with God and, later, had an encounter with each other that they would never forget. These encounters would impact the entire Body of Christ and set in motion a mandate and a direction for reaching the leaders and peoples of the earth with the Kingdom of God, in all areas of life and culture.

Lance Wallnau, who, later, had a direct conversation with Loren Cunningham about his encounter with Bill Bright, describes their conversation this way:

> *"My first encounter with the revelation of the seven mountains of culture goes back to a conversation I had with Loren Cunningham in the year 2000. Loren is the esteemed founder of Youth With A Mission (YWAM), a global missionary organization with an emphasis on enlisting young people in the call to serve Jesus. He shared how, in 1975, he was praying about how to turn the world around for Jesus and saw seven areas. He said, "I saw that we were to focus on these categories to turn around nations to God. I wrote them down and stuck the paper in my pocket." This was his list:*
>
> 1. *Church*
> 2. *Family*
> 3. *Education*
> 4. *Government and law*
> 5. *Media (television, radio, newspaper, Internet)*

6. *Arts, entertainment, sports*
7. *Commerce, science, and technology*

> *The day after this revelation, he had a divine appointment. As he put it, "I met with a dear brother, Dr. Bill Bright, leader of Campus Crusade for Christ. He shared with me how God had given him a message, and he felt he needed to share it with me. God had identified areas to concentrate on to turn the nations back to Him! They were the same areas with different wording. Bill was stunned when I took the same notes out of my pocket and showed them to him."* [343]

It was later discovered that during this same period of time, Francis Schaeffer, a Presbyterian pastor and founder of the *L'Abri* Christian community in Switzerland, received a similar message of these seven cultural categories.

Three prominent, influential and visionary leaders in the Body of Christ receiving the same message from God at the same point in time…….coincidence? Two of the three men are leaders and visionaries of worldwide youth movements and the other is a leader and visionary of Christian community…….coincidence? I don't think so. God gave these three men a prophetic message with a mandate and direction for the Body of Christ, to proclaim the good news of the Kingdom of God throughout the world, in all the cultural kingdoms of the world, as a witness.

These seven "cultural kingdoms" of this world have existed with us and have been an ever-present reality among us, in one form or another, since the early days of humanity. Their powerful influences have shaped us and their grasp on even the most routine areas of our lives have established them as fundamental to our existence.

Today, the systems associated with some of these kingdoms are so globally and intricately connected, the slightest "glitch" or "hiccup" can affect the livelihoods of millions of people worldwide. The communication capabilities of some of these kingdoms are so sophisticated and responsive, an event taking place in a remote part of the earth can be simultaneously broadcast and viewed by billions of people throughout the world, at that very moment. Other kingdoms can manipulate data and information, which used to take rooms full of equipment to contain and hours to process and transmit, by storing it on microchips and processing and transmitting it in a matter of seconds.

[343] Wallnau, Lance (2013-07-16). Invading Babylon: The 7 Mountain Mandate (pp. 53-54). Destiny Image, Inc.. Kindle Edition

These kingdoms are engrained in our lives and these kingdoms have kings and rulers who preside over them. Yes, there are kings and rulers in the political realm but there are also kings and rulers in the cultural realms. These are the kings and rulers of the kingdoms of this world. These kingdoms were established to serve and promote the existence, growth, and expansion of the human race and all that pertains to the earth. They were put in place to assist humanity in ruling the earth and subduing it, as God established in creation. These kingdoms were established as good for humanity and for this purpose. As we mentioned before, *kingdom* is the sovereignty and authority one possesses to rule a domain, and the nature, personality, character and integrity of the king (or lack thereof) determines the nature, personality, character and integrity resident within the domain.

When humanity (Adam) sinned and gave the governance of this world to Satan, Satan exercised control and has ruled these kingdoms ever since. These seven cultural kingdoms comprise the kingdoms of this world's system of operation and Satan is the god of this world's system. In His death, burial and resurrection, Jesus stripped Satan of his power. Yet, Jesus has not yet brought all things in this world under His Kingdom rule. The followers of Jesus have been left here to take the good news of the Kingdom of God into these kingdoms and endeavor to establish the seed of the Kingdom of God culture within them. The culture of the Kingdom of God is to significantly influence and impact these cultural kingdoms of the earth, in this age, especially the people who rule, live and labor within these kingdoms.

The followers of Jesus are to live their lives, infiltrate these cultural kingdoms with the good news of the Kingdom of God, and cooperate with the Holy Spirit in His prophetic Kingdom activities within these kingdom environments. As Jesus taught in His parables, explaining the presence and activity of the Kingdom of God in this age, the culture of the Kingdom of God and the culture of darkness will dwell together in these kingdoms until Jesus returns at the end of the age, to bring all of them completely under His Kingdom rule during His Millennial reign.

To better understand the dynamics of this relationship between the Kingdom of God and the kingdom of darkness, in this present age, let's take a look at Matthew 13:24-30, where Jesus tells us a parable of the wheat and the tares.

"Jesus presented another parable to them, saying, "The kingdom of heaven may be compared to a man who sowed good seed in his field. But while his men were sleeping, his enemy came and sowed tares among the wheat, and went away. But when the wheat

*sprouted and bore grain, then the tares became evident also. The slaves of the landowner came and said to him, 'Sir, did you not sow good seed in your field? How then does it have tares?' And he said to them, 'An enemy has done this!' The slaves *said to him, 'Do you want us, then, to go and gather them up?' But he said, 'No; for while you are gathering up the tares, you may uproot the wheat with them. Allow both to grow together until the harvest; and in the time of the harvest I will say to the reapers, "First gather up the tares and bind them in bundles to burn them up; but gather the wheat into my barn."'"*

Jesus said the two kingdoms would remain on the earth, together, until He returned to manifest and establish His Kingdom completely on the earth at the end of the age. The Kingdom of God is to significantly impact these cultural kingdoms, now, through the spreading of the good news of the Kingdom of God, the disciple-making activities of those who believe in Jesus, and the prophetic activities of the Kingdom of God taking place within these kingdoms. We should see the Kingdom of God having an impact in the lives of individuals and the cultures within these kingdoms, as these Kingdom activities are taking place.

Yet, do we see such influence? Do we see this disciple-making and the prophetic activity of the Kingdom taking place, demonstrating the reality and presence of the Kingdom of God within these kingdoms? I don't believe we see as much as we should and as much as Jesus would like to see. Why is this?

One reason is that Satan has done an effective job of strongly exercising his kingdom's influence within these cultural kingdoms. He has placed strong, strategic leaders within these kingdoms who willingly (knowingly or ignorantly) rule and govern within these kingdoms according to the agenda and power of the domain of darkness. Why do we see such a strong influence of darkness and its agenda and not as strong of a presence of the influence and agenda of the Kingdom of God?

It is because the Church has laid down her most effective spiritual weapons and has focused her attention on only one of these seven cultural kingdoms. The Church, for the most part, has laid aside her prophetic, spiritual weapons and has focused almost exclusively on the cultural kingdom of Religion. Over the centuries, the cultural, organized church has theologically stripped the Body of Christ of her prophetic identity and place on the earth through heresy and unbelief, while demanding almost exclusive attention, loyalty and service to its own needs and desires. By demanding singular attention and service to its own kingdom, the Religion kingdom, including the cultural, organized church, has labeled the other six kingdoms as profane and not worthy of our attention and the focus of our Kingdom service.

As a result, what the true Church, the Body of Christ, has surrendered and deemed profane and unworthy of our focus, the domain of darkness has invaded and established strongholds within, worldwide. The Church has taken out of context, the scriptures encouraging us to not be conformed to this world [344] and to come out and be separate from the world, [345] as instructions to consider everything outside of the church to be profane, evil, and unworthy of our time, attention and Kingdom service. We have considered ministry within the world's culture as being for the Evangelist and the occasional mission trip. What God instructs us to do, in regard to our affections and passions, the Church has taken to the extreme to include our ministry focus and Kingdom service. We have focused our ministry attention and Kingdom service within the church building, itself.

For the most part, we have developed a "hunker down" mentality where we predominantly engage in church activities and ministry to one another, while trying to "hold on" until Jesus comes to take us out of here. Daily, we go to our jobs within these cultural kingdoms but we have little vision or energy for what God wants to do within these kingdoms, and how He wants to impact these kingdoms through His prophetic Kingdom activities and His Kingdom people. Thus far, we have, for all intents and purposes, surrendered the seven cultural kingdoms to the agenda and activities of the domain of darkness.

For centuries, this has been our orientation as Christians. This is how most of us have been raised within the church. This is what we have been taught in our seminaries and Bible schools, and have been instructed from our pulpits, for centuries. We tell people to come into our church buildings and they will hear about Jesus because we can't go out to them or we will become polluted, like them. There has been a tremendous spiritual stronghold built within the church culture over the centuries that keeps us from realistically envisioning anything other than this "protective", "hunker down" orientation and ministry model.

Scriptural commands from Jesus have been lost or de-emphasized over these same centuries, which go hand in hand with the development of this spiritual stronghold and orientation within the Church. We need to resurrect or re-emphasize these scriptural commands. The Church needs to tear down this stronghold, individually and corporately, and catch the

[344] Romans 12:1-2
[345] 2Corinthians 6:11-18

"Kingdom vision" for what God wants to see happen through us, as it relates to taking the Kingdom of God to these seven cultural kingdoms, in our day.

Jesus tells us to go to the highways and by-ways and *compel* people to come into His Kingdom. He didn't tell us to invite them to come to us, where we are, so we can engage them in a philosophical discussion about Jesus. He told us to go to them and bear witness to them of the reality and presence of the Kingdom of God…to compel them with the verbal witness and the demonstration of the prophetic activities of the Kingdom of God.[346] Paul, for his part, emphasized this aspect of his and our ministry to unbelievers by reminding the Corinthians that he didn't come to them with persuasive words of wisdom but with the demonstration of the Spirit's presence and with power. [347]

Jesus went to the villages, roads, hillsides, wells and other public venues and compelled people to come to the Kingdom of God, through His verbal witness and the prophetic demonstration of the reality and presence of the Kingdom of God.[348] Paul, likewise, went to the cities and villages of the Gentiles (the non-Jews), giving verbal witness and prophetic demonstration of the reality and presence of the Kingdom of God, as a means of compelling them to come into the Kingdom.[349] Paul didn't use words only but also the prophetic activities of the Kingdom of God.

We are to go into the world proclaiming and demonstrating the reality and presence of the Kingdom of God. Our verbal testimony of the good news of the Kingdom of God is to be accompanied by the prophetic demonstration of the reality and presence of the Kingdom of God. The New Testament is filled with this activity in instruction and by example. Inviting and expecting unbelievers to come to our churches in order to hear a persuasive, philosophical sermon on the merits of believing in Jesus is not a New Testament-inspired method. It is a method espoused and practiced by the Greek and Roman philosophers and their cultural practices.[350] Our western culture is heavily influenced by the Greek and Roman cultures which inhabited most of Europe throughout the centuries, and this "philosophical orientation" has greatly influenced the Church in the West and the way we conduct our ministry activities and communicate our message.

---

[346] Matthew 10:5-8; Mark 16:15-18

[347] 1Corinthians 2:1-5

[348] Mark 6:53-65; Mark 10:46-52; Luke 6:12-19; John 4:7-26; Luke 5:17-26

[349] Acts 14:1-3, 8-10; Acts 19:8-12

[350] Acts 17:16-21

The good news of the reality and presence of the Kingdom of God is not an intellectual philosophy to be bantered about in philosophical discussions. It is a truth that we are to give verbal witness to with the prophetic activities of the Kingdom of God bearing witness to its present reality; compelling people to enter the Kingdom with great passion and commitment. We should not expect those who do not follow Jesus to come into our church buildings to hear about following Jesus. The New Testament "norm", the "model" espoused by Jesus and the other New Testament writers through their instructions and examples, is to give verbal witness to the reality and presence of the Kingdom of God, accompanied by the prophetic demonstration of the reality and presence of the Kingdom, "compelling" people to enter it.

We should not and cannot expect to significantly influence and impact the seven cultural kingdoms of this world with persuasive words of wisdom, alone. We need the power of the Holy Spirit demonstrating the reality and presence of the Kingdom of God, as we give verbal witness to it. This is why we need to embrace the prophetic activities of the Kingdom of God and integrate them into the life of the local church. This is why we must tear down the spiritual stronghold that has been established over the centuries, in all of our minds and lives as followers of Jesus, so we can embrace and pursue these Kingdom activities in real faith. We must embrace the Kingdom of God with great passion and energy, as Jesus continues to move forward with great passion and energy on the earth.

We need the Holy Spirit to renew our minds and build our faith so we can effectively embrace and integrate the prophetic activity of the Kingdom of God into our lives and the life of our churches. The scriptures tell us that a generation of Jesus followers is coming who will embrace, experience and demonstrate the reality and presence of the Kingdom of God. They will know God, they will be spiritually strong, and they will do prophetic exploits. They will arise at the time of the end, just before the antichrist comes on the scene at the end of the age. [351]

Those of us who have been raised in the Church or have been influenced by the cultural, organized church for any length of time have been exposed to theology and activities which contradict much of what I have been saying in this book about the Kingdom of God and the prophetic activities associated with its reality and presence on the earth today. We've been taught that these prophetic activities aren't valid and relevant anymore. Even if we have discovered the truth and have embraced the Kingdom and its prophetic activities, we still have considerable obstacles to overcome in order to

---

[351] Daniel 11:29-35

effectively experience these activities in our lives, consistently, on an ongoing basis.

One of the biggest obstacles we face is what James refers to as being double-minded or being of two minds. The Holy Spirit reveals truth to our spirits which gives us hope and faith to believe and act on that truth. Yet, our minds have been filled with contradictory information that, when faced with the decision as to how to respond in a given situation, we are pulled in two different directions. Our spirits want to respond to what the Holy Spirit has imparted to us but our minds want to respond according to what it has been taught. The one is influenced by the other to the point that we can't respond confidently and in faith because of our doubt.[352] James says, *"For that man ought not to expect that he will receive anything from the Lord, being a double-minded man, unstable in all his ways."*

Though most of us believe the Kingdom of God is real and present among us and that He wants us to experience His Kingdom realities in our lives, we see and experience little of these prophetic realities. What we have been taught over the years has raised considerable doubt in our minds so we find it difficult to respond in faith to the truth that the Spirit has revealed to us. We are not confident in our belief and, therefore, waiver when it comes to responding to the Spirit's influence. We can give mental ascent to the truth but we have difficulty responding in faith to His influence.

Yet, there is hope for overcoming our double-mindedness so we can walk by faith in the truth the Holy Spirit reveals to us. God has given us the means to resolve this double-mindedness we all experience in one way or another. He has provided us with the ability to renew our mind, or to restart or refurbish our mind. Paul tells us, *"…do not be conformed to this world, but* ***be transformed by the renewing of your mind****, so* ***that you may prove what the will of God is****, that which is good and acceptable and perfect."* [353]

Allowing the Holy Spirit to renew our minds with the truth provides the confidence and faith to respond appropriately to His influence when the opportunity arises. Our minds and our spirits agree; they are not divided. This is a spiritual process that takes time but the Spirit is faithful to perform this process in us if we ask Him and faithfully respond to Him. Even though this scripture is not talking about our mind and our spirit being in agreement, the principle is still accurate; *"Can two people walk together without agreeing on the direction?* [354]

---

[352] James 1:5-8
[353] Romans 12:2 (emphasis mine)
[354] Amos 3:3

Can we respond in faith to the Holy Spirit if our mind and spirit do not agree on how to respond? The answer is simple but it is not as simple to implement the renewing process. To experience the joy of living life with our mind and spirit in agreement with the influence of the Holy Spirit and the reality and presence of the Kingdom of God, takes time and the work of the Holy Spirit. He is able to bring our minds and our spirits into agreement so we can effectively respond to and experience the realty of His Kingdom and its prophetic activities.

As I previously mentioned, do I think it is a coincidence that God revealed the mandate of the 7 Cultural Kingdoms to two men who led worldwide youth movements and to another man who led an international Christian community movement? I don't think it is a coincidence at all. I think it is very strategic, and here is why.

Children have a tremendous capacity for comprehending and experiencing spiritual realities. They are able to grasp spiritual truth and respond in a very simple, childlike faith. In fact, Jesus tells us, *"Truly I say to you, unless you are converted and become like children, you will not enter the kingdom of heaven. Whoever then humbles himself as this child, he is the greatest in the kingdom of heaven."* [355] Children do not have the intellectual and theological hang-ups we adults do. They haven't been raised with religious and theological influences that may not be scriptural and beneficial to a life of effectual faith. Their minds and spirits are a "blank slate" to be written on and we, as their parents and elders, need to be faithful to write on these slates with the truth of God's word and the realities of the Kingdom of God.

God is raising up a generation that will be spiritually strong and who will do prophetic exploits for the Kingdom of God.[356] This particular generation must go beyond the previous generations in faith, spiritual strength, and experiencing the prophetic activities of the Kingdom of God. Historically, the Church hasn't done a very good job of training and mentoring our younger generation in these truths and realties of the Kingdom. Therefore, one generation has not been able to go beyond the previous generation when it comes to walking in these realties.

For the most part, each generation has had to "start from scratch" - to learn and grow in these realties on their own with little input or assistance from their elders. As a result, growth and progress in these prophetic realities and

---

[355] Matthew 18:3-4
[356] Daniel 11:29-35

in their personal experience has been slow, with many losing heart along the way due to a general resistance to them by other Christians around them.

Since the 1950s, God has been stressing the reality of the presence of His Kingdom in the world and the prophetic activities that accompany this reality. This generation has made tremendous strides in realizing and experiencing these realties, even in the midst of opposition and resistance. Yes, there have been abuses. Yes, mistakes have been made for various reasons including spiritual immaturity. You can't pour new wine into old wineskins without some tearing and spilling. Yet, since the 1950s, God has prepared and raised up a generation that is developing a new "wineskin" which can hold the "new wine" God is and will be pouring out. It will be able to "agree and cooperate with" the requirements these "new" Kingdom manifestations and activities place upon it, without breaking.

Your Father Has Chosen Gladly To Give You The Kingdom

Many of us, today, as individual followers of Jesus, especially the younger generations among us, do not know or understand what the prophetic activities of the Kingdom entail from a Biblical perspective. Therefore, we do not understand that walking in the prophetic, to some degree of competency, is vital to our personal spiritual experience and life with God. We do not understand that these prophetic activities are intended to affect our lives on a very deep spiritual level, while at the same time finding its outward expression in very practical ways, affecting the lives of people around us. We need to be taught and trained in how to operate in the prophetic activity of the Kingdom of God in such a way as to be able to cooperate with the Holy Spirit as He works His will in and through us.

We need to understand that every believer is to operate in these prophetic activities at some level of competency, according to the will and calling of the Holy Spirit for them; with some operating at a higher level than others because of their calling and ministry within the Body of Christ and the plan of God. If we do not grasp this fact, many of us will lack real spiritual fulfillment in regard to our personal, intimate experience with God. At the same time, others of us will experience a lack of direction and understanding regarding our ministry calling and, therefore, will experience a sense of failure in relation to God's purpose for our lives.

If we look at the timing and methods of God, in reestablishing the prophetic activities of His Kingdom within the lives of His Kingdom people, the Church, we will see several relatively recent spiritual events where God seemed to "reintroduce" these Kingdom activities into the Church on a grand scale. Many followers of Jesus identify events toward the beginning of the 20th century as the time when these spiritual activities, operations, and manifestations were, in essence, "restored" to the Church after centuries of ignorance and neglect on the part of the Church leadership.

Likewise, in the 1960s, a revival took place among the young people. This revival gave rise to the "Jesus People" or "Jesus Movement", which became the catalyst for what we now call the "Charismatic Movement" or "Charismatic Renewal". It was referred to as "Charismatic" because of the proliferation of the "spiritual" or "charisma" gifts of the Holy Spirit, as mentioned in I Corinthians 12-14. As these charisma gifts began to proliferate, Christians from every walk of life began to flock to see and experience for themselves what was taking place.

As a result of this "restoration" of the prophetic activities of the Kingdom of God, Pentecostal, neo-Pentecostal and charismatic churches began springing up. Since the great majority of seminaries and Bible schools at the time did not believe in or provide training in the operation of these Kingdom activities, the pastors of these churches had, either, no formal training in the ministry at all or didn't have formal training in this area of ministry. These Kingdom activities were being experienced by full-time ministers as well as the average church member. Yet, there was little Biblical understanding of these activities and operations, how to train people in these activities, and how these activities should function within the local church.

The notoriety surrounding the operation of these Kingdom activities brought people, not only from traditional denominations to these churches, but the unchurched as well. Because of the lack of formal training and practical ministry experience of many of these "charismatic" pastors, they leaned heavily on these manifestations of the Spirit to build their ministries and churches, at the expense of solid Bible teaching and exposition. As a result, their churches were filled with people who were seeking to "move in the Spirit" but had little or no Biblical knowledge or understanding as a foundation for their faith and practice. Not surprising, we had immature leaders leading immature believers in the exercise of powerful spiritual activities that had a tremendous impact on churches and individuals.

It was at this time that God began to raise up individuals with strong prophetic gifts and ministries. But in the same way as the local churches were filled with immature believers seeking to operate in powerful spiritual manifestations, so these prophetic individuals, for the most part, exercised strong prophetic gifts and manifestations of the Spirit but were scripturally immature; possessing very little Bible knowledge and understanding to temper and support their gifts. As a result, there was a certain amount of "showmanship" to go along with the activities of the Spirit. There was unscriptural teaching being proliferated from these individuals to go along with the Spirit's operation. They often "blew in" to these churches, "upset the apple cart" by bringing confusion to the congregation, then they would "blow back out" leaving the pastor to pick up the pieces after they were gone.

There were also instances where the pastors of these churches were looking to grow by adding people to their congregations. One of the methods they discovered for "bringing them in" was to have one of these prophetic ministries at their church for a period of time, in much the same way as a circus advertises its unusual sideshows in order to draw the gawking crowds to their tent. This caused the prophetic ministry to feel used, abused, and taken advantage of, in order to build a bigger congregation for the pastor.

In other words, many of the actions taking place by the prophetic people, the local church leadership, and within the church's congregation were causing people to be offended by the prophetic activities of the Kingdom of God, and was the result of scriptural and spiritual immaturity. We had spiritually immature individuals receiving wonderful and valuable gifts, who did not have the spiritual and scriptural understanding and maturity to handle the gifts appropriately. Plus, we had pastors who were more interested in having bigger churches, at the cost of spiritual stability and maturity within their congregations.

If we look at the combination of: 1) immature believers in the church seeking to operate in these spiritual manifestations with little or no training or Biblical foundation; 2) immature pastors possessing little or no ministry training or experience, trying to "hold things together" while all of these manifestations (spiritual and carnal) were taking place within their church; 3) the prophetic ministries "blowing" into local churches, bringing powerful manifestations of the Spirit along with carnal manifestations and false teaching, upsetting entire churches while leaving the pastor to clean up the mess; and 4) local church pastors taking advantage of these prophetic ministries in order to add numbers to their churches; it is not surprising that we see such reluctance on the part of individuals and churches, today, to embrace and pursue the prophetic activity of the Kingdom of God.

In more recent history, some pastors who have endeavored to integrate the prophetic activities of the Kingdom into their churches have met with significant obstacles ranging from jealousy and competition between people exercising these prophetic gifts and activities, to everyone wanting to be a Prophet. There is also a misconception among some believers that if you experience these activities in your life, you must be a Prophet. This often brings with it "super-spiritual" behavior (in other words, acting spooky or eccentric). This sort of misunderstanding of the purpose for the prophetic activity of the Kingdom of God, and its resulting behavior, has increased the hesitancy on the part of many churches to embrace and integrate these prophetic activities.

In spite of this carnal and immature behavior that has surrounded these Kingdom activities, many local church pastors and leaders need to understand that God is at work to bring spiritual maturity to His people and our ability to effectively operate in these Kingdom activities, on His behalf. God doesn't "pour the baby out with the bath water" when He sees His people acting and operating immaturely in regard to His Kingdom tools, resources and activities. We can't get frustrated and give up on the Church because God isn't frustrated and giving up on her. He is working to bring spiritual maturity to our lives so we can handle His Kingdom activities in a mature manner.

This has been the main focus of this book; to give a strong scriptural and theological foundation and framework for the prophetic activities of the Kingdom of God, and its acceptance and practice in the lives of God's people individually and within the local church environment. As a wise man once said, *"Where no oxen are, the manger is clean, but much increase comes by the strength of the ox."* [357] Naturally, we want everything neat and tidy; everything working like clockwork with no loose ends and nothing to clean up afterwards. Yet, God has a way of "upsetting our apple cart" because He wants us to trust Him and not our ability to control and manage everything ourselves. Spiritual growth can be messy at times but God can handle the mess that sometimes comes in order to achieve the spiritual growth He desires.

The history of the prophetic activity of God and His Kingdom has been anything but neat and tidy; with no loose ends and nothing to clean up. Elisha the prophet told an Aramian captain (a non-Jew) to take a bath in a muddy river, to get rid of his leprosy.[358] God told the prophet Hosea to marry a prostitute and to have children with this prostitute.[359] God told the prophet Isaiah to go around naked for three years.[360] Even Jesus raised a

---

[357] Proverbs 14:4
[358] 2Kings 5:1-14
[359] Hosea 1:2-3

few eyebrows when He made mud with his spit and put it on a blind man's eyes,[361] and raised a man from the dead when he had been dead for three days.[362]

God knows what is needed in every situation, when working in the lives of people, in order to influence their lives with His Kingdom activities. He isn't afraid to offend the mind in order to get to the heart. He doesn't apologize and has no regrets after the fact. He's not afraid to do what He has to do, to touch a life for His Kingdom, even if it causes a mess that has to be cleaned up afterward. Look at the mess He has to deal with and clean up each time a person responds to Him and becomes a follower of Jesus.

He has to clean up that person's life and it doesn't happen in a few hours or days; it takes a lifetime to clean up and requires great patience, love and compassion to do so. That is our God and that is what He often requires of us, especially as leaders. There is no easy road for God or for us, to bring people from immaturity to maturity in any area of life and ministry, including teaching, training and mentoring people in the prophetic activity of the Kingdom of God. Children will be children, whether they are physical or spiritual.

As a result, this new "wineskin" of coming alongside to instruct, train and mentor in the prophetic activities of the Kingdom of God, which God has reintroduced into the Church, is necessary if we are to see a generation raised up that will go beyond the generation of its elders. They must not only understand the truth and reality of the Kingdom of God but experience its prophetic realties and activities. They will know God to a greater level, possess a greater level of spiritual strength, and do the prophetic exploits of the Kingdom to a greater level, in order to accomplish what Daniel saw thousands of years ago.

God has been preparing a generation of elders who have experienced these Kingdom realties at a level high enough to come alongside of their spiritual children in order to teach, train and mentor them in these same realities. We have had a tendency over the centuries, within the culture and ministry of our local churches, to place our senior believers, our true elders, on the proverbial shelf. We often consider them to be too old and lack the necessary energy and passion to engage in the church's ministries, effectively.

---

[360] Isaiah 20:2-4
[361] John 9:1-7
[362] John 11:38-44

Having this attitude and taking these actions has robbed the Church of some of her greatest gifts, the spiritual experience and wisdom of these seasoned saints. In actuality, God has been preparing these elder saints their entire lives, to come alongside of the younger generations, in order to train and prepare them, effectively. As pastors and leaders, we cut ourselves off from God's blessing and provision when we take it upon ourselves to put these older saints on the shelf, and wonder why God doesn't seem to be working within our congregations. It is, often, our own fault.

If you look within many of our churches, you will find the positions of church "Elder" being filled by individuals in their thirties and early forties. This is not to say that a person in their thirties or forties can't possess significant spiritual maturity but the scriptures identify a particular church leadership position as an "Elder" for a reason. There is wisdom in grey hair; the spiritual and practical wisdom that God imparts and develops within a person's life over a period of decades, through life's struggles and experiences. Our churches can't afford to "write off" and ignore that level of seasoned wisdom just because the world's response to people of age is to retire them. We make a grave mistake if we have that attitude and take that course of action, within the Church, with the true elders God has placed in our midst.

Christian community is where our children will be raised up by our true elders to walk in these Kingdom realities. Our children won't be raised with the same religious and theological hindrances we were raised with. Our children won't be raised with the level of double-mindedness we grew up with and must overcome through the renewing of our minds. Our children will take less time to learn, grow and experience these Kingdom realities than we have, and our children will experience them to a greater degree and regularity.

Whether it is our children, today, or our children's children, God is raising up a generation that will fulfill what Daniel saw thousands of years ago. It all began with three men in 1975 who received a mandate from God to take the Kingdom of God to the seven cultural kingdoms of this world. That is how God works. He begins with a seed.[363]

I have experienced a level of the reality of the Kingdom of God and its prophetic activity in my life. Now, I am teaching, training and mentoring our spiritual children and other followers of Jesus so they can go beyond previous generations in these Kingdom realities. We who are leaders and elders don't stop learning and experiencing. We need to continue growing

---

[363] Mark 4:26-29

by tearing down this spiritual stronghold that has been built within the Church and in our individual lives over the years, through the renewing of our minds. This is why contemplative prayer, developing a vital, active relationship with the Holy Spirit, and allowing the Spirit to impart the certainty and reality of the word of God into our lives is so important. When we allow the Kingdom of God to engage and influence us as His Kingdom people, we place ourselves in a position to agree and cooperate with Him in what He is doing around us.

These seven cultural kingdoms need the reality of the Kingdom of God to confront them and influence them. This will only be done through the agency of God's Kingdom people. We need to take the Kingdom outside of the church building and take it to the kings and the people who are in these cultural kingdoms. Again, this is not what this scripture is specifically referring to but the principle is still valid; *"Do you see a man skilled in his work? He will stand before kings; he will not stand before obscure men."* [364] Our children need to become knowledgeable, skilled and proficient in the reality and activities of the Kingdom of God so they aren't double-minded when the Spirit leads and instructs them in what He wants them to do, as they engage these seven cultural kingdoms.

These seven cultural kingdoms do exist into the millennium. They become the kingdoms of our Lord and of His Christ. The earth and all people on it are not destroyed when Jesus returns. Unbelievers will live into the millennium and they will have children throughout the millennium. The seven cultural kingdoms have their evil kings removed and the millennial administration of Jesus takes over governance when He returns to setup His Kingdom on the earth.

These seven cultural kingdoms continue to serve humanity and to assist in ruling and subduing the earth, even into the millennium, only under a different ruler – Jesus. Even in the millennium, people will have natural bodies and will need to become followers of Jesus, by faith, even though Jesus is present on the earth and ruling over the earth. There will even be people with natural bodies rebelling against Jesus and the Kingdom of God at the end of the millennium, being led by Satan who is released from prison for a short period.[365]

Today, we see the antichrist spirit working in the world much as we did in the days when Jesus was born. We saw the activities of Satan set on destroying Jesus as a child, when he moved Herod to kill all of the infant

[364] Proverbs 22:29
[365] Revelation 20:7-10

boys under two years old. Satan knew what was happening and he tried to hinder the plan of God before it was able to be implemented and completed. The antichrist spirit, Satan, is doing the same thing today. He sees what God is doing and what is coming. He recognizes that God is preparing a generation that will confront his activities of darkness in this world with the activities of the Kingdom of God. In an effort to thwart the plan of God from being implemented and completed in these last days, Satan has moved to destroy as much of this generation as possible before they are ever born.

Since 1973, when abortion on demand was legalized in the US (about the same time God gave the seven cultural kingdoms mandate to these three men, by the way), along with the efforts of other countries like China and their "One Child Law", hundreds of millions of unborn children have been aborted in an effort to derail God's plan to confront this evil age with the prophetic activities of the Kingdom of God. A dynamic, powerful generation of Jesus followers is coming and if the activities of Satan are any indication, it may be present in the world right now.

But, just as God was able to thwart Satan's attempt to destroy Jesus before He could accomplish His work, using the prophetic activities of the His Kingdom (dreams, visions, angelic visitations, etc.), God will thwart the devises of Satan in these last days so this final prophetic generation can accomplish its work for the Kingdom of God in regard to the seven cultural kingdoms. Satan cannot and does not win. God cannot and does not lose. The activities of Satan through abortion, terrorism, and other activities which strike fear and hopelessness in the hearts of people, will not keep the Kingdom people of God from taking their place on the earth and confronting Satan and his activities.

Regardless of age, all believers must pursue the reality of the Kingdom of God, the prophetic activities of God, and their places within the Body of Christ. Those of us who are this generation's elders have a generation of children to raise up and prepare so they can fulfill what Daniel saw and prophesied thousands of years ago.

Chapter Questions & Notes

Talk It Over….

1) The kingdoms of this world consist of more than geographical or political kingdoms. There are kingdoms and rulers within every sphere of human existence and culture. They assist humanity with executing the mandate God gave us when He created us – to rule over all aspects pertaining to the earth and to subdue it. Only one of the seven kingdoms has to do with religion. If the remaining kingdoms comprise what we consider to be "secular" culture and God wants us to take the Kingdom of God to these remaining kingdoms, what must we do, as followers of Jesus, to accomplish this task? How does this change the focus of the Church and the local church in particular, and what changes are necessary within the local church environment to effectively reach these earthly kingdoms with the Kingdom of God?

2) Jesus wants us to extend beyond our own natural, human abilities and attributes in order to take the Kingdom of God to these seven cultural kingdoms. He wants to demonstrate the reality and presence of His Kingdom to the world through His Kingdom people, just as the Father did through the ministry of Jesus. Renewing our minds to overcome double-mindedness is necessary if we are to truly walk by faith and engage with the prophetic activities of the Kingdom. In your group, discuss what this means, how we go about renewing our minds, and how the community of Jesus followers can be a tremendous benefit in pursuing these activities.

(9)

Make Room For The Prophetic Activity Of The Kingdom Of God

"And no one puts new wine into old wineskins; otherwise the new wine will burst the skins, and it will be spilled out, and the skins will be ruined. But ***new wine must be put into fresh wineskins.****"* Luke 5:37-38 (emphasis mine)

It is very important, as we embrace and pursue the prophetic activities of the Kingdom of God, to make room for it within our own individual lives and in the life and functions of our churches. This may seem like a fairly simple thing to do but anytime we embrace change, we embrace something that will require flexibility and adjustment. Sometimes these changes take little effort and adjustment on our part in order to implement them. But other changes, such as embracing and pursuing this prophetic activity of God, will require a greater level of flexibility, adjustment, and patience. This is because the operation of the Kingdom of God and its activities is completely different from the manner in which most of us have lived our lives since the day we were born.

We grew up being trained by our spiritual orientation (sin) and the society and culture in which we live (natural instead of spiritual) in order to approach our life and the world around us through the physical filters we call our five senses. These five senses allow us to contact and interact with the world around us in different ways. The information gathered by these physical senses is sent to our brain which then processes the information and forms conclusions based on this input. This sensual process is not exact but through practice and the course of time, we have become fairly adept at this continual information-gathering and decision-making.

The prophetic process for gathering information from the Kingdom of God is not a process where we can simply transfer our already-developed sensual process skills to this new spiritual process and expect to become adept at it quickly. In fact, the prophetic process for gathering information from the Kingdom of God is completely different from our sensual process. Just like the sensual process, the prophetic process is not an exact science.

Competency and expertise in regard to its operation and exercise is acquired through a process of diligent pursuit, instruction, training, and trial and error over an extended period of time, just like the sensual process.

Not only is the prophetic process, itself, something that takes time to grow in and adjust to but most of our theological institutions, local church organizational structures, and religious affiliations (denominations) are not trained and organized in such a way as to administrate and manage these prophetic activities of the Kingdom operating in their midst. Therefore, understanding and accepting this will help us identify how we as individual believers, leaders in the local church, and organizational leaders can prepare ourselves to embrace, pursue, and make room for the prophetic in our midst.

Before we look at a scripture from Luke 5, it is important to understand some of the background of the passage. In this scripture, Jesus is addressing a group of Jewish religious leaders known as the Pharisees. To better understand what Jesus said to them and why He said it, I want to go back and trace the origin of the Pharisees to see how, when and why they were established and how they evolved as a group, over time.

The Pharisees, a religious sect of the Jews, trace their history back to the time of Ezra and the rebuilding of the temple in Jerusalem, in approximately 450 BC. At that time, they referred to themselves as the "Nivdalim" or "those who had separated themselves from the filthiness of the heathen", and placed upon themselves specific vows and obligatory practices. This "separation" espoused by the "Nivdalim" was very sincere as a result of the spiritual revival that took place in Israel when God allowed them to return from exile to rebuild the temple. Over time, the "Nivdalim" evolved. Along this evolutionary journey, these individuals gradually strayed from the spirit of "separateness" brought about by revival, to engage in outward observances, practices, and appearances only.[366]

In 200 BC the Syrian Empire dominated much of the southern part of Europe and began to spread into the area of Palestine. They forced much of their culture and religion on the people of Palestine, including the Jews. As a result, these Jewish religious "separatists" provided the initial resistance to the Syrian domination of Palestine, resulting in the eventual revolt led by the Maccabees against the Syrians in 167 BC.

---

[366] *Sketches of Jewish Social Life*, by Alfred Edersheim, pages 210-218. Copyright 1994 by Hendrickson Publishers, Inc., P.O. Box 3473, Peabody, MA 01961-3473

The revolt was successful and the Syrians were defeated and removed. Not long after the overthrow of Syria, the Maccabees began corrupting the Jewish priesthood with the activities of secular ruling and governing. In response, these religious "separatists" withdrew their support from the Maccabees and eventually stood in resistance to them in order to restore the priesthood to its proper function, as the Law of Moses intended. As a result, many of these "separatists" suffered martyrdom at the hands of the Maccabees for their convictions and resistance.

During this time, many of the "separatists" became sidetracked from their original spiritual separateness by focusing on the outward ritualistic observances of the Law, specifically tithing and purification. Soon they began practicing outward separation but the inward spiritual condition and motivation were being ignored and lost. This group not only focused on the outward observance of the Law's rituals but also became loyal to the many supplements to the Law that were handed down by the elders in the group. Over time these supplements became known as "the traditions of the elders". This group, which deviated from the original "separatists" to focus on and practice these outward observances and rituals, became known as the Pharisees.

As a result of this deviation from the truth, the Pharisees became overly zealous and preoccupied with outward religious appearances. Personal spirituality and personal standing before God became synonymous with the observances of the Law's rituals and the traditions of the elders. Personal piety was now based on the ritual itself and how well and often it was performed, instead of on their devotion to God and the resulting spiritual motivation.

They became self-absorbed and self-righteous as a result of the importance of their outward appearance to themselves and to those around them. They became inward-focused as a group, becoming judges of one another while losing sight of their true Judge, God, and the truth of His word. They lost all sense of spiritual reality and began living in a world they themselves had created; physically separated from those labeled as sinners but not separated from the influences, dangers, and effects of sin in their own personal lives.

The Pharisees established synagogues within the various towns and settlements in Palestine, as well as religious courts used for judging the activities of the people in regards to the Mosaic Law. These courts gave rise to the supreme religious court in Jerusalem known as the Sanhedrin. They also established schools of study and for training future Pharisees.[367] The

[367] *Sketches of Jewish Social Life*, by Alfred Edersheim, page 195. Copyright 1994 by Hendrickson

Pharisees became so powerful from a religious and theological perspective that the term "Pharisee" became synonymous with the established theological direction the Jews would embrace and practice as a people.[368]

Over time, the preoccupation of the Pharisees with outward religious appearance and works of the Law gave place to extreme class behavior. They established four levels of attainment, recognition, and privilege within the fraternity of the Pharisees. This included modes of religious dress that would identify each level in order to provide a greater means for self-gratification and a sense of religious and social achievement. This combination of extreme class sensitivity, a desire for physical separateness from sinners, and the focus on outward observance of the Jewish Law and traditions provided a foundation for spiritual leadership that was blind to the needs of the common people, blind to the spiritual atmosphere of the times in which they lived, and blind to the truth of the Person of God and the relevance of His word.

With this as a backdrop, let's look at Jesus' conversation with the Pharisees in Luke 5. Here, the Pharisees came to Jesus while He was eating at the home of Levi (Matthew), with Levi's friends, other tax collectors, and the common people. During this conversation with Jesus, the Pharisees asked Him two questions that reveal their spiritual and theological orientation. These two questions are, *"Why do you eat and drink with the tax-gatherers and sinners?"* and, *"The disciples of John often fast and offer prayers; the disciples of the Pharisees also do the same; but yours eat and drink."* These are two areas where the Pharisees, over the last four hundred years, had chosen to separate themselves from the common people as part of their religious practices. Not that these practices are wrong in and of themselves,[369] but the Pharisees allowed these practices, over time, to become a personal measuring stick for their own self-imposed spiritual achievement and pride.

In response to their questions, Jesus told them a parable that compared a patch of new cloth being sewn onto an old garment, and new wine being stored in old wineskins. In both examples, Jesus highlights the incompatibility of the new with the old. The new patch was incompatible with the old garment and the new wine was incompatible with the old wineskin. What did Jesus say to the Pharisees in this parable? He told them that the present purpose and activities of the Kingdom of God (represented

---

Publishers, Inc.

[368] *Sketches of Jewish Social Life*, by Alfred Edersheim, page 223. Copyright 1994 by Hendrickson Publishers, Inc., P.O. Box 3473, Peabody, MA 01961-3473

[369] Hebrews 7:25-26; Matthew 17:20-21

by the new patch and the new wine) were incompatible with the current theological and religious systems and structures.

There was no room for the present activities of the Kingdom of God in the established Pharisaical paradigm. The current Pharisaical "wine skin" and "garment" could not agree and cooperate with the "new wine" and "new patch" of the present activities of God and His Kingdom. There needed to be considerable changes made to their current structure and systems. There needed to be a paradigm shift in regard to how God's people related to, came into agreement with, cooperated with, and obediently carried out the activities of the Kingdom of God.

What we need to recognize and understand from this parable is that the sect of the Pharisees was born out of a revival movement of God. Yet, what began by the Spirit had deteriorated to where they were no longer able to distinguish between what was of God and what was of man. That is why Jesus said to the Pharisees again, in Matthew 16:2-3, *"When it is evening, you say, 'It will be fair weather, for the sky is red', and in the morning, 'There will be a storm today, for the sky is red and threatening.'* ***Do you know how to discern the appearance of the sky, but cannot discern the signs of the times?"*** (emphasis mine) The Pharisees possessed a tremendous amount of religious tradition, theological knowledge, and training in the Law but they had no spiritual eyes and ears to discern what God was presently doing and saying in regard to His Kingdom activities on the earth.

When Jesus came on the scene, they were amazed by the miraculous works that He did. Yet, at the same time, they were perplexed by the fact that all of this was happening without their involvement. *"Haven't we been the spiritual leaders of God's people for hundreds of years?" "Weren't we born out of a revival?" "Aren't we God's men of faith in these days?" "How could someone like Jesus come along without us knowing about it?" "If this is of God, it would have certainly come through one of us since we are the spiritual leaders among God's people?" "If this man and these works are from God, why are we on the outside looking in?"*

The Perils Of Pride & Short-Sightedness

To better illustrate the situation the Pharisees found themselves in, at the time Jesus came on the scene, let me use a modern-day business analogy. The "Computer Revolution", which began with the birth of the modern computer in the mid-1900s, gave rise to a number of world-class computer companies that dominated the business landscape for many years. Companies like NCR, Univac, Sperry, Burroughs, Honeywell, Control Data, Wang Labs, Digital Equipment, and IBM competed for the multiple billions of dollars being spent on computer hardware and software worldwide.

Then in the early 1980s, a paradigm shift occurred in our society as a result of the miniaturization of electronic components used in making computers. The "new wine" known as the Personal Computer was introduced in 1981.

Many of these large "mainframe" computer companies balked at the PC, refusing to focus their planning and resources on this irrelevant "toy" that was emerging on the scene. As a result, since 1981, virtually all of these multi-billion dollar companies have vanished from the computer industry landscape except for IBM, who was one of the original inventors of the Personal Computer. These companies assumed that because they had been born in the midst of a "computer revolution", their international status, size, and cultural influence would guarantee their strong, prolonged relevance and prominence in the marketplace, regardless of the impact of this "new wine" called the PC. Yet, only IBM was able to make the timely and necessary decisions to transition their "wineskin" or operating model to come into agreement with and to cooperate with this "new wine" PC and the resulting societal revolution it initiated.

Yet, even IBM did not fully grasp the impact this "new wine" PC would have upon the culture. Once they introduced their Personal Computer into the marketplace in 1981, IBM decided that they would strictly be a hardware company, as it related to the PC segment of the computer industry. They chose not to pursue the PC Operating System and Central Processing Unit (CPU) business. As a result, IBM relinquished the original PC DOS operating system business to a small company run by a young kid named Bill Gates. Thus Microsoft and the eventual Windows operating system was born. IBM also relinquished the PC's CPU business to a small fledgling company named Intel. For the first ten years of this PC revolution, the mainstream PC was also referred to as the "IBM Compatible" PC. But as the 1990s came around, the functional role or position of PC hardware in the overall scheme of things became less and less unique and prominent. In fact, the PC itself became much more of a commodity item.

More and more PC manufacturers came onto the scene to compete with IBM, making the PC hardware itself an afterthought. What was most important, now, was the application software that would run on the PC's Windows operating system, as well as the CPU that did the actual processing of the information within the PC. As a result, what was once referred to as "IBM Compatible" was now referred to as "WinTel Compatible" (Windows/Intel). The IBM-dominated hardware architecture, and its prominence, gave way to the Windows/Intel prominence.

Now, the new products being developed for the PC by other hardware and software companies must be "WinTel compatible". Even though IBM was an original participant in the "PC Revolution", their short-sightedness, lack of humility in the marketplace, and inability to discern "the signs of the times" led them to unknowingly relinquish their PC industry leadership to a couple of "nobodies", even though this change of leadership took as much as ten years to manifest itself in the marketplace. IBM tried to regain this PC prominence and relevance by introducing a new PC hardware and software platform, known as the PS/2 personal computer running the OS/2 operating system on an IBM CPU. This effort failed because the original PC with the Windows operating system running on the Intel CPU had become so heavily entrenched within the business and home computing environments, it was nearly impossible to displace.

As a result of the PC Revolution, a new group of computer 'super companies' joined IBM as worldwide names. Microsoft, Intel, Hewlett Packard, Apple, Toshiba, Compaq, Dell and many other companies made names for themselves because they "caught the vision" and made for themselves compatible "wineskins" for the "new wine" called the PC. Later, a new paradigm shift or "new wine" emerged on the scene, called the Internet. Many of these new, established computer giants scurried to "transition their wineskin" in such a way as to be compatible with this "new wine" called the internet. Many of them found it difficult to find their place because: 1) they did not discern "the signs of the times" until it was too late, or 2) they did not rightly discern the nature and purpose of the "new wine" called the Internet, and therefore did not understand how to come into agreement with it and how to cooperate with it.

As a result, other companies emerged as the leaders in Internet computing, such as AOL, Netscape, Amazon, Google, and Yahoo because they were able to establish a "wineskin" that was flexible and compatible with this "new wine". Being able to see and evaluate "what is coming", develop an effective wineskin for the emerging "new wine", and to effectively observe "the signs of the times" is critical to the ongoing success and relevance of any organization or individual. Resting on past successes and current leadership positions, and assuming "the way we have always done it" is good enough, will not ensure future leadership, relevance, and effectiveness.

This is what Jesus was trying to tell the Pharisees and it is what He is telling us today. Many of us attend churches whose denominations were born out of revival or renewal, whether it is Lutheran, Methodist, Baptist, Presbyterian, Assemblies of God, or one of many others. In fact, many of our non-denominational churches also identify themselves with past spiritual revivals, renewals, and movements. What Jesus is saying to us is this. What we did in the past does not ensure our continued relevance in the present, nor in the future.

Our present orientation and mode of operation ("wineskin") is not guaranteed to be compatible with future moves and activities of the Kingdom of God. To think so is to be out of touch with the plans, purposes, and activities of God. The Holy Spirit is the presence, voice, and activity of God on the earth and He is continually speaking and acting to accomplish His will. If we don't know Him and don't know what He is saying and doing, we run the risk of not being engaged with His present and future activities.

We must develop and maintain our spiritual eyes and ears in order to see and hear what God is doing and saying. We must continually discern the "signs of the times", otherwise we will end up like the Pharisees who were convincing one another that they were still relevant and still the chosen instrument of God for the hour but were, in reality, the major persecutors of Jesus and the ones who opposed the current activities of the Kingdom of God on the earth. They had relinquished their spiritual leadership many years before but it did not manifest itself in their immediate circumstances until the "new wine" came on the scene, in the person of Jesus of Nazareth, and in the new prophetic activities of the Kingdom of God.

If we are not willing to make the necessary changes to our own wineskins (our hearts, as well as to the theological and organizational structures of which we are a part), we will not be able to contain the new wine of the Spirit when it comes. Remember, the purpose and plans of the Kingdom of God are constantly moving forward and God is communicating His strategies and plans to those who have eyes to see and ears to hear.

In order to make our personal and organizational "wineskins" compatible with God's "new wine", it is possible that some of us may need to tear out the "old foundation" on which our personal life and church life have been built, and establish a new one that is flexible enough and scriptural enough to recognize and incorporate what God is doing right now, as well as what He will be doing in the future.

Inflexible, closed systems, whether in our personal life or in our church, will cause us to stagnate. Flexible, open systems will allow us to transition, grow, mature, and change when we see God moving and implementing a new phase of His plan. We need to be able to "follow the cloud" when it moves. [370] This changing of our spiritual orientation will not come easy but we will be blessed as He pours His new wine into our compatible wineskin. Recognizing, developing and exercising our prophetic nature and capabilities

---

[370] Numbers 9:15-23

will help us discern and respond to the "new wine" brought about by the Holy Spirit and the activities of the Kingdom.

Gaining the commitment and cooperation of the leaders in our churches, regarding our alignment with and the pursuit of the prophetic activities of the Kingdom, is extremely important to our Kingdom success. If our leaders are not in agreement and committed to this endeavor, we will not succeed. Securing the agreement and commitment of the leaders must be our first priority when embracing the prophetic as a church. Once the leadership is committed and in agreement, it will be easier to gain the commitment and agreement from the members of the congregation.

There will be some in leadership, as well as in the congregation, who will choose not to pursue this prophetic Kingdom orientation, for various reasons. The same thing happened to Jesus throughout His ministry and He allowed these individuals to stop walking with Him.[371] Pleasing the Father and accomplishing the Father's work was more important to Him than pleasing those who were leading with and following Him. It must be the same for us. We must make room for the prophetic activities of the Kingdom in our churches and the first step in doing so is for the church leaders to make sure that they are walking down this path together, committed and in agreement among themselves and with God.

---

371. John 6:60-66

Chapter Questions & Notes

Talk It Over….

1) When we read accounts of Jesus' interactions with the Pharisees and other religious leaders, we tend to voice our amazement at how unaware and unreceptive they were to Jesus and what He was doing. In reality, spiritual pride and engaging in religious habits and rituals is very easy to slip into if we are not actively pursuing a relationship with the Holy Spirit, where we consistently endeavor to hear what He is saying and to see what He is doing. Why is slipping into spiritual pride and engaging in religious activities and habits much easier than developing an active, vital relationship with Jesus?

(10)

Run With A Vision

"Where there is no vision, the people are unrestrained, but happy is he who keeps the law." Proverbs 29:18

Most of us have seen or heard the first part of this verse from Proverbs many times throughout our lives. It is a foundational principle of leadership that is taught in both secular and Christian leadership courses. We all know that having a clear vision for what we do is critical to our pursuit and eventual success in achieving our goal. Vision can be as grandiose as all that we desire to accomplish within our careers or ministries, or it may be as tactical as what we want to accomplish over the next few years. Regardless of the scope of that vision, it is necessary to have a vision if we expect to achieve our purpose in an effective manner.

What we seldom think about or consider is that God, Himself, casts vision for what He wants to do. Why would He tell us to have a vision so people know what we want to do, if He doesn't have a vision for what He wants to do? The purposes and plans associated with His vision may take millennia or centuries to complete, or He may want to complete them in a matter of decades or years. Regardless, God has a vision for what He wants to accomplish and He casts that vision to us, along with the plans and purposes He has put in place to achieve that vision, so we can know what He is doing and what He is saying, in that regard.

The reality is many of us don't realize God is casting vision, so we aren't listening and watching to what He is saying and doing through the prophetic resources and activities of His Kingdom. God casts vision for what He wants to do in this world through the Holy Spirit. But, it requires spiritual resources and capabilities to hear and see Him that many of us are ignorant of or don't make ourselves available to.

As a result of not hearing the voice of the Spirit, we are "unrestrained" in that we may be engaged in a lot of activities that may not be the activities He wants us engaged in or to accomplish for Him. They are our own plans and activities. We are "unrestrained", not because God isn't casting the vision for what He wants to do but because we aren't "listening" and "catching" the vision He is casting. The Kingdom of God is prophetic in its nature and activities in this age, and we have to function prophetically, as His Kingdom people, if we are going to hear, see and interact with Him.

The scope of our vision for leadership and ministry, individually and corporately, is strongly influenced by and connected to the overall purpose and plans of God and His Kingdom. That is why we cannot forget or ignore the last part of this verse which says, *"…but happy is he who keeps the law."* Our purpose must be strongly linked and dependent upon His overall purpose for His Kingdom. The unique vision God reveals for each of us will correspond to the overall vision He has for His Kingdom.

Therefore, what we do or don't do has an impact on the Kingdom of God. If we don't receive and act on His vision for us, it doesn't hinder the success of God's Kingdom purpose and plans but it does impact our particular contributions to it. We don't have the luxury, as God's Kingdom representatives on the earth, of being able to establish our own vision based on what we want to accomplish and how it will benefit us as individuals or as a church.

Our vision must be tied to God's revealed will and purpose for us otherwise our vision is a self-imposed vision, devoid of the Spirit and anointing of God. Even if we do what we and others consider to be "good things", they may not benefit us in eternity because they are not in accordance with His purpose and plan for His Kingdom and for us. There is a reward system in heaven. It is not based on what *we* think is the good and right thing to do. It is based on the purpose, plans and desire of God and His Kingdom, and our willingness and ability to recognize, pursue, and accomplish what He has planned for us to accomplish, as part of His Kingdom activities.[372] His vision for us and the activities associated with that vision will always be good because they spring from the vision He, Himself, has for the expansion of His Kingdom.

We must remember that when we enter into our relationship with the Kingdom of God, through Jesus Christ, we enter it as the representative party. He is the principal and we are His representatives. Being the representative party doesn't mean we are viewed as second-class or are

[372] 1Corinthians 3:10-15; Luke 19:12-26

disrespected by the principal party (God) in the relationship. All it means is that God determines what He wants to do and how He wants to do it. Then, we get the information, strategies and plans from Him and carry it out for Him, using the resources and capabilities he provides to us. This all happens prophetically because the nature, presence and operation of the Kingdom of God, in this age, take place prophetically. This is why, as God's prophetic people, we need to embrace and learn how to function prophetically in or lives.

Therefore, it is our responsibility and privilege to seek the Lord regarding His purpose and vision for us as His people. If we go about our lives without securing His unique purpose or vision for us, or if we choose to pursue our own vision based on our own personal desires and agenda, God is not obligated to assist us, even if we say we are doing it for God or in the name of God. We can't do anything for God or in the name of God unless it is something He wants to do and that He wants to do through us as His representatives. Even then, we do it according to His plan and with the provision He gives us to accomplish it.

We must not forget that this is His deal, not ours. If we are in a place of leadership among God's people, we represent Jesus as if He was here engaging in these ministry activities, Himself. It is not, simply, our career or job. It is a special and unique calling and appointment that is closely aligned with the purpose and plans of Jesus and His Kingdom activities on the earth. Therefore, it is not to be entered into lightly or treated flippantly.[373]

Once we seek the Lord and secure His unique vision for us, which is often revealed in phases over time (regardless of how small or insignificant it may seem to us), we can set our sights on achieving that purpose, knowing that all of the resources of God and His Kingdom are behind us to accomplish the work.[374] What may seem small and insignificant to us may be the very activity which proves to Jesus that He can trust us with greater responsibility.

No vision or activity is so small that it is insignificant to Jesus. It's not the size or magnitude of the activity He gives us to accomplish that is important. It's our faithful obedience and passion with which we engage and accomplish the activity that is important. Jesus sees everything and every faithful response we make toward Him is noticed, appreciated, and credited to our reward account. It isn't what we do for Jesus, as much as it

---

[373] 1Corinthians 1:1 Galatians 1:15-16
[374] 2Peter 13

is our willingness to obey and cooperate with Jesus in what He is already doing, that is important.

As we go about obediently responding to and cooperating with Jesus in His Kingdom activities, a tremendous resource He has made available to us is the prophetic activity of His Kingdom, empowered by the person of the Holy Spirit. This is a very powerful and engaging resource that is designed to dramatically arrest the attention of people and draw them to God and to His Kingdom. Paul confirms this aspect of the prophetic activity of the Kingdom, when he says, *"And my message and my preaching were not in persuasive words of wisdom, but in demonstration of the Spirit and of power,* ***that your faith should not rest on the wisdom of men, but on the power of God.****"*[375] The Holy Spirit's prophetic activity is our God-given resource and method for getting people's attention regarding the reality, presence and message of the Kingdom of God.

Jesus' Vision For The Local Church

Now that we have committed ourselves to embrace, introduce, and integrate the prophetic into our church, and we have gained the commitment and energy of the leadership of our church for this endeavor, it is time to cast the vision for the prophetic into our church. Casting the vision for the prophetic into the church is the means by which we allow the Holy Spirit to "infect" the individual members of the congregation with the same vision for, desire for, and energy to pursue the prophetic as the leaders possess. If the vision for embracing the prophetic is from God then the same conviction, anointing, and energy the Holy Spirit has placed upon the leadership will be placed upon the members of the congregation in order that the entire church can "walk together" in the prophetic activities of God.

When a church's leaders and individual members are committed to and in agreement with the will of God for that particular church (even as it relates to the operation of the prophetic in their midst), they will endeavor to develop their wineskin (church) in such a way that they can both receive and contain the wine of the Spirit that God makes available to them so they can pursue and achieve their vision from God.

Therefore, only through a Holy Spirit-orchestrated agreement between the leaders and the congregation, will the Holy Spirit accomplish His prophetic

---

[375] 1Corinthians 2:4-5 (emphasis mine)

purpose for the local church. Again, just as some leaders in the church may not choose to join themselves to this pursuit of God's prophetic activity, there may be members of the congregation who will choose not to join the pursuit. God has another church for them, where they can be affective for Him and where they can serve in agreement with the leadership of that local church.

In regard to the spiritual and mental attitudes of the leaders and individuals in the local church, the pursuit of the prophetic must be accompanied by true humility and a servant-attitude between the leaders and among the members of the church. The exercise of the prophetic in our midst will, most likely, bring with it the temptation to *"think more highly of ourselves than we ought to think."* [376] Many will experience the temptation to be prideful and selfish, which may surprise and humble us, both, as individuals and as a church.

That is why we must make the decision as leaders and as a church, before we ever embark on pursuing these prophetic activities, that we endeavor to exercise humility, patience and grace toward one another and to *"do nothing from selfishness or empty conceit, but with humility of mind, regard one another as more important than ourselves; not merely looking out for our own personal interests, but also for the interests of others."* [377]

Experiencing the supernatural prophetic activity of God's Kingdom in and through our lives can be, both, exciting and a little daunting. But the prophetic is not to be feared or rejected because of this. Instead, we must *"...be of sober spirit, be on the alert. Our adversary, the devil, prowls about like a roaring lion, seeking someone to devour. But we must resist him, firm in our faith, knowing that the same experiences of suffering are being accomplished by our brethren who are in the world."* [378]

The same temptations that we will encounter while engaging in the prophetic activities of the Kingdom are the same temptations that everyone else who has ever experienced these same activities of God has encountered. That is why we must see Jesus and the way He lived and operated on the earth, as our example because He, *"...existed in the form of God, but did not regard equality with God a thing to be grasped, but He emptied Himself, taking the form of a bond-servant, being made in the likeness of men. And being found in appearance as a man, He humbled Himself by becoming obedient to the point of death, even death on a cross."* [379]

---

[376] Romans 12:3
[377] Philippians 2:3-4
[378] 1Peter 5:8-9

Even though Jesus knew He was the single most important resource God had in His arsenal when it came to accomplishing His purpose and plans for redeeming humanity, Jesus chose not to consider that or let it distract or sidetrack Him from what He was here to do. Instead, He chose to adopt the perspective, as the Father's agent representative to humanity, that this was not about Him but it was all about the Father and humanity and bringing humanity back into a relationship with God. It was this attitude working in and through Jesus that dictated the attitudes, activities and actions of Jesus, even as the most dramatic and powerful prophetic events humanity has ever experienced were taking place by His hands.

In the same way, we too must adopt this perspective of God and His Kingdom as we engage in the prophetic activities of the Kingdom of God. Each of us has a unique and important purpose within the overall purpose and plans of the Kingdom. Experiencing the prophetic activity of God in and through our lives is one method by which God will work through us to achieve that purpose. Yet, we must keep in mind that this is not about us; it is about God and His desire to bring all people to Him.

This is not about my ministry or your ministry. This is about God's eternal plan for humanity. Therefore, everything we do should be focused on bringing people into the Kingdom and preparing God's people to dwell with Him in the manifest presence of His Kingdom forever. There are many things that need to be done to accomplish this goal but at the same time, everything we do should have this goal in mind.

When we begin to cast the vision for the prophetic into the church, we must be able to articulate the vision including the strategy, objectives and plans that will be executed, if we are going to be successful. We all know that strategies, objectives, and plans are important to keep things focused and on track but we also know that God wants us to keep our eyes on Him and to trust in His power, not in our planning. Therefore, we will sometimes experience "adjustments" that God chooses to make in our plans in order that we continue to walk by faith and not totally by our plans. Even so, God is working His plan and as long as we are seeking Him to ensure our plans are in lock-step with His plans, we will find His grace is sufficient for any obstacles or circumstances which arise, for His power is sufficient in our weakness.[380]

---

[379] Philippians 2:6-8
[380] 2Corinthians 12:9

A few of the necessary strategies, objectives, and plans we should put in place have to do with building the proper spiritual, scriptural, and administrative foundations for the prophetic in the church. Our strategy for the prophetic should interlock with the overall vision or purpose God has given us for the church. Look at the various areas of ministry operating within the church and begin to ask God to reveal to us how He may use the prophetic activity of His Kingdom to help drive the effectiveness of these ministries over the long-term.

This is intended to be a time when we ask God to increase our own vision for what is actually possible through these ministries and any other ministries He may want us to implement, as He initiates His prophetic activities through us. He may actually tell us to pull out of some of these ministries and to initiate others. We are not trying to control God and His working.

We are trying to put ourselves in a position to be actively involved with what He wants to do, and is already doing. Remember, this is His deal, not ours. It is also important to develop a plan for instructing the congregation in the operation of the prophetic. This should include both scriptural instruction and practical application. As I mentioned earlier, God has introduced and will probably continue to introduce, the prophetic differently into each of His churches.

What is important for us to understand here is God will not allow more to take place within our congregations than what we are able to effectively oversee and administrate. God is all for order in the church,[381] yet He wants to stretch us and take us to the place where we either have to trust Him or we fail. It is highly probable that as soon as you commit yourself to embrace and pursue the prophetic as leaders and as a church, you will begin to see the prophetic break out within your midst in some fashion. It could come through dreams, visions, prophecy, angelic visitations, or even gifts of healings and miracles. God is looking for obedience on our part and as soon as He sees it, He will begin to initiate the prophetic in our midst. Again, He is not looking for perfection, just a willing heart to obey. His grace will be sufficient in every situation.

As we see the prophetic take place in our churches, we must remember it is breaking out among people who are, for the most part, immature in this area. Operating in the prophetic is not a sign of maturity but it is a necessary ingredient if a church is going to achieve the level of maturity God desires. If we are leaders, we must be patient with those we lead because

---

[381] 1Corinthians 14:39-40

God is patient with us, as leaders, as we seek to grow in these activities. We don't overly discipline our children when they make a mistake based on immaturity. We encourage them to keep going and keep trying until they get it right. We administrate the prophetic in much the same way.

A very effective way to introduce the congregation to the prophetic is for leaders to meet with smaller groups of members over a pre-determined period of time. A leader may meet informally with a group of members at a member's home or some other smaller, intimate location in order to cast the vision for the prophetic. This will allow for a more personal time for sharing, for answering questions, and for addressing any apprehension or fear that may arise from introducing the prophetic. Many individuals have encountered negative experiences in regard to the prophetic in the past, and may have to work through these issues before they can fully embrace the vision.

This is especially important for the church's leaders since they will be involved with casting the vision themselves, and therefore must be free from any negative attitudes that can hinder the operation of the prophetic in the church. As those responsible for leading and administrating the prophetic in the church, leaders must deal with any issues they have involving the prophetic before the vision is cast to the rest of the congregation. This is also a good time to provide introductory instruction in order that the members can see there is a scriptural and practical way to operate in the prophetic, as well as to administrate it when it does take place. If people can see that the leaders have prepared themselves as much as possible for the operation of the prophetic in their church, they are more willing to embrace the vision and to go along with it, knowing the leaders will do all that they can to lead in the correct way.

Instruction and initial training in the prophetic in home group meetings and other formal church gatherings is also a good way to prepare the people and introduce the prophetic into the church. They can gain a basic understanding of what the scriptures say regarding the prophetic, plus they can understand basic prophetic etiquette (scriptural methods for operating in and administrating the prophetic). There is much more that can be said regarding casting the vision for the prophetic. Hopefully this has provided some practical guidelines for doing so.

Chapter Questions & Notes

Talk It Over....

1) God is a vision-caster. He wants His people to know what He is doing, where He is going, and what He wants to accomplish. He is a revealer, not a withholder. How can we place ourselves in a position to develop a relationship with the Holy Spirit; to hear Him, see what He is doing, and receive the vision Jesus is casting, regarding His activities on the earth?

2) As followers of Jesus and His Kingdom representatives on the earth, it is important to realize that our personal ministry vision, as well as the ministry vision for our local church, is closely aligned and linked to the overall vision that Jesus has for the Church, as a whole. The Holy Spirit communicates and imparts our vision, individually and as a church, and trains us to cooperate with Him to execute that vision. Discuss how the local church leadership can embrace and facilitate these training and preparation activities for individuals and for the church.

(11)

Leading, Governing & Administrating God's Prophetic People

"Do not quench the Spirit; do not despise prophetic utterances. But examine everything carefully; hold fast to that which is good."
1Thessalonians 5:19-21

"...and the spirits of prophets are subject to prophets; for God is not a God of confusion but of peace, as in all the churches of the saints"
1Corinthians 14:33-33

"Therefore, my brethren, desire earnestly to prophesy, and do not forbid to speak in tongues. But let all things be done properly and in an orderly manner." 1Corinthians 14:39-40

It is my personal opinion that the manner in which we approach and execute this next aspect of the prophetic activities of the Kingdom of God will determine the level of success and integration we will experience in our churches. There are two reasons why I believe this: 1) Most, if not all of us, have a deep desire for more than an intellectual orientation to our personal relationship with God. We want to truly experience the reality of the presence of God in our lives, as well as in the outward workings of God through our lives; 2) Many of us possess an unhealthy, almost crippling fear and intimidation when it comes to engaging ourselves in the work of God, especially as it relates to the prophetic gifts and manifestations of the Spirit as identified by Paul in 1Corinthians 12-14.

God has placed the desire to be intimately acquainted and involved with Him, on a deeply personal level, within each one of us because He created us in His image. The writer of Ecclesiastes puts it this way, *"I have seen the task which God has given the sons of men with which to occupy themselves. He has made everything appropriate in its time.* ***He has also set eternity in their heart****..."*[382]

God has set an eternal awareness and purpose in the heart of every human being, and that eternal awareness and purpose is crying out within us, wanting to find expression because it will not be satisfied with intellectual exercises or physical and natural accomplishments. We will only discover and accomplish our God-given purpose when we set our hearts on the Kingdom of God and allow the Kingdom to operate in and through us, to manifest itself and its presence to the people we encounter in our day-to-day lives.

David put it this way, *"…I remember You from the land of the Jordan and the peaks of Hermon, from Mount Mizar.* ***Deep calls to deep at the sound of Your waterfalls; All Your breakers and Your waves have rolled over me.****"*[383] Regardless of how long we have been a follower of Jesus and how mature we have become, spiritually, there is more to God than we have known and have experienced. Therefore, from the depths of God Himself, He will call to the depths of our own being, drawing us ever deeper into Him. In Revelation 1, the Apostle John saw a vision of the exalted Jesus standing in front of him. As John described Jesus, he tells us that when Jesus spoke, it was like the sound of many waters…like the powerful sound of a waterfall.[384]

If you've ever witnessed and heard the powerful sound of Niagara Falls, this is the description John gave to the voice of Jesus. "Deep calls to deep at the sound of Your waterfalls," literally means that the powerful voice of God calls from the depths of His being to the depths of our being. As we experience the spiritual reality of God calling from the depths of His being to ours, and as we respond to that by gazing and contemplating Him in personal experience and prayer, it creates a fascination and a sense of awe in our hearts toward Him. This communion and communication with God creates in us, both, a satisfaction and contentment, as well as a dissatisfaction and discontentment regarding our personal experience with Him. We are at peace and content with Him but we never seem to get enough of our experience with Him to satisfy our desire for Him.

This paradox is also part of the divine plan of God for humanity. This entire experience of deep calling unto deep is a prophetic experience, in and of itself. It is the essence of prayer. It is the prophetic nature and presence of God and His Kingdom breaking into the natural world in which we live,

---

[382] Ecclesiastes 3:10-11
[383] Psalm 42:6-8
[384] Revelation 1:15

into our own personal lives, and engaging us in prophetic communication. It is this type of prophetic activity that first leads us to the new birth in Christ, and then affects our life from that moment forward, through every other prophetic event that we experience, by the Spirit.

In contrast to this prophetic relationship and experience, many of us are living and operating within a religious paradigm that is predominantly intellectual and humanitarian in nature, ignoring or dismissing the supernatural aspect that brings the sense of connection with God and His Kingdom. We possess a distorted image of God that does not allow for a healthy development of spiritual self-identification with His Kingdom, nor does it allow for a consistent process of spiritual maturation and fulfillment. Therefore, we feel a sense of spiritual disconnectedness with God and His Kingdom and a sense of spiritual frustration because we "know" that we are not where we should be, and need to be, in regard to spiritual experience and maturity.

There are many of us who experience a deep sense of frustration and disconnection in our Christian life because we know that, no matter how much we endeavor to live fulfilling lives before God, there is a sense of direction and mission missing from our lives. We give intellectual ascent to the idea that God is at work in our lives and we have a strong desire to serve God through our lives but there is a "disconnect" between our theoretical acknowledgement and our practical experience that leads to confusion and frustration on the inside. In our quiet moments, when we are away from everyone else and it is just our own thoughts and God, we know that there is something missing that would bring that "connected" satisfaction.

We know there is something that we were created to be and to do but we can't seem to put our finger on what it is. Yet, we know that it is bigger than we are and that it will have eternal ramifications when we are finally able to pinpoint it and do it. That is why so many people are spending billions of dollars on psychics, mediums, and New Age channeling and paraphernalia. They are seeking to satisfy that longing for spiritual connection and significance that only a deep experience with God and His Kingdom can bring.

I believe that a healthy and scriptural understanding of and experience with the prophetic activities of the Kingdom will go a long way in bringing each of us to a sense of connectedness with God and His Kingdom, and in giving each of us a sense of deep satisfaction that we are engaging in those things for which God created us in the first place. The prophetic is the supernatural element of our experience with God and His Kingdom that will transform every believer and, therefore, every local church into the spiritual force that God called us to be before the foundation of the world.

Therefore, the manner in which we as leaders lead, instruct, and administrate the prophetic in the lives of individual believers and of the church will determine our effectiveness in the world for years to come. As a result, we need to clearly understand what the scriptures say regarding the prophetic and how we are to lead others, instruct others, and administrate the prophetic effectively among others within the church. Let's start our discussion in the New Testament book where we are encouraged and instructed the most in regard to its operation - 1Corinthians 12-14.

The Apostle Paul is writing this first letter to the church in Corinth in order to address several behavioral issues that are affecting the spiritual condition and outward witness of the church. These major behavioral issues are: 1) unhealthy divisions or cliques in the church[385], sexual immorality[386], lawsuits between believers[387], partaking of the Lord's Supper in an unworthy manner[388], and operating in the manifestations of the Holy Spirit in a manner that is unruly, out of order, and selfishly motivated[389]. Paul makes a statement that sums up the overall spiritual condition of the Corinthian believers, by saying, *"And I, brethren, could not speak to you as to spiritual men, but as to men of flesh, as to babes in Christ. I gave you milk to drink, not solid food; for you were not yet able to receive it. Indeed, even now you are not yet able, for you are still fleshly."*[390] Paul summed up the condition of the Corinthian church at this time by telling them that they are carnal or fleshly. They did not have control over their physical and soulish desires. They were spiritually immature.

Yet, even in the midst of their spiritual immaturity and carnal over-indulgence, Paul speaks some amazing things to them about what they have going for them, spiritually, and what he wants them to do as they move forward toward spiritual maturity, as a church. First, Paul tells them that they are tremendously blessed by God because they are not lacking in the function and operation of any of the manifestations of the Spirit (grace gifts) as a church.[391]

Second, Paul tells them that, even though they have a lot of behavioral issues to work through as a church, he does not want them to de-emphasize

---

[385] 1Corinthians 1:10-13
[386] 1Corinthians 5:1-5
[387] 1Corinthians 6:1-7
[388] 1Corinthians 11:20-22
[389] 1Corinthians 12-14
[390] 1Corinthians 3:1-3
[391] 1Corinthians 1:4-8

their activities regarding the prophetic manifestations of the Holy Spirit in their church. In fact, Paul specifically tells them to "*desire earnestly*" the prophetic manifestations of the Spirit, especially that they may prophesy.[392] Again, the phrase translated "*desire earnestly*" actually means "*to covet or lust for*". Paul is telling the Corinthians to lust for the prophetic manifestations of the Spirit, especially that they may prophesy. He goes on to tell them that they may ALL prophesy, as long as it is done in order and to encourage the Body.[393]

When we see an individual or a group of people acting in an immature manner, spiritually, our first tendency, as leaders, is to "back off" of that activity or have the "perpetrators" "back off" from engaging in that activity, until we see more spiritual maturity from them. Then, when we see them behaving more maturely, we let them get involved again in that previous activity. Yet here, we see Paul doing just the opposite. When Paul hears about how carnal and immature the Corinthians are, in regard to the operation of the prophetic manifestations of the Spirit, he doesn't tell them to "back off" until they gain more maturity. Instead, he tells them to continue lusting after the prophetic. He tells them not to stop desiring it or operating in it.

He tells them to pursue these things like never before. What he also does, however, is assist them in that maturing process by giving them practical instruction in the nature of the prophetic, the purpose for the prophetic, and how to operate in and administrate the prophetic within the church. That is why we must use this letter to the Corinthians as a model for our own churches. Our churches are immature in many areas, especially the prophetic, just as the Corinthians were. Paul gives us very practical wisdom in how to "lust after" the prophetic but also in how to do it right and how to administrate it correctly.

Paul, in 1 Corinthians 12-14, instructs us in the "*charisma*" of the Spirit or the manifestations of God's "*grace*" by the Holy Spirit in the lives of believers individually and corporately. These manifestations of the Spirit are manifestations of God's grace toward His people that, both, minister to them as individuals and operate through them to minister to the needs of others. These prophetic manifestations of God's grace are intended to go beyond the human ability, talents, and attributes of individuals and to allow the power of God and His Kingdom to manifest in the life and circumstances of people.

---

[392] 1Corinthians 12:31; 14:1, 39
[393] 1Corinthians 14:24, 31

Paul also instructs us that as individual believers with unique callings and ministries from God within the Body of Christ, we should "lust for" the prophetic manifestations of God's grace that He has appointed to operate within each of our lives, so that we may accomplish those callings and ministries. This "gift mix" is the set of specific prophetic manifestations that we should lust for and expect to see function through our lives as we pursue our relationship with God and the ministry God has given us within the Body.

At the same time, we should not rule out the desire of the Spirit to manifest any or all of these prophetic manifestations through us, at one time or another, in order to minister to the needs of people around us. God desires to minister to people and if we are open and available to be used by Him, He will do it, even if it is not in our normal "gift mix".

We need to be sensitive to the Spirit at all times and "go with the flow" if we discern the Spirit wanting to do something like this. Remember, this is not about us and what we can or can't do. We can't do any of this apart from the working of the Holy Spirit in our lives. It is about God and what He wants to do through us, to help people. We are simply vessels of honor that He flows through, by His grace, to accomplish His purpose and plans in the earth. Therefore, we must understand how to cooperate and work with Him in the area of the prophetic activities of His Kingdom so that He can use us at any time for any reason, in order to accomplish His purposes on the earth.

What we need to observe from what Paul is telling us in this letter to the Corinthians is that the prophetic activities of the Kingdom are very important to the spiritual life of the individual believer, the local church, and to the purpose and plan of God for the world around us. Just because an individual believer or a local church may be immature in the way they operate in the prophetic, doesn't mean we shut the whole thing down and wait to mature before we seek to operate in it again.

Paul understood that neither an individual nor a local church can mature effectively without the prophetic activities of the Kingdom operating in their lives. He knew that the answer was not to stop the prophetic activity of God from manifesting just because the people were not exercising it in a mature manner. Therefore, we as leaders need to heed Paul's example in this regard. We need to be able to lead, instruct, train, and administrate in the prophetic even as the individual believers and the church grow and mature spiritually and in these prophetic activities, over time. We need to be patient and approach this as spiritual fathers and mothers.

We have to remember how God continually exercises patience with each of us in all of our shortcomings and immature activities. As we see Him father us in our lives, we need to shepherd the people He gives us to lead and care for.

Chapter Questions & Notes

Talk It Over….

1) An individual's relationship with God must be prophetic if it is to be active, vital and growing. The Holy Spirit actively engages with our human spirits in order to fellowship, reveal, instruct, train and guide us. The depth of God calls out to the depths of our being in order to engage and interact. This is the essence of prayer. Discuss this prayer dynamic and give examples of when you have experienced this "deep calling" in your relationship with God.

2) Jesus doesn't want us backing off of our pursuit of the Kingdom of God, and the prophetic aspects of the Kingdom of God, because we make mistakes or don't always have our "spiritual act together". Paul tells us to lust after the prophetic manifestations of the Kingdom of God. How does this encouragement make you feel and what motivation does it give you, if any, to embrace and pursue a vital, active relationship with the Holy Spirit, as an individual and as a church?

About The Author

Tom Casey graduated from the University of Missouri in St. Louis with a Bachelor of Science degree in Business Administration, and graduated from Regent University School of Divinity with a Master of Arts degree in Practical Theology. Tom and his wife, Andrea, reside in the St. Louis, Missouri area and are active members of Destiny Church.

Tom has been a successful businessman and manager in the field of innovative and emerging technology with companies such as IBM and Toshiba America. Tom has been a local church leader, speaker and Bible teacher for over 35 years, having engaged in youth ministry, street and event evangelism, adult education and training, intercessory prayer ministry, and mentoring and training in prayer. In addition to "Studies In The Kingdom Of God", Tom has authored many other teaching resources and aids to assist in the communication and understanding of the Kingdom of God and other important Bible truths relevant to Christians today.

Author's Contact Information

Tom Casey
PO Box 822
Ballwin, MO 63011

tcasey.stl@gmail.com

Made in the USA
Middletown, DE
04 March 2021